A Class Act

Studies in Education/Politics
Volume 8
Garland Reference Library of Social Science
Volume 1445

STUDIES IN EDUCATIONAL POLITICS
MARK B. GINSBURG, *Series Editor*

A CLASS ACT

CHANGING TEACHERS' WORK, GLOBALISATION AND THE STATE

SUSAN L. ROBERTSON

FALMER PRESS
A MEMBER OF THE TAYLOR & FRANCIS GROUP
NEW YORK AND LONDON
2000

Published in 2000 by
Falmer Press
A member of the Taylor & Francis Group
29 West 35th Street
New York, NY 10001

10 9 8 7 6 5 4 3 2 1

Library of Congress Cataloging-in-Publication Data
is available from the Library of Congress

Printed on acid-free, 250-year-life paper
Manufactured in the United States of America

To Roger, Bianca-Jade and Nick
—for everything

Contents

Acknowledgments

It has always felt something of an irony that in writing this book about teachers as a class, and the changing political and economic conditions that have framed and shaped their work over time, it in no small way reflects my own life over the past decade. My academic career over this time has spanned four countries all in various states of restructuring—Australia, Canada, New Zealand and England. For that reason, the completion of this book has been both frustratingly slow and yet, at the same time, considerably enriched because of the different contexts that I found myself trying to understand and write about. Each of these experiences has been particularly important in underlining for me the similarities and differences between countries as they have responded to changes arising from the collapse of the post–World War II settlement and the pressures of globalisation and regionalisation. More important, these different locations and experiences have pressed me toward a theory frame for critically analysing teachers as a class, the way in which teachers have acted and continue to act, and the changing nature of teachers' work and professional projects across time, space and place. The arguments and analysis within this book are an attempt in that direction.

Few endeavours are ever the sole effort of an individual: rather, they rest upon the initiatives, insights and accommodations of others. This book is no different, and, indeed, for both its inception and its completion I am indebted to many individuals. The genesis of the book owes a great deal to the initial encouragement of Ivor Goodson and Andy Hargreaves, whom I would like to thank publicly. Its successful conclusion owes an enormous amount to Mark Ginsburg, the series editor for

Falmer/Garland; Michael Spurlock, education editor, and staff at Falmer/Garland; and Frank Seth at the University of Auckland, who, on numerous occasions, rescued my words because of my own technological inadequacies. Mark Ginsburg's insightful reading and always helpful suggestions added considerably to the book. My own analysis of globalisation, educational restructuring and teachers and their work is also indebted not only to the many teachers whom over the years I have observed, engaged with, and studied in depth, but to the many seminal conversations with friends, colleagues and students over the years in different settings. In particular, I would like to thank Victor Soucek, Raj Pannu, Michael Apple, Harry Smaller, Mark Ginsburg, Terri Seddon, Janina Trotman, Rod Chadbourne, Bruce Haynes, Martin Thrupp, Mark Olssen, Eve Coxon, Joce Jesson, Elizabeth Rata and Nesta Devine.

There are also several special acknowledgements to make. First, to Nick and Bianca Jade, my two wonderful children. This book was always accommodated with the grace and understanding shown to the intrusions of my work into your lives. Somehow you always understood this book was about the lives of real people, in real places, with real consequences. Second, to my father and mother, Peter and Sybille. They have constantly made possible many things in my life that ought to have been impossible, even when oceans separated us. In myriad ways that mattered, they were there. Finally, to Roger Dale: my dearest of friends, my colleague, my teacher, my husband. I can't describe how much you have continued to inspire me with your acute insight into the social world, your constant commitment to understanding and how that might be captured in words. The arguments in this book have gained so much from our wide-ranging and intense conversations, and from your perceptive and constructive critiques of various drafts. Finally, over the past four years, you have continually encouraged me with the view that what I had to say was important, and you always, generously, created the spaces that enabled me to finish. Thank you.

All the World's a Stage: Who Should Direct the Play?

Series Editor's Introduction to
A Class Act: Changing Teachers' Work, Globalilzation and the State

MARK B. GINSBURG
University of Pittsburgh

"Take education out of politics!" "Education should not be a political football!" "Keep politics out of the schools!" "Educators should not be political!" These and similar warnings have been sounded at various times in a variety of societies. Such warnings, however, miss (or misconstrue) the point that education *is* political. Not only is education constituted by and constitutive of struggles over the distribution of symbolic and material resources, but education implies and confers structural and ideological power used to control the means of producing, reproducing, consuming, and accumulating symbolic and material resources (see Ginsburg 1995; Ginsburg and Lindsay 1995).

Political struggles about and through education occur in classrooms and nonformal education settings; school and university campuses; education systems; and local, national, and global communities. Different groups of students, educators, parents, business owners, organized labor leaders, government and international organization officials, and other worker-consumer-citizens participate (actively or passively) in such political activity. These struggles not only shape educational policy and practice; they also are dialectically related to more general relations of power among social classes, racial/ethnic groups, gender groups, nations, and regional/multinational blocs. Thus, the politics of education and the political work accomplished through education are ways in which existing social relations are reproduced, legitimated, challenged, or transformed.

The "Studies in Education/Politics" series is designed to include books that examine how in different historical periods and in various local and national contexts education is political. The focus is on what groups are involved in political struggles in, through and about education; what material and symbolic resources are of concern; how ideological and structural power are implicated; and what consequences obtain for the people directly involved and for social relations more generally.

The purpose of this series, however, is not only to help educators and other people understand the nexus of education and politics. It is also concerned with facilitating their active involvement in the politics of and through education. Thus, the issue is not whether education should be taken out of politics, nor whether politics should be kept out of schools, nor whether educators should be apolitical. Rather the questions are toward what ends, by what means, and in whose interests should educators and other worker-consumer-citizens engage in political work in and about education.

This volume by Susan Robertson, the sixth book to appear in the "Studies in Education/Politics" series, examines what I believe is at the core of education/politics—teachers' labor. I would thus include *A Class Act* in league with other important book-length analyses of how power as well as material and symbolic resources are struggled over as a part of teacher's work in classrooms, schools, union/professional organizations, and communities. Here I would mention in chronological order: Willard Waller's (1932) *The Sociology of Teaching*; Albert Blum's (1969) *Teacher Unions and Associations*; Dan Lortie's (1975) *Schoolteacher: A Sociological Study*; Paul Mattingly's (1975) *The Classless Profession American Schoolmen in the Nineteenth Century;* Michael Apple's (1982) *Education and Power*; Kevin Harris' (1982) *Teachers and Classes: A Marxist Analysis*; Robert Connell's (1985) *Teacher's Work*; Martin Lawn's (1985) *The Politics of Teacher Unionism*; Linda Dove (1986) *Teachers and Teacher Education in Developing Countries*; Martin Lawn's and Gerald Grace's (1987) *Teachers: The Culture and Politics of Work*; Patricia Smuck's (1987) *Women Educators: Employees of Schools in Western Countries*; Madeleine Grumet's (1988) *Bitter Milk: Women and Teaching*; Jenny Ozga's (1980) *Schoolwork: Approaches to the Labor Process of Teaching*; Kathleen Weiler's (1988) *Women Teaching for Change: Gender, Class and Power*; Sandra Acker's (1989) *Teachers, Gender and Careers*; Hilary De Lyon's and Frances Migniuolo's (1989) *Women Teachers: Issues and Experiences*; Bruce Cooper's (1992) *Labor Relations in Education: An International Perspective*; and my own (1995) *The Politics of Teachers' Work and Lives*.

Robertson's book, however, takes the scholarly and political project further by more fully and more explicitly contextualizing teachers' labor not only at the level of classrooms and schools, nor only within national education systems and political economies, but also within a global and globalizing political, economic, and cultural dynamics. One of the major theses of *A Class Act* thus calls to mind Jaques' well-known soliloquy in Shakespeare's *As You Like It* that "All the world's a stage" (Act 2, Scene 7; http://tech-two.mit.edu/Shakekspeare/Comedy/asyoulikit/asyoulikeit.2.7.html). The volume makes a significant contribution, extending other efforts to examine education as a global as well as local phenomenon (e.g., see Arnove and Torres, 1999; Ginsburg, 1991; Meyer and Hannan, 1979), by inserting teachers' work into the heart of such discussions. Robertson accomplishes this masterfully, highlighting the experience of public school teachers in England and the United States but locating "teachers and their work within wider social formations and their underlying social relations" as part of a local-global analysis. In part this is achieved by examining teachers' relation to the state as it changes across "settlements"—*Laissez Faire Liberalism* (1850-1900), *Keynesian Welfare Statism* (1945-1970), and the currently emerging *Competitive Contractual State*. In this latter settlement she draws our attention to how teacher's labor is being (re)organized in the context of "fast capitalism" and "fast schools." Thus, despite the common notion that teachers' work has remained the same (e.g., see Sarason, 1982), even in the face of educational reform movements, Robertson's longer term, "conjunctural time" perspective illuminates the changing nature of teachers' work.

In contrast to Jaques world, however, Robertson argues persuasively that teachers "are not *merely* players" (emphasis added); teachers' acts — their identities and their work—are not fully determined (i.e., scripted) by institutional, state, and global political economic structures. Robertson theorizes effectively and documents extensively how teachers' class (and, it would be appropriate to add, gender, race, and national) acts are not directed only from above. Individually and collectivity teachers are performing on a world stage of struggle in which they make claims to and seek to use economic, cultural, social, and organizational assets. This is not to say that such claims and strategies are always successful, and that teachers should be conceived as autonomous or somehow outside of power relations. The point is that teachers' roles on the world stage are worked out through negotiation and struggle in which teachers have degrees of freedom (partly depending on their assets) to define how they will play their parts. Thus, in drawing attention to agency as well as structure (see also Giddens, 1979), Robertson provides us with an approach for both understanding teachers' performances in various societal and historical contexts and informing teachers in their contemporary struggles over the nature, organization, and consequences teachers' labor. I hope that this book will provoke and challenge teachers and others to reflect more deeply on what is happening in teachers' work and lives, why it is happening, and how one can become involved with other worker-consumer-citizens to literally "set the stage" for a new settlement, hopefully one that is characterized by peace, justice, and environmental sanity.

As I was reviewing a draft of this book, I was performing as a teacher on "stage" that was floating around the world. Along with approximately 26 other faculty members, 50 non-academic staff, 610 undergraduate students, 45 senior adult passengers, 15 faculty/staff family members, and 200 crew, I was sailing on the S.S. Universe Explorer in conjunction with the Spring 1999 Semester at Sea "voyage of discovery." Teaching courses (e.g., Wealth and Power, Work and Occupations) while at sea and coordinating seminars, site visits, and other field experiences when in ports (in Cuba, Brazil, South Africa, Kenya, India, Malaysia, Vietnam, China, and Japan), I had incredible opportunities to reflect on local-global dynamics and compare the situation of teachers. It was instructive to note, for example, how privatization and tourism, respectively were creating disincentives for Cubans and Chinese to enter or remain in teaching and how moves toward equalizing educational resources between blacks and whites in South Africa presented a dilemma for teacher organizations because part of the process of equalizing resources involves reassigning teachers to historically "disadvantaged" schools.

One thing that stands out in my memory of the experience is the lived—though, for some, barely livable—reality of people I encountered. Although there were some economic differences among the students participating in the Semester at Sea program, the students were much more similar in their economic standing than the citizens of Brazil, India and other countries whom we did (or could have) observed, interviewed, and interacted with. As Braun's (1997, p. 73) in *The Rich Get Richer* notes, globally "358 billionaires have a combined net worth of $760 billion, which equals the net worth of the poorest 45%" of the world's population. This economic and political reality, I would argue, has profound implications for the work and lives of educators and other worker-consumer-citizens.

More recently, as I was in the final stages of crafting this editor's introduction, protest marches and rallies against the World Trade Organization (WTO) erupted onto the world's stage, and not only in Seattle, Washington, where the WTO was meeting in late November and early December of this year (1999). The events, which mobilized thousands of people, indicate that people in many walks of life and from many countries are concerned about the issue of whose interests are being (and will be) served by the process of globalization. In my remarks at one such event, which I helped to organize at the University of Pittsburgh, I stated that the issue was not whether one is for or against trade or other forms of interaction between people of different nations, but how we evaluate and deal with the tendency for multinational corporations' (and their profit motive) to take center stage within and to write the script for the WTO. For instance, I believe that the image of trade among nations does not capture the reality that "[m]ore than a quarter of the world's economic activity now stems from only two hundred corporations, while approximately one-third of world trade takes place *among different units of a single global company*" (Braun, 1997, p. 143; emphasis added).

It is interesting and important to speculate whether concerns about constraining "free trade" could be used as a rationale for restructuring the work of teachers. What if teachers and other citizens of a given country worked to have legislated a law restricting the amount of instructional time that could be devoted to internet-based programs developed by citizens from other countries? Would this be challenged in the WTO? What if teachers and other citizens in a variety of countries lobbied successfully to have mandated curriculum that promoted the idea people should only consume products and services that were produced and distributed in ways that insured living wages for the workers, protected the health of the workers and other people, and sustained the physical and biological environment? Could the dissemination of such knowledge be viewed as undercutting the capability of some corporations in some countries from engaging in selling their products and services to individuals or organizations in that country?

The recent developments in Seattle—both the WTO meeting and the protest actions—encourage us to recall Jaques' statement that "all the world's a stage." For me this means that teachers and other worker-consumer-citizens need to think and act locally but with profound awareness of the global "play" in which we find ourselves. Moreover, we should not accept the script that someone else has written for us; neither should we assume that the government or international organization officials, who seek to "direct" or "performance," are necessarily working in line with human interest. Rather teachers and other worker-consumer-citizens need to redefine their lives and meet the challenge of being more than "merely players." With this goal in mind, we are fortunate to have sophisticated analyses like the one developed by Susan Robertson in *A Class Act*.

A Class Act

A Class Act: Teachers and Change

CHANGING TEACHERS' WORK

Teachers are an important occupational group in modern industrialised societies. They make up around 3 percent of the workforce and perform critical work for the state, economy and civil society, although the precise details of that work and the conditions under which it is performed have clearly changed over time, and such changes will inevitably continue. Change is what teachers are *engaged* in with students. Put simply, change is the outcome of their labour. Teachers also *experience* change, not only as daily events but as disruptions to the broader patterns that come to define who they are and their life in classrooms and schools.

Teaching as an occupation is important for other reasons. Historically, it has been an important avenue of social mobility and employment for working- and middle-class (typically white) women, although claims to being a legitimate 'profession' have, over the long haul, largely been mediated and marginalized by both gender and race. Any major policy change directed at teachers as an occupational group, and in particular the contexts and conditions under which teachers work, must surely be an important concern of those scholars interested in labour issues, in the restructuring of the professions in modern societies, in women's work and in the analysis of education.

At one level, teachers' work and their workplaces have an enduring quality, epitomised, for example, in the image of a single (often female) teacher working with a classroom full of students with its familiar organisation of space and its disciplinary assumptions. Aside from changes in government nomenclature and the length of the school week, Miss McGuire's contract with the government of Quebec, Canada, dated June 1, 1880 (Danylewycz and Prentice 1988, 61), could very well have been written more than a century later: in 1990. Danylewycz and Prentice record how Miss McGuire, as a schoolmistress in District School 13, had agreed to:

> ... exercise an efficient supervision over the pupils attending the school; to teach such subjects as are authorised and to make use only of duly approved school books; to fill up all blank forms which may be sent her by the Department of Public Instruction, the Inspectors or Commissioners; to keep all registers required; to preserve amongst the archives of the school such copy books and other works of the pupils which she may be ordered to put aside; to keep the school rooms in good order and not to allow them to be used for any other purpose without permission to that effect; to follow such rules as may be established for discipline and punishment; to preserve carefully the *Journal of Education:* in a word to fulfill all the duties of a good teacher; to hold school every day, except on Sundays, and festivals and on the holidays authorised by the Commissioners or granted by proper authority.

While there has, over time, clearly been considerable weakening in the moral attitudes that have constructed 'the good teacher', it has, nonetheless, continually struck me that the outward appearance and the sense of familiarity of teachers teaching, like Miss McGuire, tends to conceal what appear to be quite fundamental transformations in the nature of their work. One reason for this occlusion lies with teachers themselves; in the fact they are (though not in any intended way) complicit in this process by maintaining the view that they can lock the door on change. Not only will it be business as usual, but, many assert—*plus ça change, plus c'est la meme chôse!*

Such a view from teachers is hardly surprising. Not only is it difficult for teachers to stand back from the daily events that define their classroom work, but in a very real sense, teachers remain committed to a notion of occupational autonomy. Closing the classroom door on the intrusions of the outside world is, for teachers, symbolic. It is the exercise of organisational power—the ability to control one's labour and the stuff of professionalism—a claim that runs the long and jagged vein of teachers' occupational history, particularly since the mid-19th century.

Controlling the terms and conditions of their labour has never been a straightforward nor, indeed, unitary process for teachers. Rather, the nature of teachers' work and their class location has been the outcome of a history of struggles which has been shaped by the politics of social class, gender and race, and which continues in myriad (albeit different) ways today. Accounts of teacher activism by writers such as Clifford (1975), Lawn (1987), Urban (1989) and Fraser (1989), among others, reveal the courage and commitment of groups of teachers as they sought to progress an agenda for change around conditions of work, pay and equity. Fraser (1989, 133), for example, reveals in wonderful detail a fascinating exchange in 1907 in New York between the Association of Men Teachers and Principals and feminist campaigners, spearheaded by Grace Strachan, over gender equity in the salary scales. The Association asserted not only that teacher salaries should be driven by market forces, and that wages for male teachers should be higher than for females to attract males into teaching for the purpose of providing male role models, but also added (not at all glibly) that it would not be good for women teachers to be paid the same as men as it would make them a celibate class who would ostensibly not need to marry! Addressing an audience of female teachers in reply, Strachan retorted:

> I am sure that we all agree that men who are men will be welcome as teachers in our public schools to serve as models for our boys; but, I believe also, that you will agree with me that the man who believes that it would be unmanly to pay his sister the same salary as is paid to him when she does the same work is not the type of man we want in our public schools, is not the sort of man we want our sons and daughters to imitate (Fraser 1989, 133).

Nearly a century later, it might appear—at least in many countries— that female teachers had won the battle for pay equity with males, and that there remained few differences between teachers. However, the divisions between teachers, and indeed their coherence as a social class, are often concealed by a complex system of stratification, not only separating elementary/primary (in many cases, largely female) teachers from secondary and early childhood teachers, but also disguising the social relations of gender and race, and teachers' location and relative power within the organisational hierarchy of schooling. Further, and equally important, any amelioration in the differences and divisions between

teachers is never secure. Rather, as the states manoeuvre toward the introduction of individual performance pay for teachers, teachers will seek
to secure their status within the community and their position in the marketplace in new and different ways.

The genesis of this book arose from an attempt to better understand
teachers' work at the end of the 20th century, in particular how and in
what ways teachers' work had changed following the demise of the post-
war settlement in the early 1970s and the imminent collapse of teachers'
professional project. However, as the project progressed, I became
acutely aware of the need to develop a more rigorous set of tools in order
to undertake this task. As Basil Bernstein (1996, 17) has noted, "[S]ocio-
logical theory is very long on metatheory and very short on specific principles of description". I agree with Bernstein on this, though I would
hope to hold onto and link particular types of metatheory to more carefully developed principles of description. In relation to mapping the
changing nature of teachers' work, though educational sociologists have
drawn upon and developed particular approaches, we are still some way
from being able to develop specific principles and descriptive categories
that enable us to undertake more systematic investigations.

To begin this task of theorising the changing nature of teachers'
work and teachers as a class of workers over time, I needed a way of
thinking about change itself, over time and across space. While the daily
events that define teachers' work are important, I was first interested in
understanding the underlying social, political and economic conditions
that gave rise to those events and practises in the first place. Second, if I
were to describe and understand the nature of the continuities, disconti-
nuities and changes in the nature of teachers' work and their social class
location over time—like the Miss McGuires of the teaching profession—then I would need to isolate the essential aspects that shape teachers' labour to begin with, and to explore how, why, under what conditions
and with what outcomes these things change. Finally, though the broad
features of teachers' work might appear similar and different across nations, I wanted to understand the conditions that gave rise to those similarities and differences. This meant developing an approach that went
beyond a comparison of broad systems and superficial similarities and
differences to understanding what gave rise to these systems in the first
place. This would have to include the part that teachers' own struggles,
like those of Grace Strachan (Fraser 1989, 133) outlined above, played in
this difference. The intention of this chapter is to sketch out some of the
key ideas that underpin the analytical approach I have developed to deal

with each of the tasks outlined above. I have envisaged this process much like a building: sketching the design, laying the foundations, building the broad structure, filling in the detail, reviewing the foundations and so on. Like any architectural project, each layer of that process is dependent upon the others. As a result, the strength of the foundations is constantly put to the test with the weight of new evidence, new conditions and new ideas.

In this book I lay out and operationalise a theoretical framework that enables us to map the consequences for teachers of their changing relationship to the state, the economy and civil society over time and in different places. This clearly is a major project and for that reason *A Class Act: Changing Teachers' Work, Globalisation and the State* must be seen as a preliminary attempt in that direction. Nonetheless, I hope that these new lines of investigation will open up new opportunities for research on teachers and new debates.

PLUS ÇA CHANGE, PLUS C'EST LA MÊME CHOSE?

A quick glance at the social indicators on teachers suggests that though we might like to believe that the more things change the more they stay the same, this does not hold true for teachers and their work. Teachers in the 1990s—across a range of countries and in comparison with their counterparts in the 1970s—are paid in some countries significantly less, work longer hours over the week (International Labour Organisation [ILO] 1996), have less security of tenure, experience increasingly difficult working conditions, have less control over the work they do and lower social status within the community. At the same time in some countries teachers' union membership has increased, despite a trend in the other direction for labour generally (Robertson and Chadbourne 1998). Furthermore, in New Zealand, for example, where teachers have experienced the sharpest end of the neoliberal experiment, teachers' associations are foremost among remaining unions to continue to represent the collective interests of workers. These *effects* on teachers provide some clues as to the precise changes in the patterning of their work. However, it ought not be inferred that teachers' changed fortunes in the 1990s represent their peripheral importance to the state and its interests. Rather, it is precisely because of teachers' importance to the work of the modern state that their work is of concern. The state has placed teachers, as producers of new forms of labour, social stability and political legitimacy yet with their own power to reason and ability to organise politically on a large scale, at the centre of state restructuring. However, focusing only on the various manifestations of the effects of restructuring on teachers' existing workplaces inevitably leads to what Robert Cox (in Cox and Sinclair 1996, 88–89) has called 'problem solving theory'. *Problem solving theory* refers to those approaches to the social world as if social practises and social institutions can be understood as discrete and unconnected events. Because problem solving theory looks at phenomena in isolation, it fails to link the manifestations of social relations (social practises) to underlying causes, and contingent conditions and contexts. The point is, however, how do we move beyond a problem solving theory approach to understanding the complex changes taking place in teachers' work and their workplaces today?

In *A Class Act: Changing Teachers' Work, Globalisation and the State* I develop an analysis that takes seriously the need to locate teachers and their work within wider social formations and their underlying social relations. In order to do this I combine a number of mutually sympathetic theoretical approaches derived largely from neo-Marxist theory with its emphasis upon historical and material forces, structures and agency (cf., Cox and Sinclair 1996). I also draw upon the work of the regulation theorists (Aglietta 1979; Lipietz 1992; Boyer 1990; Jessop 1993) who have sought to articulate a relationship between the complex and dynamic interrelation between forms of economic development, nationally specific institutional structures and social relationships. Though I will have a lot more to say about regulation theory as a framework for analysing the changing relationship between teachers and the state in chapter 2, I concur with David Harvey (1990, 22) when he notes the value of this approach is that it focuses our attention on "the complex interrelations, habits, political practises, and cultural forms that allow a highly dynamic, and consequently unstable, capitalist system to acquire sufficient semblance of order to function coherently at least for a certain period of time". This clearly and inevitably has consequences for teachers and their work in modern capitalist economies.

In the book I examine in detail two settlements: laissez-faire liberalism 1850–1900, Keynesian welfare statism 1945–1970, and sketch out the conditions and emerging architecture of the 'competitive contractual state settlement' (Dale and Robertson 1998) which we tentatively propose is replacing Keynesian welfare statism. This new settlement, framed by the politics of globalisation and regionalisation, is marked by a fundamental remaking of structures and relationships between individuals, civil society, the state and the economy. These are not confined to the education sector; rather, they involve all levels within a social formation from the global and local to the self. This new social settlement is a complex and highly mediated relationship between what I have rhetorically called 'fast capitalism' and new social and state structures. This involves teachers in schools in a new multi-level set of politics which challenges notions of local community, traditional conceptions of professional service and altruism, teachers' privileged knowledge, and forms of bureaucratic organisation.

These challenges are not confined to one country. Though acknowledging that we must be attentive to the specifics of local difference, there is a remarkable degree of similarity across a number of countries in the patterns of change that arise from the pressure for states to adapt to what states themselves describe as 'global realities'. One line of analysis might be to accept the theoretical arguments presented by John Meyer and his colleagues (cf., 1979; 1992; 1997) which Dale (forthcoming) has described as "a common world educational culture" perspective. In this view the activities of states are shaped by a dominant world ideology based upon universal norms and culture. Such a perspective, while useful, is confined to isolating the broad knowledge categories that define schooling. As I have already suggested, I am interested in more than the broad categories that define the knowledge upon which teachers labour. Moreover, I believe that we need to be able to describe not just the knowledge categories on which teachers labour, but how they labour, under which conditions and with which outcomes The perspective that informs my own analysis in this book views patterns of similarity (and differences) in teachers' labour within and across nation states as arising from the changing nature of the capitalist economy as a driving force of globalisation and which seeks to establish its effects, though highly mediated, on education systems (cf., Cox and Sinclair 1996; Dale [forthcoming]). This latter conception involves political struggle over meaning and affect. As Philip Cerny has recently observed, globalisation is also a political phenomenon that operates at a number of levels, with the result that "the shaping of the playing field of politics itself is increasingly determined not within insulated units, i.e., relatively autonomous and hierarchically organised structures called states; rather it derives from a complex congeries of multi-level playing fields, above and across, as well as within, state boundaries" (1997, 253).

CRITICAL THEORY AND CHANGE

Change can be understood as comprising three levels of experience: (1) the world of events, (2) conjunctural time, and (3) the *"longue duree"*

(Braudel 1994). All three levels of time/space experience are necessarily central to this book. The experience of change at the level of the *world of events* refers to the day-to-day changes that affect teachers directly as individuals. Describing change at this level involves the systematic collection of 'events'. These changes and continuities can be documented, interpreted and acted upon. The focus here is on describing what it is that teachers do, how they manage and cope with the complexities of classroom and staff-room life, and so on. By implication, an examination of changing teachers' work focuses our attention on how teachers cope with, manage, resist or transform the changes taking place around them.

In the main, the continuities and changes in those 'events' which make up teachers' work tend to be theorised within a *problem-solving* framework. The social world of the teachers is conceived as if it were relatively fixed—like a continuing present. This mode of reasoning suggests that "with respect to essentials, the future will always be like the past" (Cox and Sinclair 1996, 92). Problems that emerge to be solved are the result of inadequate solutions to problems within the system. For example, teachers' isolation might be understood as the result of the lack of collegial structures, while problems of school effectiveness might be viewed as arising from problems of school leadership or, alternatively, the lack of clearly stated learning objectives for students. Clearly these 'events' matter and have an impact on teachers' work. However, looking at them in isolation provides little theoretical leverage as to why teachers' work is organised in the way in which it is, or indeed why it is reorganised in particular ways. On the other hand, a *critical theory approach* according to Robert Cox (op. cit.) locates the world of events within a wider historical, political and social setting, and asks, What are the wider social relations and frameworks that give rise to particular practises and events? As already suggested, at one level such a framework can be viewed as an historical structure or settlement—a particular combination of thought patterns, material conditions and human institutions which have a certain coherence among its elements. These structures do not predetermine actions; rather, they constitute the framework within which actions are shaped and take place.

Historical structures can be linked to *conjunctural time,* for instance, as settlements that come to define a social formation for an extended period of time—it is the history of gentle and not so gentle rhythms that may last for a period of several decades or more, as in the Keynesian Welfare State settlement. Given that I will have a great deal to say about settlements in the following chapters I will limit my remarks here to suggesting that this is something of what Gramsci had in mind when he defined a particular period of time as an historic bloc: "a unity between nature and spirit (structure and superstructure), a unity of opposites and of distincts" (1971, 137). Beyond a notion of conjunctural time, there is the *longue duree* covering a century or more and which focuses on the broadest of patterns and structures. It is useful to see teachers' work against a longer canvas in time in order to understand better the enduring features of teachers' labour over the long haul. In this book I work across all of these three levels of time experience. Beginning in the 1850s, I explore teachers' increasingly formal and ongoing relationship with the state, tracing the detail of this relationship in two illustrative country studies. Inside this broader framework I examine the detail of two social settlements and their crisis and transition years, which are central to understanding the broad features of teachers' work. These periods can be viewed separately as settlements that have their own internal dynamic; in combination and in contrasting countries they chart the fortunes for teachers against the backdrop of the changing relationships between the state, economy and civil society. Over time, they describe the broad patterning of teachers' labour as well as the enduring and disrupted features of schooling life.

PHILOSOPHICAL REALISM AS METHODOLOGY

So far I have argued for the importance of a critical theory approach to the analysis of teachers' labour, largely because it takes seriously the social relations arising within a system of capitalist production and patriarchy and the ways these are central to understanding teachers' work. However, while a critical theory approach gives us some clue as to what might form the basis of critique (i.e., by examining the complex and contradictory relationship between teachers and the state), it is little more than a set of signposts to what might constitute an adequate *methodology* for analysing the causes, underlying conditions and the consequences of such changes. Roy Bhaskar's work on what he calls scientific realism (1975) and which others have called critical realism bridges that gap. Scientific realism became influential as a possible solution to the theoretical problems raised by the critique of positivism—'realism' directs attention not only to events but also to the underlying processes and mechanisms which produce them (cf., Bhaskar 1975, 1986; Sayer 1992).

According to Bhaskar (1975), to base one's analysis on the constant conjunction of events is to conflate three domains: (1) the *empirical—*

consisting of experiences and sense impressions, (2) the *actual*—consisting of events, and (3) the *real,* which consists of entities and structures that produce events. Ernest House usefully summarises Bhaskar's position for us:

> Events themselves are not the ultimate focus of scientific analysis. Rather events are to be explained by examining the causal-structures that produce the events, and events are produced by complex interactions of a multitude of underlying causal entities. Reality consists not only of what we can see but also of the underlying causal entities that are not always directly discernible. Reality, then, is stratified. Events are explained by underlying structures which may be explained eventually by other structures at still greater levels. Hence the process of scientific discovery is continuous (1991, 4).

According to Bagguley et al., the value of realist models of the social world is that they ". . . distinguish between relatively enduring social entities which have causal properties, and specific, contingent entities to which the social entities give rise" (1990, 3). The relationships between causal entities are highly complex, however, in that the *realisation* of the causal entities or properties is not guaranteed. Rather, realisation, their partial realisation, or indeed the blocking of their realisation, is highly dependent on other properties. Bagguley (ibid.) continues: "The way in which empirical phenomena arise, then, reflects the intricate relations

Table I.1 Realism and Research

Domain	Focus	
Empirical	Experiences and Sense Impressions	
Actual	Events	Problem solving theory
Real	Entities and structures	critical theory

between entities, the mutual realisation, part-realisation or blocking of their causal powers". The emphasis is on the contingency of the realisation of particular causal powers. In practise, this means that empirical accounts of class structure must be developed within a framework that is multi-dimensional.

Realism is a powerful methodology for examining the social world of teachers' work. A central idea within realism is that the regularity model is replaced with one in which objects and social relations have causal powers and which are transformed over time. For instance, and as I argue in Chapter 2 where I develop a framework for exploring the relationship between teachers and class, social class (viewed as a configuration of assets) has causal properties that may be realised in particular events or social entities. A second key idea within realism is that the world is differentiated and stratified, consisting not only of events, but objects (including structures) which have powers and liabilities capable of generating events. For instance, the gendered division of labour and the reality of social classes give rise to a particular patterning of events over time. Realism, like critical theory, thus directs our attention not only to events but to the underlying processes and mechanisms that produce them. This gives us a much more powerful way of thinking about the complex interrelation between *causal entities* such as class, *contexts and contingent condition* such as the highly gendered nature of teachers' work and Keynesian ideas, and *forms of realisation* or *events* such as teachers' market or status positions. The value of realist models of the social world is that they enable us to "distinguish between relatively enduring social entities which have causal properties and specific contingent entities to which the social entities give rise" (Bagguley et al. 1990, 3). Most important, the relationships between causal entities are highly complex and the realisation of the causal entities or properties is not guaranteed.

CRITICAL REALISM AND TEACHERS' LABOUR

Combining critical theory with a realist methodology for understanding teachers' work results in several things that I would like to spell out briefly. The first is that the world of events in teachers' work world must be connected to 'conjunctural time', and as Bourdieu observes (1996), accumulated history. This is not to suggest that history itself is an inevitable accumulation of events; rather, that history is a way of recording and understanding particular sets of political, economic and social relationships at particular times and in particular settings and how these are connected through time. This sinewy vein of path dependency thus sets limits on new possibilities and new institutional structures.

Second, critical realism takes the view that capital accumulation both creates and is dependent upon the production and reproduction of the social relations of capitalism and patriarchy over time. The modern state, as collective capitalist and as guarantor of the long-term interests of capital and patriarchy, is central in this process (Poulantzas 1978). Throughout the book, I examine the way in which this interdependent and exploitative relationship between teachers as members of a social class, and social classes and groups is reproduced through forms of cultural and social capital.

Third, critical realism directs our attention to the resources that teachers seek to utilise and make claim to. Hogan (1996, 132–3) calls these potential resources "a bundle of market capacities". A 'bundle' alerts us to the fact that there is more than one resource that might be used. 'Capacities' suggests that such resources are only potential and that their realisation will only take place through an agent though mediated by particular conditions. Finally, 'market' highlights the twin notions of value and exchange. I will refer to this bundle of market capacities for teachers as 'assets'. I will argue that the history of teachers' work is a history of struggle with the state over the realisation of this bundle of class assets. It is, therefore, a history of teachers' class struggle. Much of the terrain of this struggle is both framed and shaped by the state. The state both employs teachers and provides education. This bundle of market capacities for teachers, as for all workers, is made up of four aspects: *economic,* such as income or housing; *cultural,* such as specialist knowledge and expertise; *social,* such as networks, unions and other forms of association; and *organisational,* for instance, position within the bureaucracy. However, what counts as an asset changes over time. It is both the object of and outcome of struggle. These struggles by teachers take place under particular material conditions and societal settings. This is not to propose a deterministic account of change and how it occurs. Rather, it is dependent upon a strong theory of agency. It involves struggle over material and symbolic resources. For teachers this has historically included their economic position (income, security), position in the division of labour, the precise nature of their work (curriculum, assessment and pedagogy), the conditions under which that work is carried out, and their social status.

Fourth, a critical realist framework proposes that understanding the changing nature of teachers' work requires us to examine the conditions and contexts that give rise to teachers as a class of workers as well as the work that teachers do. Further, this must be located historically and over time in order to understand more precisely the shifting terrain on which that struggle takes place as well as to specify the consequences for teachers.

Fifth, given the progressive incorporation of teachers into the state through various combinations of state funding, provision and regulation over this century, any systematic analysis of the changing nature of teachers' work requires us to explore both the dynamic and changing nature of the relationship between the state, economy and civil society as well as grasp the way the state both mediates and is transformed by social and political change. As Colin Hay has recently observed, this also means the way in which "social change itself becomes reflected in transformations in the structures, boundaries and responsibilities of the state" (1996, 26). For example, the ability of teachers in England in the 1920s to mobilise with other labour groups around a socialist agenda led to important transformations within the state and eventually to the way in which teachers were regulated.

Finally, critical realism linked to regulation theory encourages us to examine the way in which relationships between the state, economy and civil society fought out during the period of crisis and transition prior to a settlement become institutionalised as an architecture of compromises and a framework for consensus. This broad architecture can be referred to as a *social settlement;* a stabilised set of structures, practises and modes of calculation which is dependent upon a 'concordat' between capital and labour, the efficient working of a particular model of economic development and the regulation of social and political life within the social formation. All settlements, however, are impermanent because within social formations settlements are vulnerable to the contradictions embedded within capitalist modes of production and the institutional structures and social relations that shape its regulatory architecture.

THIS BOOK

The arguments in this book are advanced in three sections. *Part 1, Conceptual Contours*, is largely theoretical and develops the foundations for the arguments advanced in the book. Chapter 1 begins by arguing that class is a viable conceptual tool for understanding teachers' labour in the 1990s. The concept of class has come under scrutiny in the past two decades largely as a result of the profound economic, political and intellectual changes that have occurred globally. While acknowledging that there have been problems with class theory, in this chapter I set out to build on the work of Erik Olin Wright (1985), Lash and Urry (1987), Lockwood (1958) and Savage et al. (1992), and outline a framework for conceptualising class which I then use to locate teachers as class actors. I argue that class location is determined by the four causal assets which in turn shape class consciousness. By mapping the consequences of the links between how teachers experience the social world and contingent conditions which shape that world, we are able to plot teachers' changing fortunes in broad terms and in particular historical and societal contexts. I argue that class is a critical feature of the terrain of struggle for teachers and is central to our understanding of the dynamics which shape the on-going politics of teachers' work. In Chapter 2 I combine several theoretical approaches to examine education, teachers' labour and social settlements. A number of levels of analysis are identified—from the local to the global—which are central to a systematic investigation of the contexts and conditions which shape the nature of teachers' work at a particular historical juncture. I draw explicitly upon the work of the regulation school to focus attention upon the complex and dynamic interrelation between forms of economic development, nationally specific institutional structures and social relationships. In the final section of this chapter, I review the adequacy of Braverman's (1974) 'proletarianization thesis' for understanding teachers' labour and suggest that, while this approach has been a means of viewing teachers' labour more critically, there are important questions that need to be raised as to its adequacy.

Part 2, Changing Contexts, operationalises the theoretical frameworks and tools developed in Part 1 through an illustrative analysis of teachers' work in two countries, America and England. Chapters 3 and 4 examine, respectively, the laissez-faire liberal settlement (1850–1900) and the Keynesian welfare state settlement (1945–1970s) in each country. Both these periods are punctuated by crises. Here I argue that these 'crisis' or 'transition' years are highly political, with intense pressure to restore the stability and unity of the accumulation process. It is also a period where the institutional structures and practices, customs and networks, institutional compromises, rules of conduct and laws are challenged and reworked. In these two chapters I examine teachers' changing market, work and status situations as they mobilise particular assets in the pursuit of their professional project.

Part 3, Contemporary Change, examines teachers' work in the 1990s. Chapter 5 begins by suggesting that 'fast capitalism'—a response to the dynamics of globalisation—has resulted in a changing politics of production and consumption. This new set of conditions has created spaces for new sets of what I broadly term 'post-Fordist' discourses about how teachers' workplaces should be restructured. Here I outline the underlying assumptions of these discourses and argue that each offers a very different analysis of society and projects a very different future. In particular, I explore the different opportunities each discourse offers for teachers as an occupational group to realise material, cultural, organisational and social assets. In Chapter 7 I examine the teacher-state-market relationship in order to understand more precisely how the ideology of the market has been used by the state as a means of disembedding the institutional structures and practises that were central to the organisation of teachers' work as welfare state professionals in the post-war years. In Chapter 8, under the heading 'fast schools', I examine the ways in which this new economic and political framework makes its appearance in teachers' work through a new set of production and consumption relations: the co-option of schools to the competitive state project; the reorganisation of schools based upon new administrative and contractual relationships; fostering school/corporate sector relationships; reconceptualising schools as lifestyle choices within the marketplace; and recasting the identity of students and teachers in the new knowledge-information world. All represent a significant change in conditions for teachers and their work.

In a brief concluding chapter, *Critical Realities Reviewed*, I bring together the key contextual elements of the contemporary landscape for teachers and their work and suggest that in important ways and in a number of countries there has been a significant and some might argue deliberate erosion of teachers' collective ability to realise economic, cultural and organisational assets. The professional project of teachers has increasingly been reshaped by the state to incorporate the sentiments of the new market-based ideology proposed by various strains of neoliberalism. There is already evidence that particular groups of individual teachers will benefit from this project of individualised market-based professionalism. However, the end result of this will be to fracture and potentially undermine the collective mobility project of teachers as a social class and as a profession, through limiting the realisation of class assets.

PART I

Conceptual Contours

CHAPTER 1

Teachers and Class: The Terrain and Stakes of Struggle

IS CLASS A VIABLE CONCEPTUAL TOOL FOR UNDERSTANDING TEACHERS' LABOUR?

In recent years the concept of class has come under increasing scrutiny as a means of explaining both the present and the past. The reasons for this, as Joyce (1995, 3) observes, lie largely in the profound economic, political and intellectual changes that mark our time. The numerical decline of the old manual or 'working class', the emergence of new forms of 'post-Fordist' production, the shift in employment and investment from production to consumption, together with the new intellectual currents centred around feminist/identity politics and the individualism of neoliberalism, have all worked to challenge the sovereignty of class and dislodge it as a fundamental analytic tool in social theory. On the one hand, the new theoretical trajectories have yielded rich insights into the nature of teachers' work, bringing to the fore the complex interplay of social forces and individual subjectivities (Middleton and May 1997). On the other hand, it has become unfashionable in academic circles to talk about class, as if class suddenly no longer mattered and the historic concerns of class theorists—such as inequality—had disappeared.

There is little doubt that there have been major theoretical problems in class theory; indeed, these issues have occupied sociologists for much of this century and the work of Marx and Weber has been extensively reinterpreted and reformulated. The challenge for theorists concerned with class analysis is how to address the multi-dimensional and permeable nature of class boundaries and relations, as well as the uncertain links that connect classes. Recent work by Erik Wright (1985; 1997) and the emergence of scientific 'realism' represented in the work of writers such as Bhaskar (1978; 1986), Sayer (1984), Lash and Urry (1987) and Savage et al. (1992) have revitalised the Marxist tradition by extending its reach with new ways of thinking about the way capitalism and class relations shape and determine outcomes in capitalist societies. Their work is central to this chapter and has been critical to my own formulation of teachers as a class and class actors. It also provides considerable scope for an assessment of the effects of the restructuring on class structure and formation. This task is particularly important if we are to comprehend fully the profound ways in which teachers' work has been transformed and also the ways in which the social and material conditions of existence as a collectivity have altered.

CLASS MATTERS

Given the fraught nature of much class analysis, as noted above, it is not surprising that the general response by many sociologists of education to questions of teachers and class is either to allocate teachers to a class arbitrarily and work forward from there or to ignore the question altogether. The difficulty with the former position is that it reduces class to little more than a label, presumably intended to explain everything but which can paradoxically explain nothing. Additionally, it offers a way of categorising teachers but does little to help in understanding the nature and significance of class for what it is that teachers do, how, under what conditions and with what consequences. Clearly, ignoring the matter of class and teachers is the least useful, largely as it unwittingly or deliberately closes off important questions about the nature of the relationships between an individual's and group's employment positions, class consciousness, social and material circumstances and other life experiences. For instance, it does not help us answer the question of how class membership shapes teachers' conceptions of themselves as workers and vice versa. Neither does it help address the question of whether teachers' class membership remains static or changes over time, and if so, under what conditions. Rather, it perpetuates the politically acceptable notion that teaching is necessarily an apolitical activity and teachers are neutral social actors. Such conceptions avoid questions of power and the ways in which teachers are implicated in the distribution of symbolic and material resources in their workplaces (Ginsburg et al. 1995, 4). As will become clear over the course of this chapter, our understandings and explanations of teachers and class matter precisely because as a social collectivity, teachers are engaged in social action and social reproduction and they do have an impact on social change. We are also able to see the effects of class in teachers' work through the way in which teachers participate in reproducing wider social relations, particularly those associated with capitalism, democracy, patriarchy and racism. At the same time we are able to record the ways in which teachers, as agents and therefore social actors, actively participate in resisting, transforming or creating discourses, practises and structures that seek to minimise or exaggerate overt exploitative behaviour.

Having decided that class matters raises further and more difficult issues—the vexed ones of how to conceptualise class and then where to locate teachers. The orthodox Marxist position has been to focus upon the two great camps that make up the class structure—capital and labour (Marx and Engels 1888). The relationship between these two opposing classes—which is essentially antagonistic—is defined as one of interdependence and therefore exploitation. Marx himself never systematically defined and elaborated the concept of class (Wright 1985, 6) but rather presented a complex picture of classes, fractions and social categories providing little by way of a set of precise concepts for "decoding rigorously the structural basis of most of those categories" (ibid. 7). Marx was sure, however, that society as a whole was moving toward greater polarisation with the two great hostile camps facing each other. However, as the record of the past one hundred years and more reveals, this tendency toward radical polarisation has not eventuated. Rather, what has emerged has been a much more complex occupational and class structure. A key element of that complexity has been the growth of professional, managerial and technical occupations. This has created new challenges for social theorists where, as Wright notes (ibid. 9), it has become more difficult to sidestep the theoretical problem of the gap between the abstract polarized concept of class relations and the complex concrete patterns of class structure, formation and struggle.

It will be helpful to our discussion of teachers as a class if we distinguish between the two core ideas within class analysis: *class structure* and *class formation*. Wright (ibid. 10) gives a succinct account of the difference, which I shall summarise for our purposes here. Class structure refers to "a set of empty places filled by individuals or families" and which "exists independently of the specific people who occupy specific positions". In that sense we can talk about the working class as an objective category that exists independent of the individuals that might occupy specific positions. Class formation, on the other hand, refers to "the formation of organised collectivities within that class structure on the basis of the interests shaped by that class structure. . . . A given class structure may be characterised by a range of possible types of class formation, varying in the extent and form of collective organisation of classes. Class-based collectivities may be organized, disorganized or reorganized within a given class structure without there necessarily being any fundamental transformation of the class structure itself" (Ibid. 10). Wright concludes: "If class structure is defined by the social relations *between* classes, class formation is defined by social relations *within* classes, social relations which forge collectivities engaged in struggle" (ibid.). We can, then, talk about classes in two ways: (1) as a class *in itself* (structure) and as a class *for itself* (agency), and (2) class as both an objective category (as in a middle class defined by its relations to the working class and to capital) and as a subjective experience (the consciousness and struggles of the middle class or fractions within it).

Much of the recent development in Marxist theory has been an attempt to bridge the theoretical gap between class structure and class formation, a gap that has become evident with the problem of the 'middle classes'. Early work had tended toward simple polarisation and toward arguing that while it might appear otherwise, these new social positions were really either part of the working class or the ruling class, creating, as Wotherspoon observes, a dichotomy between 'professionalism' and 'proletarianisation' (1996, 120). An alternative tendency, where occupational groups seem ill-fitted to either of these (such as many of the professional, managerial and service classes), was to cast them like unruly subjects into occupying a contradictory class location with a foot in both camps. The difficulty here was that one was left looking for the mechanisms by which the interests and concerns of the middle class could be attributed to a different class—for instance, that the middle class was a functionary of the ruling class. In the case of teachers, this led to early conceptualisations by writers such as Kevin Harris (1980) of teachers as lieutenants of the ruling class and agents of a larger system with no independent power, a position that he was later to refute largely for the same reasons that Connell was also to note:

> It is not surprising that teacher activists, when they encountered this writing, were taken aback. They could respond to the social radicalism that underlay social reproduction theory, the protest against social injustice conveyed by this powerful image of the conservative society. But the theory gave them nowhere to go as teachers (Connell 1995, 92).

Clearly, this particular type of framing of teachers, with little if any independent social and political power, did not sit well with the reality many teachers experienced. The alternative explanation was to argue that as a result of teachers' contradictory class location, they were less predictable agents of the system. "Such moves certainly lightened the burden of theoretically informed teachers, who now at least had room to wiggle", notes Connell, "but it did not change the fundamental logic of their situation" (ibid.).

A number of theorists have argued that the middle class is a class in and of itself, distinct from either the working or ruling classes. This new or middle class has emerged largely as a result of industrialisation and post-industrialisation (Gouldner 1979; Goldthorpe 1982, Lash and Urry 1987). They argue that the expansion of the professions and semi-professions, managers and intellectually trained labour, all point to a class that looks decidedly different from either of the existing two classes. However, it is not sufficient to argue that a class is a class for itself because this provides a convenient means of categorising particular groups with similar occupations. To study a consciousness of class, as David Lockwood (1958) notes, one must be concerned with a sense of identification with, or alienation from, a class and the way in which the social relations within that class forges a social collectivity on the basis of the interests shaped by that class structure.

It might crudely be argued that the middle class, as a formation, is a social group of people with shared levels of income and remuneration, lifestyles, cultures and political orientations. However, while these few insights are useful starting points, they do not take us too far in thinking about the distinctiveness of one class in relation to another, nor indeed what the properties are that define membership of one class rather than another. If, as Savage et al. argue, a social class is stable social collectivity (1992, 5) where class difference from other classes is rooted in particular types of exploitative relationships, then within this framework we need an account of how class might be broadly conceptualised, what might be distinctive about a middle class as a class for itself, the axis of exploitation which defines class difference and—following from that— the basis of teachers' class membership.

A REALIST FRAMEWORK FOR CLASS ANALYSIS: CAUSES AND CONDITIONS

Savage et al.'s (1992) analysis of middle-class formation draws on a wide range of empirical material to suggest how relatively stable social collectivities have emerged in contemporary Britain and provides a particularly useful starting point for this task. They develop a *realist* account of class analysis; that is, that class analysis should take place within a *realist* framework which takes seriously the conjunction of theoretical and empirical research. Scientific or critical realism sees classes as having causal powers which are then realised in the struggle with other classes. Explaining the formation of the middle class and teachers' location in that class is therefore dependent upon identifying and mapping the causal properties and distinguishing these from what we might call specific and contingent events. Realism, then, becomes a way of conceptualising the complexity of causal and contingent elements; for instance, the interactions of institutions such as the state and relations such as gender, race and class, and the way in which these work with and against each other. In the case of teachers, a realist framework enables a more sophisticated analysis of the interactions between causal and contingent elements within particular historical and social and spatial circumstances and the ways in which these combinations change over time. We are able to see, for instance, the ways in which school teaching itself (as opposed to school administration) came to be regarded as women's work and became, as Altenbaugh (1995) observes, sandwiched between the public and the private worlds of women's lives, between the experiences of home and the experiences of the classroom.

STARTING POINTS: ECONOMIC, ORGANISATIONAL AND CULTURAL ASSETS

Working within a realist methodological framework and drawing on the work of Erik Olin Wright (1985) and Pierre Bourdieu (1984), Savage et al. (1992) posit that middle-class formation in Britain is based around what they term three causal entities or assets: *property, bureaucracy* and *culture*. Each of these three assets can be defined in terms of an axis of exploitation; they depend in each case upon the capacity of the asset holders to deprive others of equal access to that asset. These causal entities have different values; property assets are the most powerful given the possibility of their being stored and therefore passed on. It is pertinent here to rehearse Wright's argument because of its centrality to that of Savage et al.'s argument.

In his book *Classes*, Wright argues there are three main types of exploitative assets around which classes are based: *property, organisation* and *skills*. Property follows the Marxist principle that economic assets are based around the ownership of the means of production and are central to enabling some classes (bourgeoisie and petite bourgeoisie) to exploit other classes (proletariat). Wright then proceeds to identify two further assets crucial to understanding class formation: *organisation* and *skill*.

The concept of organisation assets is used by Wright to point to the significance of power relations *within* organisations as a major axis of class formation. School managers, administrators and teachers working in bureaucratic organisations, for instance, use their hierarchical position of power to secure advantages for themselves in relation to their subordinates within the same organisation. In other words, organisations are vehicles and sites for power struggles and relationships. Rather than being seen as the 'natural' way of organising people, as in Weberian social theory (for clearly there are other forms of organisation, including networks), this particular perspective argues that organisations embody particular types of power relations and inequalities. Bidwell, Frank and Quiroz (1997), for instance, provide evidence to show how particular aspects which define the nature of schools, such as size and client power, can be correlated with a particular configuration of workplace controls over teachers and resultant power relations. The critical point to be made here is that the value of the asset is significant to the particular organisation; that is to say, they are organisation-specific. As a result, the value of organisation assets is less likely (though not necessarily) to be recognised at a wider level, for instance through the credentialling system.

Teachers engage in a particular form of labour which involves students (see Connell's [1995] discussion of labour). It takes place alongside other teachers, is largely managed by school administrators, and is regulated by numerous agencies. Within this framework, teachers' organisational relationship to other workers within the lower ranks of the division of labour (such as the school custodian, the school secretary, the working class in general or unpaid labourers in schools such as mothers), can be viewed as objectively exploitative and as examples of where they have interests that are opposed to workers in general. Yet teachers labour under particular sets of conditions, including having their work administered by an ascending and rigid hierarchy of patriarchal authority—the subject head, the school principal, the district superintendent and so on. Teachers are also exploited by a range of other more invisible mechanisms; for instance, when their labour is incorporated into curriculum materials (see Apple 1982; 1993), or where the nature of the curriculum is determined by groups with a vested interest in the development of a particular perspective, or in profit, or in silencing the voice of the teacher within the classroom. In such instances, being excluded from ownership of the means of production and alienated from their labour, teachers can best be described as having similar interests to workers in general.

Wright's third asset is based around *skill*. Wright argues that skill takes two forms: 'credentialism', which limits the number of people able to exercise the use of particular skills, thus influencing wages; and 'natural talent'—as in a gifted singer—which can be used to secure increased income. In Wright's terms, professional workers, like teachers or lawyers, rely on skill assets which can, under particular circumstances, be realised to give them a privileged position when the profession is able to secure professional closure (Parkin 1974) and the attribution of monopoly of competence from the state (Larson 1977).

Wright's conceptualisation of the assets involved in class formation takes us a considerable distance in being able to establish the causal powers of different class assets, and in particular the way in which wage earners such as teachers might be distinguished by the two subordinate relations of exploitation characteristic of capitalistic societies—organisation and skill/credential assets. For instance, organisational assets—because they involve a particular form of exploitation—place super-ordinates such as school principals in an exploitative relationship to subordinates such as teachers. The crucial point here is that exploitation in organisations is context-specific; that is to say, it ties the exploiter to the particular organisation or institution involved. Because the assets cannot be stored outside the organisational context, it does not allow class formation as readily as in the case of the ownership of property. Teachers who leave the profession, for instance, cannot take their organisational assets with them. Teachers also depend upon the state for the attestation of 'skill'; the attestation also provides evidence for other employers that the skill/credential is not wholly occupationally specific. Teaching credentials, for example, are a cultural asset in that they may be used as 'evidence' of 'people management skills' enabling teachers to move into a range of service industries outside of teaching.

Wright's conceptualisation enables us to see how positions within organisations and the ownership of particular skills/credentials may result in contradictory interests with respect to the primary forms of class struggle within a social formation. On the one hand, like workers, teachers are excluded from ownership of the means of production; on the other, teachers have interests opposed to the worker because of the effective control over organisation and skill assets. This reconceptualisation of the middle class also means that, as Wright notes (1985, 89), "it is no longer axiomatic that the proletariat is the unique or even universally the central rival to the capitalist class for class power in capitalist society. There are other class forces within capitalism that have the potential to pose an alternative to capitalism". This gives some conceptual space to Gouldner's (1979) argument that a third—or new class—has emerged with its own distinctive consciousness. I will return to this argument in Chapter 2, for it has important things to say about the nature of teachers' intellectual work during the post-war period in England.

A further important point is that conceptualising class in this way suggests that the class assets of a particular occupational group, such as teachers, will vary over time and will depend upon the particular combinations of exploitation relations within a given society. As I will argue in the following chapters, the erosion of the traditional procedural bureaucracy with its hierarchical relations, the attempt to limit the extent to which credentials are used as a means of determining selected entry to the profession and the attempt to routinise and codify teachers' work create the conditions for a new configuration of assets in middle-class formation.

CULTURAL CAPITAL AS A CULTURAL ASSET

However, if we return to the earlier proposition—that social classes are stable social collectivities rooted in particular types of exploitative relationships—Wright's concept of skill assets presents us with a major empirical and theoretical problem, largely as it is not easy to see how a person with skills—such as a professional—*exploits* the unskilled. That is, as Savage et al. note (1992, 16), it is not the skill itself—such as the skill of the teacher to teach reading—but rather the cultural fields that legitimise particular types of skills. In particular, it is the ability to exclude others from that field through credentials and other forms of closure that is likely to give this asset its value. Savage et al. turn to Pierre Bourdieu (1984) and his work on 'cultural capital' as a means of overcoming the problems posed by Wright's third category. Cultural capital, they argue, is a cultural asset; it has its own value and can be converted into social power independent of income. Cultural capital is based on the contested legitimation of cultural forms, such as particular types of taste, experience and knowledge where, as Savage et al. propose (1992, 16), it is a process through which mutually antagonistic classes are formed as each attempts to legitimise its own culture. Cultural assets thus serve to buttress and perpetuate structures of power and advantage. Teachers both embody and transmit the aptitudes and knowledge which represent legitimate culture. Like other professionals, they are also able to store cultural assets in their bodies (e.g., form of dress, walk, speech) and their mind (e.g., way of thinking, speech patterns), all of which can be both passed on to their offspring as well as being crucial in reproducing the social relations of the social formation.

There has been a considerable body of work in the social theory of education applying Bourdieu's notion of cultural capital. Theorists build on his argument that educational institutions are not socially neutral but rather are part of a larger universe of symbolic institutions that reproduce existing power relations. In other words, the culture that is transmitted and rewarded by the educational system reflects the culture of the dominant class. Thus, while teachers labour with students, as we have already noted, they labour on the curriculum in particular settings, which reinforces and rewards particular types of linguistic competence, authority relations and curricular knowledge (Bernstein 1996). Children from more privileged social and cultural backgrounds enter schools with sets of cultural resources that enable them either to feel familiar with or to 'decode' the dominant culture of schooling.

There are two crucial points here in respect of teachers' cultural assets. First, teachers as an occupational group possess a particular level of cultural capital largely as this capital has been objectified as a form of academic qualification which they have been able to convert into some form of economic capital (through the monetary value of a given academic capital). This enables teachers to use this cultural capital as an immediate form of exchange, or as Gouldner has argued (1979), to use that knowledge to further their own social projects as a form of class legitimacy (equity, welfarism, education as a public good) as well as to derive the material or economic benefits as well (state-employed professionals). I will develop Gouldner's argument in Chapter 2 when I examine the theoretical resources that have been used to explain teachers' work, for it is important to our thinking about the particular moral and political basis from which teachers' collective social consciousness and power arose during the post-war period. Second, by actively or uncritically participating in a system that privileges and legitimates particular knowledge forms and practises, teachers engage in what Bourdieu calls *symbolic violence*. In other words, we can now argue that the axis of exploitation in relation to cultural assets is defined by the way in which they can be used in particular organisational, institutional and social settings to reap particular types of economic rewards.

TAKING THE ANALYSIS FURTHER: SOCIAL CAPITAL AND SOCIAL ASSETS IN CLASS FORMATION

So far we have argued, following Wright and Savage, that class formation can be seen as arising from the ability to acquire and convert particular types of assets: economic, organisational and cultural. In the case of teachers, as members of the middle class, we can use this framework to examine the ways in which teachers convert cultural capital into organisational and economic assets through which they 'objectively' exploit those who do not possess such cultural capital.

I want to take the analysis a little further and suggest that there is a fourth type of asset that is ignored by Savage et al. and Wright—social assets—that is crucial to understanding class formation. The work of Bourdieu is again fruitful in this regard. Bourdieu (1997) argues that *social capital* is an important form of capital. Social capital is defined as "the aggregate of the actual or potential resources which are linked to possession of a durable network of more or less institutionalised relationships of mutual acquaintance and recognition—in other words—membership in a group—which provides each of its members with the backing of collectively owned capital, a 'credential' which entitles them to credit, in the various senses of the word" (1986, 248). We can, I believe, call social capital a *social asset*. Social assets consist of social obligations or 'connections' that are able to facilitate the realisation or achievement of certain ends that would be unattainable in its absence.

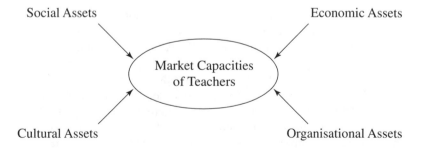

Social Assets   Economic Assets

Market Capacities of Teachers

Cultural Assets   Organisational Assets

Social assets for teachers, as institutionalised social relationships, may take a number of forms: (1) particular institutional arrangements such as teachers' unions or subject associations; (2) sets of obligations like the old school tie network; (3) information channels, for instance electronic networks; and (4) norms and sanctions, as in the ethic of professionalism for teachers and what it implies in particular settings. Social assets also operate along an axis of exploitation. Like credentials, they are what Hirsch (1977) calls a positional good; that is to say, their value depends as much on others not having them as on the possession itself. Having a network open to all 'users' would not provide any particular advantage to any group as presumably all who want to can access the network and derive precisely the same sort of information or benefit from that network. In the same way, too, the benefits of membership in a teacher union are only available to those who are 'entitled' to membership and which could not be realised without membership—such as the weight of the collective bargaining agent as opposed to the voice of the individual. Entitlement is clearly a contested issue, as are the conditions of membership itself. Social assets are critical in class formation because they can become the means for members of that class to further or maintain their advantaged position for themselves and that advantage is only gained when others are excluded from acquiring the same information or when they are able to influence the outcome of a decision in a particular way. Hirsch (1977) notes that the value of a good or service is not entirely economic but has a social value which is shaped both by individual valuations and by the differential between those who seek access to the positional pie and those who are excluded from it. Social assets, when mobilised, can enable differential access to the various positional pies; for instance, schooling, the labour market or the social arena.

Social assets have three features. First, rather than working in isolation, they act as a 'multiplier', creating even further advantages for the holder. For instance, the research on school choice in New Zealand shows that working-class parents require particular types of information to make the optimal choice of school. Where they have that information, they are advantaged if they have particular types of cultural capital (which they are unlikely to have) to convert that preference into a choice. Second, social assets operate in institutional settings and contexts where power relations and the exercise of power is likely to be less visible; it is more personal, less formal and uncodified, and as a result takes on the appearance of mystique. As I shall argue later in the book, social assets are particularly important in being able to release the potential of network-based forms of organisation. A different and more obvious example of this occurs where schools may seek sponsorship from the corporate sector—as in the current type of market organisation of schooling—decisions taken that include some players and exclude others cannot easily be contested because both the nature of the game and its rules for realisation are no longer visible. Third, social assets can be stored and passed on, for instance where membership of a particular 'old boys' network might be passed on to the offspring, enabling them to convert that membership into some form of advantage at a later date.

REALISM AS METHODOLOGY: 'CONSEQUENCES' AND THE CONTRIBUTION OF LOCKWOOD

I now want to extend the framework developed so far with its focus on causes and conditions to include what I have called the *consequences* of teachers' class membership at a particular historical juncture; that is, a way of identifying the outcomes for teachers and their situation of the extent to which they are able to realise, as a consequence of struggle, particular configurations of assets under particular sets of contingent conditions and in particular contexts. In Bhaskar's (1978) terms, these consequences might be viewed at the level of *events*.

David Lockwood (1958), in his classic account of a white-collar occupation, offers us a way of thinking about the realisation of assets in terms of a set of outcomes or consequences; that is, the situation of the worker. Lockwood (ibid., 15–16) proposes that class situation comprises three factors: market, work and status situations which together produce a particular type of class consciousness and disposition for class action. *Market situation* refers to the economic position of the worker, source and size of income, degree of job security and opportunity for job mobility. *Work situation,* on the other hand, is the set of relationships that one is involved in at work by virtue of his or her position in the division of labour. Finally, *status situation* refers to the position of the individual in the hierarchy of prestige in the society at large. These situations—work, market and status—provide us with some clues as to how we might identify economic, cultural, organisational and social assets. That is, we are able to describe aspects of teachers' work in terms such as source and size of income (economic assets); relationships within the division of labour (cultural and organisational assets); the social status and standing of teachers within a community and nation (social and cultural assets); and the ways in which these combine at particular points in time, for particular groups of teachers, in particular places. An important aspect of Lockwood's work is his elaboration of the notion of variations in view within a particular occupation arising from their class situation. These variations arise because of the way in which both individuals and groups within an occupational category come to visualise the structure of their society from the vantage point of their own milieux and how the perceptions of the larger society vary according to their experiences in the smaller society. For example, secondary teachers' perceptions of the world are quite different from those of primary teachers. We might also venture to say that urban teachers' views of society will be different than those of rural teachers. In both cases the perception of the world out there will be shaped in significant ways by the experience of the world in their milieu. This is evident among teachers (cf., Middleton and May 1997); these variations arise not only as a result of geographic milieux, but also organisational and gendered milieux.

CONCLUSION

I have argued here that a realist methodological framework enables us to develop a more complex account of teachers' class membership and class consciousness. I have also argued that four causal assets can be identified, which determine class location and which shape class formation. By mapping the linkages between causes, contingent conditions and real consequences for how teachers experience the social world, we are able plot class formation and the location of particular occupational groups within that class as a dynamic and changing process, both in broad terms and in particular historical and societal contexts. Class is a critical aspect of the terrain and stakes of struggle and is central to our understanding of the dynamics that shape both the politics of education and the nature of education politics. The changing terrain, the nature of the stakes and the material and ideological battles to be fought, won and lost are central to our understanding of the changing nature of teachers' work over the course of what Hobsbawm has more recently called *the age of extremes* (1994).

CHAPTER 2

Teachers, the State and Social Settlements

> *[The aim of the state] is always that of creating new and higher types of civilization; of adapting the 'civilization' and morality of the broadest popular masses to the necessities of the continuous development of the economic apparatus of production; hence of evolving even physically new types of humanity.*
>
> —GRAMSCI 1971, 242

SETTLEMENTS, CRISIS AND TRANSFORMATION

In the previous chapter I outlined an approach to understanding teachers as class actors where class itself is both the terrain and the stakes of struggle. This approach embraced a strong theory of agency. I argued that teachers' class interests might best be conceptualised around their struggle over the realisation of a set of assets: economic, social, cultural and organisational. I also proposed that the precise value of these assets results from the struggle between teachers and other social interests waged under particular political, economic and social conditions.

I now want to extend the line of analysis developed in the previous chapter by outlining a number of levels of analytical focus, from the global to the local, that are central to a systematic investigation of the contexts and conditions that shape the nature of teachers' work at a particular historical juncture. For this purpose, two further lines of analysis are developed in this chapter which structure the arguments developed in the rest of the book. They are centred upon (1) theorizing teachers' struggles within a framework that on the one hand examines settlements, crisis and transformation, and on the other hand sees social settlements as marked by continuity and discontinuity, similarity and difference across space, place and time; and (2) the adequacy of the key theoretical approaches that have been used to examine teachers' work in these social settlements. In order to undertake the first task, I draw upon the work of the regulation theory school, which focuses attention upon the complex and dynamic interrelation between forms of economic development, nationally specific institutional structures and social relationships. Their approach is helpful in theorising the changing nature of the relationship between teachers and the state over time. In relation to the second task, that is, reviewing the adequacy of the theoretical approaches that have been used to understand and analyse teachers' labour, I begin by quoting Robert Cox (Cox and Sinclair 1996) on the matter:

> All theories have a perspective. Perspectives derive from a position in time and space, specifically social and political time and space. . . . Of course sophisticated theory is never just the expression of a perspective. The more sophisticated a theory is, the more it reflects upon and transcends its own perspective; but the initial perspective is always contained within a theory and is relevant to its explication. There is, accordingly, no such thing as theory in itself, divorced from a standpoint in time and space (1996, 87).

The two theoretical discussions will then be drawn together to examine two distinctive social and sectoral settlements in education in Chapters 3 and 4. There I undertake an illustrative investigation of the changing nature of teachers' work within two settlements: laissez-faire liberalism (1850s to 1900s) and Fordist Keynesian state welfarism (1945–1970s).

In the final section of this chapter I address the question of how far labour process theory can provide sufficient analytic purchase over understanding the changing nature of teachers' work in different social formations and across social settlements. Using Basil Bernstein's (1996) distinction between power and control, I argue that this then enables us to distinguish the contributions of Braverman (1974) and the 'proletarianisation thesis' from that of Gouldner (1979) and the 'new class thesis' at a number of levels. The work of Gouldner and Braverman together give us much greater insight into the different and complex nature of teachers' work within and across time. My intention is not so much to set one of these theorists against the other as to cast some light on the ways in which their different positions also arise as a result of their particular locations in time and space.

REGULATION THEORY—THE
ACCUMULATION/INSTITUTION RELATION

The emergence of the regulation theory school is usually linked to the publication of Aglietta's *Theory of Capitalist Regulation* in 1979. It was followed later by a range of writers including Alain Lipietz (1992), Robert Boyer (1990) and Bob Jessop (1989; 1990; 1993). Though there are differences among these theorists, they commonly propose that capitalism has experienced a sequence of 'regimes of accumulation', each associated with a particular 'mode of regulation'. These two concepts, 'regime of accumulation' and 'mode of regulation', are key ideas within regulation theory. According to Lipietz (1992), a regime of accumulation is essentially a reproduction scheme which might operate either nationally or internationally; it involves the long-term stabilisation of the relationship between accumulation and consumption. For instance, Fordist mass production, together with mass consumption facilitated by a high wage and Keynesian state interventionism within the economy and the social sphere, stabilised itself around a particular configuration of social relations between the economy, state and civil society which constituted the Fordist Keynesian welfare state settlement. In essence, what regulation theorists argue is that a particular system of accumulation can exist as long as its schema of reproduction, that is the accumulation/institution relation, is coherent. This is no simple task, as David Harvey (1989, 121) observes. The problem is how to bring the behaviours of all kinds of individuals—capitalists, workers, state employees, financiers and all manner of other political-economic agents—into some kind of configuration that will keep the regime of accumulation functioning, primarily as there must exist "an internalization of the regime of accumulation taking the form of norms, habits, laws, regulating networks, and so on that ensures the unity of the process. This body of interiorized rules and social processes and institutional structures is called the mode of regulation" (Lipietz 1986, 19).

Regulation theorists themselves have very little, if anything, to say about the way in which education, as an institutional site, is involved in this process of reproduction. This is partly the result of the fact—as I have argued elsewhere—that the state itself is only weakly problematised as a specific type of institution with very particular functions within a capitalist economy (see Dale and Robertson 1998). It also arises from regulation theorists prioritising those social institutions more directly connected to the economy, especially labour markets. Neither do regulationists focus much attention either on the completeness of the interiorisation of the social settlement or the importance of struggle between competing interests within and between settlements. However, a central claim in this book is that education *is* a critical institutional site which, over the course of the last century and a half, has been increasingly regulated (and typically funded and provided) by the state, that as a state institution it is the agent of and subject to pressures from civil society and the economy and therefore a site of struggle, and that the social relations within education arising from both knowledge production itself and contradictory social relations open up the possibility for contradiction and instability within the social settlement.

It will be useful at this point to define the common features of the work of the regulation theory perspective and begin to apply these to developing a framework for analysis of education in general and teachers' work in particular across social formations. To begin, the regulation school views capitalism as moving through a series of stages, each characterised by a specific form of the accumulation process which is itself embedded in a particular set of institutionalised sites: state-economy-civil society. We might call this triad of sites and the particular 'arrangement' of relationships between these sites a settlement; that is, a particular accumulation/ institutional architecture which is embodied in individuals and institutions—albeit partially—as a way of living, thinking and feeling. Teachers' work, and the way it changes, therefore must be located and theorised within this framework of institutionalised sites and settlements.

Second, not only are settlements articulations of specific accumulation/institutional arrangements, but they are nationally specific. The specificity of the institutional arrangements set in motion, according to Boyer (1997, 76), a "path dependence . . . since an institutional framework is constructed on the basis of an architecture that is more or less specific to each social pattern". Andy Green (1993), for example, provides a very rich account of the ways in which the relations between the state and education in social formations such as the United States and England were the result of different social and economic histories (for example, the landed gentry in England were still very powerful in determining the nature of educational provision—as compared to the sentiments of small American frontier capitalists who sought limited state interventionism in their affairs, including education). These histories resulted in a particular set of institutional structures and practises that are central in determining what is educationally feasible within a social formation today. Having said that, however, it is important to note that because institutional frameworks and individual sensibilities are also shaped by developments within the cultural and economic spheres and by national and international dynamics, these result in a pattern of similarity and difference in the nature of teachers' work within and across nations, dependent upon the strength of global, regional and local dynamics.

Third, Marx's concept of economic crisis is used by regulation theorists as a prelude to the transition between stages of the accumulation/institution relation. That is, the accumulation/institution relation undergoes a birth-growth-decay transformation cycle, as does the mode of production. Economic crisis can occur at two levels. At one level crises may be *synchronic*—that is, they arise as a result of imbalances which cause periodic crises but which can be corrected within the existing institutional arrangements. Alternatively, crises may be *diachronic;* that is, a long-term or structural crisis much as we have seen over the past two decades in much of the English-speaking world. This second level of crisis arises as a result of a significant decline in the rate of profitability and productivity over a prolonged period of time. This causes serious problems in the accumulation/institution relation, ultimately involving—as we have seen with the restructuring of schools and the work that teachers do—a transformation in this relation. However, the basic institutions do not change (that is, state, labour markets, education and so on), only their specific forms. In other words, the specific form of teacher-state-economy-civil society relation is reworked rather than being displaced altogether. This is similar to Dale's (1982) arguments regarding the core problems facing the capitalist state—these core problems (accumulation/legitimation/control) do not disappear; rather, the precise form of the problems and the temporary solutions which emerge are what constitute the state's reform agenda.

Fourth, according to regulation theorists, the labour process in each social settlement is different as a consequence of the nature of accumulation. For example, Lipietz (1986) suggests that in the period 1848–1914 the labour process was characterised by a simple extension of productive capacity and employment without changes in the organic composition of capital or labour. This period, Lipietz observes, can be described as *extensive accumulation.* It was replaced in the early part of the 20th century by an *intensive regime of accumulation* typified by Taylorist and Fordist forms of work organisation. These new complex technologies of control emerged to extract greater levels of productivity from workers, including teachers. Callahan (1962), for example, documents the way in which Taylor's ideas about scientific management were taken up by key educators across the United States and systematically implemented. These new ideas were widely acclaimed for their ability to promote greater efficiency in teaching and learning in America's schools. This period of intensive accumulation was later stabilised with mass consumption, enabling greater realisation of and broadly defining the period of Fordism/Keynesian welfare statism.

Finally, as I have already implied, states must be located within an international regime. Like Boyer (1990, 40), I argue that this is essential for the analysis of their socioeconomic dynamics. The problems facing a nation are defined at an objective level by the rules which organise a nation's articulations and regulations with the rest of the world. It is precisely because of each state's location within the international regime of accumulation—with its own attendant institutional structures (as in the Bretton Woods Agreement, the Atlantic Alliance and in more recent times the European Union [EU] or the North American Free Trade Agreement [NAFTA])—that we might observe some points of similarity across nations in the accumulation/institution relation and therefore in the pattern of education.

Clearly these articulations between a social formation and the international or global regime have consequences for how education and teachers' work are conceived within particular nations and for how states should best organise themselves (structurally and ideologically) to deliver this. Dale (1987) usefully refers to these two dimensions of education as 'mandate' and 'capacity'. Each state's educational mandate and the capacity to deliver will vary according to the balance of social forces that shape the social formation—global, national, regional and local—as well as the relative prominence and power of the coordinating institutions—the state, market and community—and their activities which make up the governance of education within a social formation. These have been systematically spelled out by Dale (1997) and will be used to identify, in quite precise ways, the levels of focus and aspects critical to a systematic analysis of teachers' work within social settlements.

A FRAMEWORK FOR ANALYSING TEACHERS' WORK IN SOCIAL SETTLEMENTS

We are now in a position to identify the key elements that might make up a specific investigation of teachers' work within and across settlements. These do not represent levels of abstraction or some kind of descending hierarchy of power; rather, they are levels of analytic focus and should be read in a dynamic way—such that pressures at the institutional level may result in changes in any or all of the other levels. Together these four levels of analysis outlined combine to specify the contexts and conditions which frame teachers' struggle over their work within a social formation and enable us to chart the transformations in teachers' work over time (see Table 2.1).

Table 2.1 A Framework for Mapping the Nature of Teachers' Work Within Social Settlements

Sphere	Level of Settlement	Articulation
Global	Global settlement	Global regime of accumulation/mode of regulation.
National	Social settlement	Regime of accumulation/mode of regulation expressed as a particular accumulation/institution relation within and between three broad spheres—*economy, state, civil society*.
Institutional	Sectoral settlement	• Mandate—purpose of education—reflects the core problems of the state (*accumulation, legitimation, control*) within the context of the global and national regimes of accumulation. • Capacity—of the education system to deliver mandate is shaped by competing interests and sets of conditions arising from the three main spheres within a social formation: *economy, state, civil society*. • Governance of education involves combinations of two distinctive axes of elements: ➢ governance activities—how education is *funded, provided* and *regulated*, through ➢ coordinating institutions—*state-market-community* engaged in these activities.
Organisational	Teachers' work	Causal assets—*economic, cultural, organisational* and *social* framed/constrained/enabled by the contexts and conditions created by level one to three and realised by teachers through struggle. These can be observed in teachers' market, work and status situations.
Self	Teachers' identity	Teacher's biography/experiences arising from their differential ability realise assets, forms of identification, alienation and so on.

CLASS AND LABOUR—POWER AND CONTROL

One of the matters I want to raise early in this book concerns the theoretical perspectives that we have used to examine and understand the nature of teachers' work. As has been noted elsewhere (Goodson 1992), teachers have often been an invisible category of workers to researchers, and if they were known, it was often through large-scale surveys or analyses of their position in society (cf., Waller 1932; Tropp 1957; Lortie 1975). Teachers were typically viewed in rather benign ways, as socialising children into adult roles and facilitating a transition from the particular values of the home to the more universal values of the wider society. The inadequacy of this particular paradigm in describing teachers and their work was made obvious with the new sociology of education, which raised important issues concerning the nature of knowledge, the relationship between knowledge and social control, and teachers' part in the production of that knowledge (Young, 1971). The interactionist approach, which grew out of the new sociology of education, emerged with the work of Delamont (1976), Hammersley and Woods (1976) and Woods (1979), among others. Those subscribing to this approach used extensive interviews with teachers and observations of their work to develop an account of the daily realities of classroom life. While valuable in highlighting the complexity of teaching as a form of labour, in Bhaskar's (1978) terms, this approach often suffered in that it focused attention upon the world of sense, impression and events rather than the underlying social relations and social structures which gave rise to these events (see Introduction).

The use of labour process theory was a huge step forward in this regard, and has indeed provided some of the most useful lines of enquiry into teachers' work over the past two decades, including my own. Inspired by the work of Harry Braverman and industrial sociology, theorists drawing on this work (cf., Apple 1982, 1985, 1993; Connell 1985, 1995; Ozga 1988; Harris 1980; Carlson 1992; Lawn 1987, 1988; Grace 1987; Seddon 1991) have made significant contributions to our understanding of teachers' work as labour. Braverman, in his important book, *Labor and Monopoly Capitalism: The Degradation of Work in the Twentieth Century* (1974), argued that the capitalist imperative responsible for the continual reformulation of jobs—whether blue- or white-collar— separated conception of work from its execution. In other words, the capitalist system strives to reduce all workers' jobs to pure execution while management has complete control over conception. In Braverman's view,

Taylor's principles of scientific management (discussed further in Chapter 4) are a logical development within a teleology of capitalism. This not only implied an underlying similarity in work (including teaching) across countries, but that there could be no end to Taylorism without an end to capitalism,

Braverman's concepts of *proletarianisation* (intensification of labour and loss of control over conception) and *deskilling* have been used to describe and understand teachers' experiences over aspects of their work in a variety of countries and educational settings and indeed has become a benchmark against which change was judged. This approach, as Bob Connell (1995, 95) noted, produced a necessarily 'messier' picture of teachers' work as theorists explored various aspects of it: workplace supervision, teacher unionism, teachers' occupational cultures and teaching as a labour process. However, though such studies were carried on across a number of countries, including the United Kingdom, Canada, the United States, Australia, Portugal and Sweden, there has been, as far as I can ascertain, no systematic account that uses labour process theory to explore teachers' work comparatively. It is precisely for this reason that in 1987 Lawn and Grace called for a comparative approach in order to develop a better understanding of the complexity of the political, economic and social relations of teachers' work in society.

I agree with Stephen Wood (1989, 9) that Braverman's key contribution to understanding labour in capitalist economics is that "the control of labour will always be a basic motive of capitalist management". However, there are difficulties that arise with Braverman's account which are of considerable importance to an analysis of the work teachers do. The first level of concern I wish to register pertains to Braverman's own account, which has been open to a number of criticisms for its (1) overly teleological account of capitalism, (2) limited conception of agency, (3) failure to acknowledge alternatives to Taylorism within capitalism, (4) excessive focus on management's labour problem, and (5) assumptions of uniformity of application across countries. In addressing the first criticism, more recent accounts of systems of capitalist development (cf., Lipietz 1992; Boyer 1997; among others) highlight the indeterminacy of capitalism rather than its determined unfolding. Critics also point to considerable evidence that workers actively participate in production systems and that they develop their own resistances to various management practises (Edwards 1979; Buroway 1985). This can also be evidenced in the research on teachers (cf., Connell 1985; Lawn 1987). In relation to alternatives to Taylorist forms of control, Martin Lawn's account has shown how the often tense relationship between teachers and the state during the period 1910–1930 resulted in the state developing an indirect form of rule that gave English teachers considerably greater degrees of autonomy over their work than American teachers (see Chapter 4 for a fuller account of this period). With regard to the assumptions of uniformity of Taylorism across countries, the proletarianisation thesis implies that, overall, the mode of control over teachers' work across the advanced capitalist economies is relatively similar, particularly if one takes seriously a teleology of capitalism. However, this view becomes quite difficult to sustain when we begin to compare the different fortunes of teachers both within and across nations.

The second level of concern arises when we ask ourselves the question: What do we miss when we use Braverman's theory as the primary theoretical framework? I believe that by focusing upon issues of control, as Braverman does, we miss an important element that characterises the history of teachers as an occupational group. That is, we fail to register teachers' ongoing struggle with the state to secure social closure and professional status. Rather, teachers and their interests are aligned with those workers with whom they may be objectively located in an exploitative relationship. Establishing state-authorised social exclusion on the basis of their 'expertise' (recognised in the form of credentials and registration) enables teachers to differentiate themselves from other workers and as a result secure particular types of advantages in relation to other categories of workers. As Larson (1977) pointed out in her seminal work on the professions, when talking about service workers like teachers—by any criteria—these jobs enjoy considerably better market and work situations than manual jobs and it is simply not the case that a *simple* proletarianisation process has taken place.

POINTS OF ANALYTICAL FOCUS—BERNSTEIN ON POWER AND CONTROL

Bernstein's (1996, 19) analytic separation of power from control provides some clues as to how we might usefully proceed on this matter of distinguishing the different facets of teachers' labour. Briefly, Bernstein (1996, 19) states that though power and control are embedded in each other, they can also be analytically distinguished from each other because they operate at different levels of analysis. The relations of *power,* Bernstein argues, "create boundaries, legitimise boundaries, reproduce boundaries between different categories of groups (gender, class, race), different categories of discourse, different categories of agents." Bernstein beautifully articulates this when he states: "Power always operates to produce dislocations, to produce punctuations in social space. . . . Power always operates on the relations between categories" (Bernstein, op. cit.). For example, teachers' power as an occupational group can be seen in their periodic ability to secure—using a variety of tactics—state support for professional closure, or where powerful factions of teachers can promote their own interests as opposed to other teachers', for instance in the case of secondary versus elementary teachers. Securing closure requires power over the discourse of difference. It also requires strategic tactical ability. *Control,* on the other hand, establishes legitimate forms of communication appropriate to the different categories. The focus here is on the relations *within* given forms of interaction; for instance, the pace of work, the content to be taught, how it might be assessed and so on. These separate but related dimensions help us identify major differences in the modalities and specificities of power and control in teachers' work across social formations. They enable us to locate teachers' power in relation to other workers (including more powerful factions of teachers in relation to other teachers) and at the same time record the particular ways in particular settings that teachers control their work. Bernstein's distinction between control and power moves our analysis of teachers' work away from the tendency to focus upon more technical aspects to one where all aspects of teachers' work—economic, cultural, organisational and social—are considered. What this requires, I believe, is a robust analysis of teachers as class actors and of their occupational power.

GOULDNER AND THE NEW CLASS THESIS

One account which offers an interesting line of enquiry and which complements the labour process approach is Alvin Gouldner's thesis that following the rise of the professions, teachers are potentially members of this 'new class' whose power rests upon a new form of capital—cultural capital. Drawing upon the work of Bernstein (1971), Gouldner argues that cultural capital is a key asset of the knowledge-bearing professional service class and central to the emergence of an identifiable and structurally differentiated autonomous social stratum. However, as Gouldner notes, "The New Class is on the one hand élitist and self-seeking and uses its special knowledge to advance its own interests and power to control its own work situation" (1979, 7) while on the other hand striving to be a new universal class committed to service and embodying the collective interest (ibid., 8). This *power-goodness paradox* encapsulates what Gouldner describes as the profoundly 'flawed' nature of this class and its interests. Gouldner's thesis extends the 'monopoly of competence' argument developed by theorists on the professions such as Larson (1977). By arguing that the professions also promote their interests as aligned with all classes, Gouldner (1979) is also able to point to the ways in which the ideology of professional workers like teachers, which is centred upon a moral set of values such as social trusteeship, appears to run counter to their own self-interest as a class in and for itself.

Teachers have historically sought to differentiate themselves from other workers, though not always successfully, by arguing that they have special expertise and to transform the value of this cultural asset into economic and organisational assets through various strategies or forms of social closure. The language of closure is thus the language of power. Parkin (1974, 5) puts this very well when he observes: "Modes of closure can be thought of as a different means of mobilising power for purposes of staking claims to resources and opportunities". Parkin identifies two forms of social closure: *solidarism* and *exclusion*. 'Solidarism' refers to strategies that pursue the interests of the collective (such as unionism) while exclusion refers to those strategies that work to protect the interests of a particular group within the collective. 'Exclusion' thus stabilises the stratification order while solidarism (for instance, unionism) threatens the social order through the threat of usurpation and where the privilege of the few is then socialised for the collective. Parkin goes on to argue that it is possible "to visualise the fundamental cleavage in the stratification order as that point where one set of closure strategies gives way to a radically different set" (1974, 5). The ambiguities in the class position of some groups occur when they adopt dual strategies; for example, one involving both exclusion (such as credentialism) and the solidaristic tactics of organised labour. As we will see in the two historical chapters that follow this one, teachers have preferred to use exclusionary strategies, but their successes in securing social closure have been the result of a dual strategy of exclusion and solidarism. Using Bernstein's conception of power, we can now broaden our frame of analysis beyond that of control and see how teachers as members of the new class use their resources to mobilise and realise economic power to create, maintain and reproduce the boundaries of distinction between teachers as 'professionals' and other workers through social closure and solidaristic strategies. At the same time, teachers are subject to the erosion of cultural and organisational assets through forms of managerial control. It is this contradictory claim to distinctiveness and universalism, expertise and social trusteeship, exclusion and solidarism, the professional and the proletariat classes—in sum the goodness/power paradox—that defines the struggles of teachers as workers and which makes them such an interesting group of study.

CONCLUSION

In this chapter I have outlined a theoretical framework for analysing teachers' struggles that examines settlements, crisis and transformation, and in which social settlements are viewed as being marked by continuity and discontinuity, and difference across space, place and time. In particular, I drew upon the work of the regulation theorists who focused attention on the complex and dynamic interrelation between forms of economic development, nationally specific institutional structures and social relationships. Their approach is helpful in charting the particular struggles waged between teachers and the state in particular places, at particular times and under particular conditions. These struggles by teachers did not occur in a vacuum. Rather, they can be understood as framed, on the one hand, by a national and international regime of accumulation (market and wage relation) (Boyer 1990) and, on the other, by particular institutionalised arrangements that reflect social and political conflicts particular to each country and which arose out of conflicting class and other social interests. This complex blend of local, national and international accumulation/institution dynamics gives rise to a dual patterning of identifiable regularities and localised specificities with regard to teachers' work. These frame the realisation of a set of assets for teachers—male and female—that ultimately determine the particular nature of their class location and their class consciousness. These theoretical frameworks will be used in the following two parts to map the changing nature of teachers' work within and across settlements.

PART II
Changing Contexts

CHAPTER 3

Laissez-faire Liberalism, Teachers and the State

INTRODUCTION

In my efforts to understand the nature of teachers' work in countries such as the United States of America, the United Kingdom, Australia, Canada and New Zealand in the 1990s, it became increasingly apparent that I would need to look backwards in time in order to answer more adequately the questions, How did this particular political order of teachers' workplace come to be? What struggles took place and under what conditions? Further, how might we explain differences in the political order of teachers' workplaces over time and across nations? In this chapter I look back over more than a century and a half, and begin an investigation of teachers' work within the laissez-faire liberal settlement 1850s–1900. It is in this period that teachers' relation to the state both increased in importance and became more formalised. In broad terms I will argue that a social settlement emerged during the 1850s, consolidated itself in a particular accumulation/institution relation in the three decades that followed, but then faced increasing pressure by the end of the century with declining profitability leading to economic and social crisis worldwide. This pressure ended in a series of ruptures in the accumulation/institution relation following the 1890s depression. During this same period and across most of the developed nations, states established national education systems for the masses, while an increasing number of teachers—many of whom were women—were employed to support the burgeoning numbers of students in urban and rural centres.

49

In Part I, *Conceptual Contours,* I developed a conceptual framework intended to produce a more fine-grained account of the changing nature of teachers' work both within and across social settlements. In combining a theory of sectoral and social settlements in education with a theory of teachers as workers and class actors, I sought to develop a framework that more adequately enabled us to trace the capacity of teachers as an occupational group to realise particular configurations of assets under particular conditions and over time and which could be seen in teachers' changing market, work and status situations.

In this chapter I operationalise that framework through an illustrative analysis of teachers' work in the laissez-faire liberal settlement in two countries—the United States and England. My focus is institutional rather than micro-political and is guided by the questions raised in Chapter 2: *Who taught what, how, under what conditions, to whom, and with what outcome? How was teachers' work governed and managed? What were the social, political and economic consequences for teachers?* As we shall see, although new institutional and organisational patterns emerged in both countries, teachers as an occupational group differed in their abilities to realise economic, organisation, social and cultural assets. In the case of England, this was shaped by an explicit class project which was mediated by gender in very particular ways. For example, males dominated middle-class secondary school teaching, while females taught in the primary or elementary school. Drawn from the working class to teach working-class elementary students, this largely female workforce took a more conservative stance on poor wages and limited organisational authority.

In the United States, teachers' fortunes and their struggles were more explicitly shaped by the politics of gender and race, occluding what were nonetheless important forms of class mediation and class outcomes. As Mattingly (1975, xiii) observes, the morally infused and market-based system of governance in the early decades of the 19th century, managed by a first generation of schoolmen and shaped by a moral rhetoric and fear of a social class obscured the importance of both morality and social class as facts of the teaching profession in the generations that followed. Mattingly continues: "[B]oth generations recognized social conflict and political partisanship as the clearest enemy of character. The first generation, however, differed in that they knew that the apolitical meaning originated from a political choice. The second generation and its successors made a habit of their apolitical thinking and treated the habit as a moral principle". In both countries, and in relation to the alternative—factory work—

teachers had some status, even though they remained poorly paid and not all teachers shared in the same level of ascribed status. However, as the settlement progressed, teaching became more closely regulated in the name of efficiency. The contexts and conditions under which these occurred, as well as the precise nature of the struggles that took place within the settlement, are at the heart of the studies that follow.

LIBERALISM AND THE 'AGE OF CAPITALISM'

In the words of the eminent historian Eric Hobsbawm (1987, 11), the period from 1850 to the early 1900s, that great 'age of capitalism', was defined by "titanic and revolutionary forces . . . which changed the world out of recognition." These developments, which extended the reach of economic capital and even local communities around the globe, were transported on what Hobsbawm describes as "a specific and historically peculiar vehicle" (ibid.): the values, beliefs and assumptions of 19th-century liberal bourgeois society. Emerging with the Enlightenment, liberal philosophy found expression in the notion of a 'social contract' between the nation-state and the individual. The new tenets of laissez-faire liberalism also meant freedom from regulations in production and trade, displacing the concern for the regulation of trading markets to suit the needs of the mercantilists with the idea that markets themselves were naturally self-regulating. This view, argues Polanyi (1944, 71), demanded nothing less than the institutional separation of society into an economic and political sphere; and a complete transformation in the structure of society and in the nature of the relationship between individuals and the state, as well as between nation-states. The new social contract implied the concept of bourgeois individuality endowed with freedom—freedom to buy or sell unhindered as far as possible by the regulatory activities of the state and organised around the three core tenets—a competitive labour market, an automatic gold standard and international trade.

For the first time the world was becoming genuinely global. Almost all parts were now approximately mapped, new forms of transportation made it possible for men and women to travel over large distances, and telegraphic communication enabled messages to be received on the other side of the globe in a matter of hours. It was also a much more densely populated world where mass migration, especially to the Americas, gave rise to dramatic increases in population in new lands. However, the confident cultural and economic conquest of the frontiers, aided by the new

technologies which fueled industrialisation and with it growing urbanisation, created a growing gap between those economies with a capitalist
economic base and those without. By the 1880s it was clear that two sectors combined together into the one economic system: "the developed
and the lagging, the dominant and the dependent, the rich and the poor"
(Hobsbawm 1987, 16).

The growing divisions between nation states were also evident within
them. The ideological reverberations of the French Revolution—liberty,
equality and fraternity—sparked unease amongst the ruling classes
across Europe as these ideas articulated with the demands from new social classes arising from the changing occupational structure (Simon
1987, 92). Amidst this ferment, differing views emerged from the
nascent social forces regarding the nature and purpose of existing social
institutions, including the forms of provision of education. These social
divisions were propelled by new sets of social relations arising from capitalism. It was now increasingly money which determined the distribution of social privilege, though differences arising from social class
origins, gender and race—as we shall see with teachers—continued to
dominate social life for all of that period and indeed during the decades
that followed.

By the 1870s and across much of the developed world, education
had been transformed from a relatively inchoate structure at the beginning of the 19th century to one comprising a much more finely differentiated and segmented set of subsystems at its close (Simon 1987, 91).
Mass education in a range of countries, including Canada, Australia,
France, the United States and England, was now secured in the form of
'universal' publicly funded primary schooling (to be distinguished from
privately funded and provided forms of education for the elite) under the
supervision of governments, though it should be noted that its universal-
ity typically did not extend to the indigenous populations who were in
some cases legislatively excluded. The emergence of this new 'secular
church' (Green 1993), while it provided mass schooling for all, nonetheless colonised other modes of learning and in doing so assumed primary
responsibility for the moral, cultural and political development of the nation. It embodied, for the first time, "a new universalism which acknowledged that education was applicable to all groups in society and should
serve a variety of social needs" (ibid., 79). Green observes that these developments were directed at an emerging concern with the national interest, even if that was largely one conceived by the dominant classes
themselves:

The national systems were designed specifically to transcend the narrow particularism of earlier forms of learning. They were to serve the nation as a whole, or rather the 'national interest' as conceived by the dominant class in society. As such, education had to become a state concern and, ultimately, an institution of the state. It could no longer be assumed that it would develop in the right ways or to the necessary extent through a process of spontaneous, molecular growth out of civil society. It had to be developed from the top downward, with the deployment of the full bureaucratic machinery of the state. The fully fledged nineteenth century education system thus became a species apart whose functions were relatively homogenous and unique and which could hardly be equated *tout court,* with those of earlier forms. It became an institution *sui generis,* an integral part of the state apparatus of the burgeoning nineteenth century nation state and a pillar of the new social order (ibid., 79).

Though by the late 1890s the main contours of education systems had been established as a result of a series of state reforms, how these were articulated within the sectoral settlement broadly defined as laissez-faire liberalism was dependent upon each state's specific political and economic history.

LAISSEZ-FAIRE LIBERALISM AND STATE PATERNALISM IN ENGLAND

The educational mandate given to mass state education in England was heavily influenced by the 'panic' which surrounded the expansion of the working class and in particular the concern with their perceived "obstinately ungovernable behaviour" (Johnson 1976, 49). State control was centred upon specific *class cultural* issues rather than more diffuse *social* ones. The educational mandate was thus directed at a particular type of cultural morality. Johnson observes:

Education was not thought of as the development of innate abilities, potentialities or skills. It was curative, regulative. Education should establish an inner restraint, a behavioural order. . . . Schooling then was intended to 'shackle minds' (1976, 48).

The emphasis on the control of the perceived crudeness and immorality of working-class culture deeply inscribed itself on the educational mandate for English state schools during this period. However, it was an education for the working class and therefore, while it might be popular, "it was to be both separate and unequal" (Bergen 1988, 41). It was a means whereby the middle class could impose its rule over the working class:

> It would be difficult to overemphasize the degree to which elementary education in England in the nineteenth century constituted an imposition of the middle class on the working class. As R. H. Tawney wrote: 'The elementary schools of 1870 were intended in the main to produce an orderly, civil, obedient population, with sufficient education to understand a command.' The state machinery of education, from the Committee of Council through the Board of Education, was primarily middle class. So also was the important and powerful Her Majesty's Inspectors. In fact, Inspectors were generally appointed directly from Oxford or Cambridge; an elementary teacher could not become an inspector, and complaints are frequent about the lack of compassion and understanding on the part of Inspectors (Bergen 1988, 48).

Meanwhile the elite private schools unofficially carried a separate and distinctive mandate which bore the stamp of the power of the landed gentry over the demands of successive waves of middle-class interests. In the first instance this was articulated by a radical coterie of industrialists, scientists and rationalist non-conformists (Green 1993, 244) whose educational thought was profoundly influenced by the progressive humanist philosophies of Rousseau, and then later through those with more utilitarian concerns whose aims for their children were determined by their own distinctive economic needs. In this latter case a good education was viewed as imparting the relevant knowledge and useful skills that would serve the children of the middle class in their future occupations.

These divisions in educational mandate were formalised during the crucial years of change—1850–1870—when a series of royal commissions were appointed which recommended the reform of all sectors of the education system—including the provision of schooling for the various strata of the middle and professional classes, gentry and aristocracy (Simon 1987, 88). By the last decades of the century, education in England, argues Simon, was a " 'trump card' in the great class competition"; it reflected the firmer grounding of the hegemony of the ruling class in a set of institutional changes within both elementary and secondary schooling brought about through direct intervention of the state. Thus,

> ... it could be said that the function of education emerging from the measures adopted in mid-century was not so much that of ensuring the *reproduction* of society with a divided social structure as the actual reinforcement and more precise refinement of an hierarchical society in which each stratum knew, was educated for, and accepted, its place (Simon 1987, 92).

Morris (1972) argues that the apparent contradiction between the individualism and anti-collectivism of laissez-faire liberalism and the successive acts of government intervention which culminated in the state's assumption of collective responsibility reflected the need to pursue accumulation, on the one hand, and to avoid social breakdown under the strain of developing urbanisation, on the other. In this regard, the state, increasingly pressed to evolve new techniques for managing the working class and in particular problems of civil discipline, found an answer in the provision of mass schooling. Morris goes on to argue that state interventionism in this context should be viewed as a form of *state paternalism,* and it was critical in maintaining the structure of English class society. This involved

> ... the control and regulation of the ranks of society and this was freely regarded as an essential part of the state's duties, concomitant with civil law and order. As an important agent of control, the education system was therefore a legitimate state interest. To leave the supply of schools to the market, according to demand, could leave a particular social class system with a deficiency of normative facilities; without a system of controls and checks as were created might also fall short of the standard of social conditioning which they were expected to purvey (Morris 1972, 283).

LIBERALISM AND CAPITALIST EXPANSION IN AMERICA

As compared with England, where matters of class were uppermost, the state's educational mandate in the United States was centrally concerned with two things: developing the basic skills of its citizens for participation in the rapidly expanding economy and securing greater forms of social cohesion amongst the successive waves of immigrants. The size of the problems posed by migration can be appreciated in the fact that between 1830 and 1920 the United States had admitted around 35.3 million immigrants (Clifford 1987, 5).

Successive waves of immigration directly altered the composition of the working class, which in turn stymied class development (Hogan 1982, 41). The outcome of the clash between first-generation industrial workers and the cultural demands of industrial capital was not the emergence of a set of institutions which reflected a growing class consciousness, but a plethora of ethnically differentiated working-class cultures which deflected attention away from the class-based nature of American society. Class development was also shaped by the unique ordering and juxtaposition of the establishment of liberal democracy and the Industrial Revolution. The appearance in America of democratic political institutions before the entrenchment of industrial capital meant various state apparatuses were viewed, not as class-based, but as "a means of preserving the democratic republic against the onslaughts of greedy monopolists, corrupt 'aristocratic tendencies' or unschooled Catholic immigrants" (Hogan 1982, 42).

This is not to suggest that there were few conflicts between groups with different social, political and religious interests. The unholy tensions between Protestants and Catholics spurred each with a missionary zeal to establish systems of schooling that extended opportunities for the development of their version of Christianity. There were also opposing views regarding the problems posed by rapid urbanisation and the growing need for municipal reform. Green notes of the United States that "there were basically two camps in the struggle over educational reform: those who supported the creation of a more uniform public education system and those who opposed greater centralisation and favoured the retention of the district system" (1993, 190). This latter position was consistent with the key values of American republicanism, which firmly rested on a belief in personal freedom, opportunity, social mobility and moral virtue. These sentiments, the essential values of small producer capitalism, cut across differences between the social classes. The result was that the state's educational mandate fell on a largely responsive community, precisely as it was legitimated by the ascendancy of popular capitalist ideology (Green 1993, 194) and its broad appeal within civil society. Differences within and between communities were seen as arising not from class, race or gender, but from the natural inclinations and aspirations of individuals such as a commitment to hard work, making use of opportunities; they were also seen as a means of personal expression. At the same time, it should be noted that the presence of truancy officers and compulsory education laws suggests that not all families (or at least the children) saw schooling as personally liberating.

Precisely for those same reasons—that is, the pervasiveness of a mythical egalitarianism and liberal bourgeois politics, which celebrated private property and capitalist accumulation—education continued to be provided in a laissez-faire manner. As accounts of teachers' careers illustrate, gender, race and place played a critical part in whether and how individual teachers could more fully realise material, social, organisational and cultural assets (cf., Labaree 1989; Clifford 1988; Altenbaugh 1995). The politics of individualism and governance of education through the market resulted in differences in educational provision across regions, despite the press for centralisation arising from the common school movement. This led to the more haphazard development of public education across states and between cities and rural communities. Thus, while the experience of schooling was not equal for different social classes, neither was it so explicitly constructed (though it was a concern of educators and those who promoted the common school and parent education)—as in England—to control the moral behaviour of the working class and to maintain class divisions. Social control over the working classes and ethnic groups rather remained a more invisible, though important, political project.

How did these differing contexts and conditions in these two nation states—England and the United States—shape the nature of teachers, their work and their struggles over the terms and conditions of their work? We can begin exploring this question by operationalising the analytic framework developed in Chapter 2, that is, examine the teachers' market, work and status situations at the time and explore the ways in which these arose from their struggle to realise economic, cultural, organisational and social assets during the laissez-faire liberal settlement. Barry Bergen's (1988), Brian Simon's (1987) and Asher Tropp's (1957) accounts provide a useful starting point here, as they respectively explore aspects of elementary and secondary teaching in England during this period.

CLASS, GENDER, SEGMENTATION AND SUBORDINATION OF TEACHERS IN ENGLAND

Bergen observes that even at the time, elementary teachers' claim to professional status was viewed as problematic and, in the view of a parliamentary committee, was the result of the failure by the state to limit entry to the profession through the application of more rigorous admission procedures. According to the committee, only those who had reached an

acceptable standard of education and training ought to be admitted to
'the profession'. Though forms of teacher certification had in fact been
put into place during the 1840s, and indeed teacher training became
more prominent through an increasingly rigorous system of selection for
pupil teachers and competitive scholarships for training college places, it
was evident that little or no policing of its enforcement took place. The
result was that there were no guarantees that teachers would know more
than the students they taught.

The establishment of the National Union of Elementary Teachers
(NUET) in 1870 was the first signal that elementary school teachers in
England sought new forms of association to further their interests. However, the NUET declared itself a non-aggressive association and set
about the task of promoting a self-improvement rather than a collective
advancement agenda for teachers (Bergen 1988, 48). One of the aims of
the NUET was to create a register of qualified teachers with authority to
teach. This was eventually established in the late 1890s but abolished
less than a decade later. Teachers' preoccupation with defining their expertise was clearly important for establishing the basis of the professionalism and seeking professional closure. Indeed, to this point teachers had
little more than rudimentary technical knowledge and no science of pedagogy that might support claims to professionalism. Without these, it
was difficult to argue the case that the state should guarantee professional closure through processes of certification and registration. This
task was made even more difficult for teachers when different curriculum
knowledge was regarded as appropriate for the schooling of different social classes.

Clearly the lower status associated with elementary teaching ran-
kled with those employed in this sector of the profession. It stood as a
daily reminder of their working 'classness' that cast a dark shadow over
their claims to status. In 1889, 'elementary' was dropped from the title
and the union was re-titled the National Union of Teachers. Elementary
teachers responded to their class origins not with direct political action
and strategic alliances with other workers, but with conservative deference and subordination to class interests. A proposal in 1895 for the
NUT to affiliate with other unions through the Trade Union Congress
was soundly defeated.

Between 1871 and 1911, while the number of male teachers in elementary schools increased three times, the number of females increased
twenty times, such that in the elementary sector of schooling, females
dominated the teaching force. However, female teachers received lower
salaries than their male colleagues, despite similar qualifications and lev-

els of service. In fact, the dramatic feminisation of teaching in elementary schools depressed salaries overall, even for males.

To what extent was the more conservative stance of elementary school teachers, particularly in the NUT, the direct outcome of the union being dominated by females? According to Bergen (op. cit.), elementary school males were far more likely than women to be members of the NUT. For example, in 1895, 83 percent of all certified male teachers were NUT members while only 35 percent of certified females were. In other words, elementary school teachers who did join the NUT were more than twice as likely to be men, though they represented only a third of the elementary school teaching population. Indeed, the NUT executive structure was dominated by males and might well explain why the NUT failed to support the 'equal pay for equal work' claim by women until more than two decades later.

By the closing decades of the 19th century, elementary school teachers were unable to establish control over the boundaries of what might constitute their work and secure state support for their rights of monopolisation—though this changed in the political ferment of the 1920s and was later consolidated in the Keynesian welfare state settlement that followed World War II. Within the laissez-faire liberal settlement, this meant that elementary school teachers in state-funded schools were not able to turn claims of special knowledge and skills (cultural assets) into social and economic rewards. Bergen (ibid., 49) shows that although wages increased for occupations such as cotton factory workers and coal miners, teachers' wages not only increased more slowly but in fact declined as a percentage of net national per capita income between 1880 and 1920. Indeed, it could be argued that elementary school teachers viewed their struggles as best waged through attempts to shore up cultural assets in the form of certification and authority to teach, rather than seeking to realise economic, organisational and social assets. This would have involved teachers in a very different set of battles over declining salaries, the inequitable pay scales between males and females, more strategic forms of association, and the level of control within the organisations they worked in.

Elementary school teachers' limited ability to convert their knowledge and skills into cultural and economic assets within the mass public schooling sector was also brought about by a combination of other events: the rapid expansion of pupil numbers in schools, the opening up of new opportunities for males within the expanding labour market and the lack of alternative work opportunities for women within the wider labour market.

Female teachers were treated differently from their male counterparts. For instance, female pupil-teachers were required to demonstrate their competency in areas such as needlework and other domestic arts during teacher training. In the training colleges (many of which were sex-segregated) female teachers were trained in 'domestic economy' while males were exposed to more scientific subjects such as geometry and economics. The dominance in elementary school education of females drawn from the working class with a mandate to deliver a basic education to working-class children was paralleled by that of males in secondary education who catered to an almost exclusive middle-class population (with only a few scholarship places open to exceptional students from working-class families).

It was the extension of working-class female labour into the public realm as class control that defined the lot of elementary school teachers during the laissez-faire liberal settlement. The bifurcation of state-funded schooling into elementary and secondary, when added to the private provision of elite schooling for the ruling classes, established three distinctive class trajectories: working, middle and upper class. In combination, these trajectories—with their different mandates and institutional and governance structures—created very different conditions and contexts for teachers and their work. These were realised in differences in income, in the way in which their labour was controlled and in status.

FROM POLITICAL PATRONAGE TO ADMINISTRATIVE EFFICIENCY IN AMERICA

We can identify similar trends in teachers' work in the United States during this same period of laissez-faire liberalism, though important variations emerged arising from differences in the education mandate and in the governance mechanisms of education. I have noted earlier that the mandate for education in America was shaped by the dual purpose of fostering social integration and the right to education as an expression of liberal democracy. Urbanisation and global migration created new pressures on existing institutional structures such as the family, church and local community which had, until this point, been the main form of social cohesion. However, this changed with the rapid expansion of markets and the economy. Hogan (1982, 46) observes: "[T]he small, decentralised, localistic, deferential, predominantly rural and relatively egalitarian society was replaced by a new society based on markets in labour, and characterised by transiency, a strident individualism, industrial production, and increasingly urban, unequal, heterogenous and interconnected". The loose congeries of district schools was eventually replaced by a new institutional apparatus of social organisation and control: common schools, high schools, normal schools (committed to teacher training) and universities (Tyack 1974).

The common-school movement, driven by Horace Mann's Protestant vision of education as a force of civilisation and democratisation (Fraser 1989, 120), came to dominate American education, eventually altering the organisational structure of schools and the institutional structure of schooling. By the 1860s, grade schools had spread to all of the large cities; in the 1870s this had become the norm:

> With the creation of the graded elementary school, with its supervising male principal and self-contained classrooms presided over by male classroom teachers, the structure of work for the nation's female teachers was fairly well set (ibid., 121).

At the institutional level, those powers that had once resided in the ward system of district schools and been managed through a system of political patronage were relocated, under the banner of administrative efficiency, to the local and the state levels.

As the laissez-faire liberal settlement progressed, the system of education became progressively more centralised and bureaucratised. While there is little doubt that, on the one hand, this arose from the demands of growing urbanisation accompanying capitalist expansion, on the other hand, the precise form of educational organisation in the United States owed a great deal to those committed to municipal reform in general and to those committed to the efficiencies to be found in the common-school movement in particular. The 'administrative progressives' (Tyack 1974) swelled their ranks with business and professional leaders and university-based advisors and, inspired by the newly emerging models of business practise and scientific management, sought to replace a system of political patronage with one based on administrative efficiency. This model combined four key ideas: a small 'appointed' school committee, a professional superintendent, the appointment of teachers on a merit-based system, and the application of scientific management to all phases of school life (Tyack 1974).

Teachers were not happy with these changes and vehemently opposed centralisation in favour of the more personal and less bureaucratic system, despite its endemic problems of political patronage and corruption (Urban

1989, 119). This was largely because while the common school embraced a new model of social organisation and set of social relations which promised greater efficiency, uniformity and less corruption; it also delivered lower levels of pay to many teachers, institutionalised the subordination of female teachers to male authority, ruptured the relationship between teachers' conceptualisation of teaching and its delivery in the classroom, and limited the way in which teachers had been able personally to mobilise local social and political networks to their own advantage. In all, the shift in governance from political patronage to the new efficiency model did little to change substantively teachers' location within the structure of power or the gender regime in which they functioned. Fraser (1989, 124) observes: "The transition from the capricious politician to hierarchical administrator did not, in its own right, significantly change the position of the elementary classroom teacher within the power structure of urban public education". Instead, teachers found themselves within a new organisational power structure with a diminished set of organisational assets at their disposal. This was despite the fact that education as a field was becoming 'professionalized', though of course this was in the areas of research and administration.

By the end of the century, education had become a dominant feature of the landscape with around 90 percent of children enrolled in public schools (Clifford 1987, 6); though this in itself had created pressures of overcrowding and inadequate resourcing. As the system of education expanded over the course of the settlement, it was dependent upon a capacity to implement that vision—an available workforce. The difficulty was that with industrial expansion, males were able to find better-paying opportunities outside rather than within teaching. Indeed, males had not viewed teaching as a legitimate career; rather, it was seen as a stepping stone to other careers such as law, medicine or ministering (Rury 1989, 14), and for very good reasons. Teaching had never provided a reasonable salary, and it was not until the lengthening of the school year in the 1850s that a teacher could earn even enough to enable some level of independence.

The solution to the problem of the growing demand for teacher labour was found among the burgeoning numbers of daughters of rural dwellers and new immigrants. The domestication of teaching was given legitimacy by arguments which suggested that women were 'natural teachers'. For example, Horace Mann argued that teaching drew on women's "natural talents" and continued the work of the family (Altenbaugh 1995, 74, citing Horace Mann's 1843 annual report as first secretary of education for the state of Massachusetts). By 1911, 27 percent of teachers were native born of foreign parents (Clifford 1987, 6). Between 1870 and 1900, the percentage of females in the teaching profession rose from 66 to 82 percent (Rury 1989), making elementary school teaching almost totally a female preserve. However, in the United States teachers were drawn primarily from the middle class, unlike in England, where elementary school teachers were drawn from the working class. This was because teachers required at least a marginally better education than the working class could access (Rury 1989, 9).

An important factor in the feminisation of teaching was that women were employed at significantly cheaper rates than men. Estimates of the earnings of men and women indicated that in 1870, women earned approximately one-third of the wages men were paid in the same position. By 1900 this differential was around half (Fraser 1989, 122). This did not alter the fact that local school boards would often go to great lengths to recruit male teachers before finally settling on a female teacher (even if the female teacher was better qualified). Teachers' wages were also significantly influenced by geographic location. Many small rural communities could not afford the costs of running a school and paying a teacher. Larry Cuban (1993) observes that rural school boards spent only half as much per pupil as did city boards, and that one-room schools staffed mainly by females received less of everything—their experience was characterised by makeshift housing and insufficient books, supplies and equipment. This created serious problems for teachers in relation to the physical conditions under which they worked and the wages they were paid, both of which had deteriorated by the 1890s (Cremin 1961, 20).

In the declining decades of the laissez-faire liberal settlement the lower wages paid to female elementary teachers became a hotly contested issue with males on one side and females on the other (Fraser 1989, 131–135). Campaigns began in earnest in the 1890s in the western states; these were followed by campaigns in Boston and New York. Despite pockets of constant and concerted male opposition and accusations of Bolshevism, women continued their struggle. By the early 1920s, though patriarchy had now become institutionalised in the hierarchical organisation of education, women had won important strategic battles on the equal wages for equal work issue. They lost ground, however, in their ability to control the form and content of their work.

Labaree (1989, 158) suggests that teachers' careers and their levels of social mobility were also affected by the ways in which their labour was coordinated through the market. This enabled a particular set of market incentives to be utilised, encouraging more entrepreneurial (typically male) teachers to move out of teaching altogether or on to a higher occupational level within the profession. These teachers "aggressively sought to improve their situation within the profession and aimed to attain two goals: better pay and better working conditions" (ibid., 163). This resulted in teachers "shuttling from one position to another and from one place to another, in a zigzag pattern which made sense mostly in monetary terms" (ibid., 164). Teachers were also seeking better living and working conditions, including having houses of their own rather than boarding; living in towns that offered social and cultural facilities; working in schools that enabled specialisation; finding positions that permitted a degree of autonomy and personal respect; and freeing themselves from arbitrary forms of dependence.

Labaree (1989) contends that three main routes for mobility for high school teachers emerged during this period of laissez-faire liberalism: geographic mobility, particularly the movement from the country to the city; movement up the schooling hierarchy, in particular from elementary to secondary; and finally, movement up the positional ladder within the schooling hierarchy, often on the basis of credentials. In all cases, however, gender and race limited a teacher's advancement. White male teachers were able to compete for positions in city schools primarily as these schools, with their better tax bases, were able to pay higher salaries. Urban city high schools—where teachers were often accorded the honorific title of 'professor' and where such teachers could also specialise, were reasonably attractive working environments for males in comparison to other occupations. Males were also more likely to be college graduates at the beginning of their careers, enabling them to move rapidly through the schooling sector and positional hierarchy. Women, on the other hand, were more likely to acquire their credentials over the course of their career, thus limiting their ability to compete with males in the educational marketplace. It is hardly surprising, given the advantages that accrued to males over females, that in the battle for equal wages, males whose credentials and mobility prospects were good should argue that salaries be driven by market forces rather than regulated through legislation by the state.

The key association to represent the interests of American teachers during the early years of the laissez-faire liberal settlement was the National Teachers' Association (NTA), established in 1857. Though the NTA claimed to represent the aspirations of all teachers, these aspirations—as in the case of their English counterparts—were mainly construed as concerned with professional expertise and credentials rather than matters of salary, working conditions in schools, or professional discretion over the curriculum. Again, also like their English counterparts, the preoccupation with credentials arose as much from the need to *build* the case for professional expertise, in order to realise its value as a cultural asset, as from the necessity to defend those assets from erosion. This was all the more difficult in the face of labour shortages, the argument that teaching was an extension of domestic labour, and Tappan's Law: the stipulation that "a teacher should have completed a level immediately above that which she aspired to teach" (Lortie 1969, 18). In other words, elementary school teachers ideally would have at least a high school education.

For much of the settlement, the institutional structures that emerged to represent teachers' interests contained and constrained them. Like teachers in England, the strategic focus for American teachers in the laissez-faire liberal settlement was on realising cultural rather than economic, social and organisational assets, leaving them at the bottom of the professional ladder. Larson (1977, 155) also advances this view, arguing that teachers were mainly concerned with the assertion and attainment of social status. Not surprisingly, these teachers saw themselves as being exploited by males, who had managed to realise organisational assets for themselves. There is little doubt, too, that the ideological campaign that had been waged through much of the settlement which asserted women's virtues as natural teachers, whose virtuousness involved accepting a low wage, had been successful. But as momentum gathered for wider social and political change and as economic productivity faltered in the final decade of the 1890s, teachers used their political muscle to place equal wages firmly on the reform agenda.

The changes to the system of political patronage that had taken place during the settlement, which profoundly affected the work of teachers in schools, were a consequence of class struggles within the wider social sphere. These changes gained momentum during the final decade of the settlement. In particular, the combined force of the municipal reform movement and the administrative efficiency experts drew together upper-class interests with professional and large business groups in a set of public policies on what had become dominant lower-class and immigrant interests amongst city leadership (Fraser 1989, 126). In other cases these struggles occurred along ethnic and religious lines, as Protestant and Catholic, working class and elites sought to align themselves in new coalitions. Whatever the configuration of alliances, all were anti-teacher in their sentiments as they sought to implement the new industrial model on teachers' workplaces.

Urban (1989) and Fraser (1989) provide instances of systematically organised dissent among teachers over their work conditions in the closing decades of the 1890s, which marked the collapse of the settlement. Unable to progress an agenda through the NTA and faced with changing work conditions and the rise of new forms of governance, women such as Margaret Haley and Ella Flagg Young (Urban 1989, 193) in Chicago spearheaded a campaign to establish teachers' councils through which teachers could advise school administrators on matters of policy. The vision for these councils was wide in scope, including pay, working conditions and curriculum matters. Though these initiatives had some support among the school hierarchy, Urban notes that often superintendents and university professors who did support these initiatives "were much more concerned with the creation of vehicles which they might use to head off attempts to organise unions and other associations independent of the local administration, than they were with establishing legitimate channels to represent the teachers' voices" (ibid., 193).

These struggles gathered momentum as the accumulation regime slowed. It was a period of intense change, contestation and struggle as the accumulation/institution relation that had underpinned laissez-faire liberalism convulsed and disintegrated. The pressure came from all sides: from female teachers seeking equal pay and greater control over the nature of their work, from male teachers seeking to maintain their market edge, and the new efficiency experts who sought to embed a new organisational and institutional structure on teachers and schools. In the short term, these struggles signalled the emergence of important alternative avenues for mobilising and channeling political dissent around the new structures that were being institutionalised. In the long term, though they delivered equal pay by gender and level of schooling (not by credentials and years of experience) to an increasing number of teachers, the price for teachers was high. In the new political climate of the post-World War I years and with the specter of socialism on the horizon, teachers were pressured to sever their links with organised labour in the struggles for equal pay and to embrace a non-political view of teaching.

A CRISIS OF PROFITABILITY AND LIBERALISM

August 1914, the start of World War I, marks the end of "the long nineteenth century . . . and the end of the world made by and for the bourgeoisie" (Hobsbawm 1987, 6). The confident conquest of the globe that had defined the early years of the laissez-faire liberal settlement, the spread of industrialisation and the expansion of world markets made it seem that bourgeois progress was unlimited. Despite the appearance of social stability and economic growth, the laissez-faire liberal settlement—with its essential feature defined by extensive accumulation—carried within it the seeds of its own eventual destruction. The tendency toward monopolisation and economic concentration which transformed the structure and operation of the capitalist enterprise led to distinctions between business and 'big' business. The tremendous growth of cities brought new problems of corruption and inefficiency, requiring an increasingly interventionist state, while the worldwide depression in prices, profits and interest rates turned national economies into more competitive rival economies (Hobsbawm 1987, 36–38). The fall in real wages created a palpable level of political sullenness which fed new forms of unrest and emerged in the development of mass movements of wage workers created by industrial capitalism that demanded the overthrow of capitalism. And while the political and cultural institutions of bourgeois liberalism—like schooling and universal suffrage—were extended to the working masses and to women, the democratisation of politics provided a mechanism for transforming society and in doing so challenged the accumulation/institution relation which had defined the laissez-faire liberal settlement.

Looking back over the latter half of the long 19th century and the laissez-faire liberal settlement in England and in the United States, a number of distinctive features and important differences emerged which defined teachers' work in these places. In both countries a complex process of industrialisation was accompanied by the expansion of education. However, in the United States, this process was complicated by the waves of immigration which brought that nation to promote nationhood and nationalism as a means of integrating the numerous disparate ethnic groups into the country's political system. In England, however, the government sought to manage the divisions between social classes by appeasing the aspirations of the middle class and managing the working class. These different educational mandates shaped the work of teachers in schools in quite a direct way. Furthermore, the ability of teachers to realise economic, social, cultural and organisational assets was mediated by both class and gender. In the United States, gender played an important part in mediating teachers' work, market and status situations. Males were able to realise greater economic rewards largely because they could command higher salaries in a system based upon market principles and in which women were encouraged to view their labour as charity rather than as recompense for a 'fair day's work'. Male teachers were also able to capitalise on college credentials and convert these into a form of cultural capital. As the settlement progressed and the new hierarchical organisational model—premised upon the legitimacy of male authority over female subordination and the efficiency of the increased division of labour—was embedded, male teachers quickly took advantage of their position of power in the new hierarchies and sought to mobilise support for their position by appeals to the 'natural order' of gender relations. Compromised by the view that teaching was an extension of family work, women found themselves unable to realise fully any economic, cultural, organisational or social assets. Though drawn from the middle class, female teachers found themselves mostly at the bottom of the organisational hierarchy, on lower pay than males, responsible to male authority, with fewer credentials. Additionally, despite spearheading the establishment of a range of organisations and associations that might give them a voice as teachers, they were not always in a position to gather the full weight of this form of social capital behind them because of the divisions between males and females. Nonetheless, the mobilisation by key female campaigners by the late 1890s was important in the collapse of the old laissez-faire liberal settlement. However, the strategic focus of campaigners on wage parity, rather than the new organisational structures that were being imposed, resulted in a failure to challenge these developments.

In contrast, teachers' market, work and status situations in England, though mediated by gender relations, were at every turn shaped by an explicit class project. Elementary school teachers were largely women drawn from the working-class, and were engaged in teaching working-class children. Their male counterparts, however, found themselves in middle-class private schools teaching middle-class students, a situation that worked to maintain the class distinctions and class hierarchies of English society. Early forms of association, for example, the National Union of Elementary Teachers, might have become a vehicle for challenging these class divisions. However, the association focused its attentions on establishing teachers' expert knowledge in order to promote the self-improvement of teachers and to gain state support for professional closure. Guarantees from the state that would have enabled elementary school teachers to derive some benefit from cultural assets failed to materialise. Elementary school teachers' struggles were also mediated by their class location. The 'cut-above' attitude of working-class female teachers created the conditions for a more conservative response to their status and work situation. They sought recognition as 'professionals' through cultural assets, rather than the collective weight of association by labour as a social asset. Bids to realise cultural assets were largely unsuccessful. The state failed to support these initiatives. The bulk of female teachers remained poorly paid in relation to other workers; they had low status, little authority in school and were unable to move across the strict divisions imposed by the class project, either into positions within the male middle-class inspectorate or into secondary schooling.

CONCLUSION

In this chapter I have shown that teachers' changing economic and political fortunes were the result of particular struggles waged by teachers both among themselves and with relation to other groups—the state and civil society—in particular places, at particular times and under particular conditions. These struggles by teachers did not occur in a vacuum. Using two illustrative studies, I have suggested that they can be understood as framed, on the one hand, by a national and international regime of accumulation (market and wage relation) (Boyer 1990) and on the other by particular institutionalised arrangements that reflect social and political conflicts peculiar to each country arising out of conflicting class and gender interests. These conditions framed the realisation of a set of assets for teachers—both male and female—which ultimately determined the particular nature of their class location and their class consciousness. These changes occurred within the Fordist/Keynesian welfare state settlement in quite significant ways, as the following chapter illustrates.

CHAPTER 4

Fordism, Welfare Statism and the Rise of Teachers as 'Professionals'

THIRTY GLORIOUS YEARS

"Most human beings operate like historians: they only recognise the nature of their experiences in retrospect", remarked Hobsbawm (1994, 257), and "it was not until the crisis years of the 1970s that observers realised that they had passed through an exceptional period of history; thirty golden years of growth and an increase in the standard of living". This 'golden age', as it nostalgically came to be known in retrospect, marked out almost three decades of unprecedented economic growth, state intervention and social stability within the developed economies— a dramatic contrast to the years of economic and political instability, chaos and ravages of war that had defined much of the first half of the century. In many respects the post-war period was also a 'golden age' for the professions as they consolidated their status and power under the auspices of the welfare state (Brint 1994).

The 'golden age' rested on the bedrock of a new model of economic and social development which, as will be elaborated further in this chapter, involved a more vigorous conception of social democracy, centralised state planning and intervention in the economy, standardised systems of social provision, Fordist mass production and extensive or mass consumption, and the consolidation of the professions in public life. In essence, this period can be characterised by the intensification of accumulation linked, for the first time, to extensive forms of consumption, including schooling. This new set of conditions underpinned a historically remarkable social settlement—the Keynesian welfare state settlement that seemed to offer, at least for a time, a solution to the endemic problems of boom and slump that has defined the history of capitalism.

How did teachers as an occupational group fare during this settlement? By the late 1960s, some improvements in teachers' wages, social status and aspects of their work situation were apparent. However, the extent of this improvement varied within the settlement itself and across nations. I will argue that this was a consequence of differences in the institution/accumulation regimes within each formation and the differential capacity of teachers as an occupational group to realise particular sets of assets that would determine their market, work and status situations. The new prosperity experienced by nations in the post-war reconstruction period, together with the power of organised labour to gain important social wage concessions did not, for reasons that will be elaborated in this chapter, always secure improvements in all aspects of teachers' work. Indeed, in England and the United States, the two countries that are compared, there were large shortfalls in the supply of trained and certified teacher labour in the face of burgeoning numbers of students in schools, though English teachers were far more successful in 'managing' the state's appointment of uncertified teachers (see Tropp 1957, 255) than their American counterparts. This meant that teachers could be appointed to schools with little or no training, which inevitably weakened the occupational group's claims to professional status. Nonetheless, there was a form of 'concordat' between teachers and the state over the nature of their relationships based upon trust that teachers, as welfare state professionals, should and would exercise their judgement in socially and politically acceptable ways. In exchange for teacher loyalty, goodwill and political neutrality, the state guaranteed teachers tenure, a secure wage and some scope for discretion over their work, though this varied across nations, for reasons that will be outlined in this chapter. Teachers generally carried on their work controlled by mechanisms such as the organisation of the curriculum (cf., Apple 1982), the official knowledge sanctioned in textbooks (Clifford 1975) and professional socialisation (cf., Ginsburg 1988; Ginsburg and Lindsay 1995).

Bessant and Spaull's (1972, v) description of Australian teachers during this settlement—as moderate, dedicated and conservative—could well have applied in both the United States and in England. However, it obscures two important developments that underpinned the Keynesian welfare state settlement. First, the dramatic changes and considerable struggles that took place between teachers and the state over the redefinition of their work occurred during the transitional and crisis years, 1900 and 1945. The gains, losses and compromises of this phase structured key aspects of the architecture of the settlement within states that followed. It is therefore critical to examine those 'crisis' or 'transition' years in each nation state that punctuate the space between laissez-faire liberalism and Keynesian welfare statism. As I have argued in Chapter 2, regulation theorists point out that crises and settlements are two sides of the same coin—a process that is both highly political and one in which there is considerable pressure to restore stability and the unity of the accumulation process. Indeed, regulation theory "confronts the paradox that capitalism has proved rather more durable than envisaged in Marxist theory, that crises may not be *only* the way stations on the path of terminal decline, but that—in terms of the actualities of capitalist development—they may also play a rejuvenation role, brutally restoring the contradictory unity of the accumulation process" (Tickell and Peck 1995, 360). It is also within this period of crisis that the modes of social regulation—carried in the institutional structures and practices, customs and networks, institutionalised compromises, rules of conduct and laws—are challenged, reworked and transformed. This process is a political process, reducible neither to the needs of capital itself nor the conscious actions of the state. What emerges is a combination of continued, new and transformed institutional forms, practises and norms that arise from multiple struggles at multiple levels, including individual, organisational, sectoral and the wider social environment (see Table 2.1).

Second, we need to look beyond the surface features of teachers' professional demeanour of ostensible 'conservatism' and 'care' and ask, What are the political, social and economic conditions and mechanisms of power and control which gave rise to and shaped this outlook? Furthermore, what are the consequences of this outlook for teachers and for students as they labour together on the curriculum? Teachers' outlook necessarily embraces two potentially contradictory elements: (1) the state's internally contradictory political project; and (2) teachers' own 'professional' project which, as Brint (1994, 7) usefully proposes, involves both a technical and a moral aspect. Technically, it promises competent performance of skilled work involving the application of broad and complex knowledge. Morally, it promises to be guided by an appreciation of the important social ends it services, or in Gouldner's (1979) terms, a particular construction of goodness. The combined effect of (1) and (2) above creates the conditions for considerable tension and contradiction for teachers, particularly in those cases where teachers' 'professional' project—as historically specific and situated action—cuts across important aspects of the state's project, as in the case of English teachers

in the first two decades of this century. These dynamics manifest themselves in different ways over the course of a settlement and reflect the
shifting relationship of power and control between teachers and the state.
The bulk of this chapter is given over to an examination of the struggle
between teachers and the state over the shape and form of the structures
and their underlying social relations which would underpin the Keynesian welfare state settlement of 1945–1970 and teachers as welfare state
professionals. Drawing on studies of teachers' work in two different national and social entities—England and the United States—I examine the
way in which historically contingent contexts and conditions, together
with the ways in which teachers mobilised particular resources, gave rise
to variations in teachers' economic, work and status situations both
within and across nation states.

As in the previous chapter on laissez-faire liberalism and teachers, I
draw upon the theoretical frameworks on class and social settlements developed in Chapters 1 and 2 and use these to continue an analysis of the
changing nature of teachers' work in the pre- and post-World War II periods in the United States and England. Within this broad framework, the
chapter proceeds as follows. I begin with an analysis of Taylorism and
Fordism and examine their convergence into a model of economic development, noting the politics of the incorporation of Taylorist practises in
education in the United States in response to the movement toward economic efficiency. This consolidated authority in the schooling hierarchy
(and embodied in the school administrators) rather than in teachers' occupational knowledge, limited teachers' control over their work. I compare this with the politics of teachers' work in England, where the state's
concern over what was perceived as teachers' missionary socialism and
their working-class roots created a rather different set of modes of governance through which teachers and their work was controlled. This enabled teachers to institutionalise occupational authority and as a result to
gain more control over the precise nature and content of their work. I
then turn to examine how these sectoral politics intersected with the rise
of Keynesian ideas and their consolidation in the Keynesian welfare state
settlement.

TAYLOR'S ALCHEMY AND THE FORDIST MODEL
OF PRODUCTION

The emergence of Fordism as a dominant model of economic development in the second half of the 20th century had its early roots in the push

toward increased workplace efficiency and productivity. The rapid decline in growth in the developed economies, which ended in the collapse of the laissez-faire liberal settlement in the 1890s, created a climate where new solutions were eagerly sought and embraced. In particular, science offered new possibilities for understanding and controlling the 'laws of nature', including human nature. Scientific management, the science of administration (organisation theory), exchanges (economy), society (sociology) and individuals (psychology) were all mobilised to shape the new institutional structures, its practises, and the individual identities within them. This applied as much to the education system as elsewhere, with the result that for much of the 20th century, the grammar of schooling life and teachers' work was determined by this new scientific rationality.

Taylor's Magic

We can begin our history of Fordism by tracing the rise of the influential American engineer Frederick Winslow Taylor and his work on the science of management. This came to be known as 'scientific management' or 'Taylorism'. In his famous book *The Principles of Scientific Management,* published in 1911, Taylor laid the foundation stones for what was widely viewed at the time as a form of magic. Using a so-called scientific approach to the organisation and management of labour, Taylor demonstrated that profitability, productivity *and* wages could all be increased *at the same time.* This solution seemed a far cry from the current orthodoxy, where profits and wages were seen as a zero-sum equation—if wages went up, profits went down and vice versa.

What were the principles underlying Taylor's approach? We can identify three key ideas (Braverman 1974). First, knowledge about each labour process would be gathered by management, which then enabled the breaking down of each craft or labour process into its component skills or parts. Second, all brain power could then be removed from the shop floor and concentrated in the hands of the management's planning department. Third, this knowledge would then be used by management to control each step of the labour process, in particular its mode of execution. Using knowledge about the labour involved in a task, machines could be designed to embody the skill of the worker, in the process redefining the worker as a cheaper appendage to the machine.

Taylor's descriptions of how he set about identifying these principles are rich insights into what was to become a hegemonic management practise for much of this century. In observing workers at the Bethlehem Steel Mill where he had been appointed engineer, Taylor noted his surprise when his calculations revealed that workers could be loading more than four times the amount of pig iron at the Bethlehem Steel Mill if they followed a more 'scientific' mode of working. In fact he was so surprised, he went over his figures several times and when he was sure this new calculation was, as he noted, a "proper day's work", he set about implementing this new schedule as a matter of 'duty'.

The distinctive feature of Taylor's approach was the role of management: to dictate to the worker the precise manner in which the work was to be performed. Though up until this point management had the right to control labour, what changed in Taylor's process of rationalisation is that 'day work' and 'piece work' were replaced with 'task work'. This involved a system of management which controlled the actual performance (or practise) of every labour activity: "The establishment of Taylorism signified a decisive intensification of exploitation, based on far-reaching deskilling processes, the destruction of traditional craft forms of workers' power and the introduction of efficient techniques of managerial control and supervision" (Hirsch 1991, 15). The separation of conception from execution, head from hands, mental from manual labour, stood in opposition to the way in which the craft or skilled trades had been traditionally organised. In each craft, the worker was presumed to be the master of a body of traditional knowledge, while the methods or procedures were left to the discretion of the worker. Braverman observes: "[I]n each such worker reposed the accumulated knowledge of materials and processes by which production was accomplished in the craft. . . . The worker combined in mind and body, the concepts and physical dexterities of the specialty" (1974, 109). According to Braverman, the separation of hand and brain was "the most decisive single step in the division of labour taken by the capitalist mode of production" (1974, 126).

Implementing scientific management was no easy task, as Taylor was to find in the years that followed. In obtaining his objective of a "proper day's work"—defined as all a worker could do without injury to his health—Taylor needed to "overcome what he saw as the greatest obstacle to the attainment of this standard" (Taylor, cited by Braverman, 1994). This he called 'soldiering', or marking time. Taylor identified two types of soldiering. One was a natural instinct he observed which could be identified among workers as simply 'taking it easy'. The other—'systematic soldiering'—was the result of "a deliberate strategy among men with the object of keeping their employers ignorant of how fast work can be done" (Taylor [cited by Braverman] 1974, 98). Taylor describes in great detail the difficulties of imposing his system of scientific manage-ment in the face of worker resistance to the intensification of their labour. Taylor engaged in a bitter struggle with workers at the Bethlehem Steel Mill; for more than three years, workers resisted both the loss of control over their work and the intensification of their labour. Taylor might have anticipated this resistance, according to Gramsci (1971, 279): "The fact that a progressive initiative has been set in train by a particular social force is not without fundamental consequences: the subaltern forces which have to be 'manipulated' and rationalised to serve new ends, natu-rally put up a resistance".

Despite worker resistance, Taylor's ideas dazzled much of the American public. His new principles were widely canvassed in the press, catching the imagination of American industrialists, politicians and re-forming schoolmen. Taylor's magic was nothing short of alchemy ac-cording to the engineers and industrial managers who testified with extraordinary fervour as witnesses to the U. S. Interstate Commerce Commission in September 1910 (Callahan 1962, 20). One of the popular magazines of the day, *Outlook,* commenting on the "magic power" of scientific management, noted that the effect upon industry "has been compared to that made by the change from the use of hand tools to the use of machinery" (ibid.). Scientific management was indeed a panacea for the economic ills that beset America—a means by which production could be increased, wages raised and prices lowered. It was also viewed as a potential panacea in international circles. By the early decades of the 20th century, Taylor's work was increasingly being disseminated in a widening public arena, including Britain, France, Germany and Russia.

Fordist Production and Extensive Consumption

Taylorism had a lasting effect on the organisation of modern industrial work. This was enhanced by the way in which car manufacturer Henry Ford of the Ford Motor Company built upon the principles developed by Taylor. Writing about these developments at the time, Gramsci (1971) linked together the new production practises emerging in the United States under the heading 'Americanism and Fordism', a development he suggested arose from an inherent necessity to achieve a planned econ-omy following the disasters arising from economic individualism and the self-regulating free-market economy.

The theoretical concept of 'Fordism' has its origins in Gramsci's (1971) analysis of the changes in economic production and the organisation of labour at the beginning of the 20th century. When Ford founded his company in 1903, building automobiles was a task reserved for craftsmen—the versatile mechanic who moved about in order to complete his work. By 1908, influenced by the work of Taylor, the production processes in the Ford plant had changed quite dramatically. A number of key elements underpinned the new production process. First, instead of 'all round men' who worked as a 'jack of all trades', 'single task men' were employed to assemble a particular component, so that each worker became responsible for a more limited set of operations. Second, Ford introduced a conveyor chain enabling car assemblies to be carried past fixed stations where men performed simple or single-task operations as the assembly line passed. Like Taylor's own innovations, the results were startling. Within three months the assembly time for the Model T Ford had been reduced to one-tenth of the time formerly taken. By 1925, Ford's factory produced as many Model T Fords in a single day as had previously been produced in an entire year. Third, Ford linked the new production method to a 'high wage'—the $5.00 per eight-hour day—in an attempt to overcome the problems imposed by the boring and monotonous assembly line work. A high wage went some way to guaranteeing the consent of workers and at the same time provided them with the material resources which enabled them to participate in the consumer society. By increasing the amount of money available for extensive or mass consumption, and combining it with the capacity to produce large numbers of any one item, Ford moved the principles of economic organisation into a new era. Finally, Ford introduced new forms of moral regulation into the workplace and beyond; a new type of 'man' suited to the new type of work and the new production process. This included the more rigorous discipline of sexual instincts, the regulation and stability of sexual relations, and the strengthening of the 'family'. According to Gramsci, the moral regulation of workers might, at first, appear a laughable idea; however, such developments were critical to the new social order:

> People who laugh at these initiatives (failures though they were) and see in them only a hypocritical manifestation of 'puritanism' thereby deny themselves any possibility of understanding the importance, significance and objective import of the American phenomenon, which is *also* the biggest collective effort to date to create, with unprecedented

speed, and with a consciousness of purpose unmatched in history, a new type of work and man (Gramsci 1971, 302).

The inquiries conducted into workers' private lives were regarded as legitimate territory by the new industrialists. For instance, Ford employed a *coterie* of welfare workers who closely monitored and sought to regulate the private behaviour of workers, including their consumption of alcohol, smoking and sexual activity, and in doing so extended the control of the workplace.

We can now see the architecture of the new social settlement emerging: a regime of accumulation and mode of regulation based upon mass production, mass consumption and a particular type of moral regulation. This involved the division between mental and manual workers, increasing mechanisation, an increase in the volume of goods produced per worker, the pursuit of scientific strategies linked to an increase in productivity, and a new morality linked to economic efficiency. At the same time, wages were increased following increases in productivity. The new social settlement was stabilised when plants were used to their full capacity, in full employment and a high level of profitability by firms. By the mid-1940s, the foundational legs of the development model of Fordism, the new economic order that underpinned the Keynesian welfare state settlement, had been cemented into place (Lipietz 1992). The state was critical in this arrangement, not only as manager of the imbalances that could and did result in periodic *synchronic* crises, but in the development of the new institutional structures which regulated the Fordist regime of accumulation. However, before examining the new Keynesian ideas that shaped the state's activities in the post-World War II period, I want first to look critically at the extent to which and in which ways Taylorism and Fordism influenced the organisation of schooling and teachers' work in America—the home of Taylor and Ford—and compare these with developments in the organisation of teachers' labour in England.

EDUCATION AND THE CULT OF EFFICIENCY IN AMERICA

By the 1890s, rapid industrialisation, urbanisation and immigration—linked to declining levels of profitability—had created the conditions for widespread political and social crisis. In the United States, rising levels of inflation and a diminished capacity for communities to raise taxes placed severe pressure on the educational system. In the cross fire that followed, reform crusaders called for a fundamental reorganisation of schooling. The crisis in American schools was not simply rhetoric. Rural and urban schools alike faced problems of overcrowding and underfunding. In urban areas, the changing class and racial/ethnic composition of urban students (particularly at the secondary level, as compulsory schooling became more routine) added further pressure to the system. Increases in the population resulted in constant demands for more classrooms and more teachers. Given the human and fiscal constraints, teachers in schools faced growing numbers of students in classes with few resources and poor physical conditions. This 'reality' in schools stood in depressing contrast to the philosophical debates centred on various forms of progressivism which focused attention on the freedom of the child (Cremin 1961, 20).

The concerns of the school reformers were not motivated entirely by issues of resourcing. Tyack (1974) points out that the crisis in schooling also disguised an attack by the new industrialists on community control and agrarian politics. In particular, advocates of the consolidation, bureaucratisation and professionalisation of (particularly rural) schooling, many of whom supported the common-school movement and were now enchanted by the new canons of business efficiency and scientific management (Tyack and Hansot 1982, 106), made their case as follows:

> The "bookish" curriculum, haphazard selection and supervision of teachers, voluntary character of school attendance, discipline problems, diversity of buildings and equipment—these were but symptoms of deeper problems, they believed. What was basically wrong with rural education was that rural folk wanted to run their schools and didn't know what was good for them in the complex new society (Tyack 1974, 21).

Local protests of the previous decades now turned into "a nation-wide torrent of criticism, and reform that took on all of the earmarks of a social movement" (Cremin 1961, 22). In this new environment of public dissatisfaction, teachers were widely constructed as self-interested, corrupt and inefficient.

Public dissatisfaction with America's schools was palpable in the first two decades of the 20th century. Critics were everywhere and investigations of school systems increased as part of a move to create a science of education that would examine numerous facets of school life

(Callahan 1962, 49). Not surprisingly, the persistent criticisms of public schooling and of teachers—carried in the popular journals—served to increase the public's clamour for change. These conditions provided fertile ground for rooting new ideas, practises and structures—in particular, those offered by science and business 'experts' (Tyack and Hansot 1982, 107). The movement for educational reform combined many voices of protest in uneasy and often contradictory unison. An attack on local political corruption and professional intransigence sat alongside calls for a more self-conscious progressivism, greater vocational emphasis, and a national system of education. The movement enlisted support from parents, teachers, crusaders and politicians so that within two generations the essential character of American education had changed.

The 'incendiary bomb' for change, according to Callahan, was thrown at teachers by educator Leonard Ayres in a book published in 1909 under the title *Laggards in Our School*. Ayres's (1909, 3) argument (cited by Callahan 1962, 15) was that most students were "retarded"; by that he meant they were overage for the grade they were in. The fault was the school, Ayres argued. Callahan reports that the diagnosis offered by Ayres was that the school programme was suited primarily to the unusually bright academically oriented students. Ayres's analysis drew explicitly on a model of factory efficiency. The "Index of Efficiency", which he derived from precise calculation of input and expected output, was then applied to school systems in fifty-eight cities (Callahan 1962, 16). Ayres discounted and ignored the social and economic conditions that contributed to the 'problem', though he deplored the overcrowding in many schools. Even these conditions were seen to arise not from a lack of adequate resourcing but the inefficient use of the resources at hand. The transformation of schooling had at its heart a new conception of modern society and how it might be governed. As Tyack and Hansot observe (1982, 107):

> The ideal of a society planned by experts and run by scientific managers rested on assumptions not only about how to govern but also about who should govern. It was a conception of leadership designed to consolidate power in large and centralized organizations, whether steel mills, large department stores, or city school systems. The process of concentrating decision-making power and delegating it to a manager in public education is most apparent in the campaign of the administrative progressives to alter the governance of urban education. There the new advocates of professional management and their allies

among elite business and professional groups waged political battles to
destroy the old ward based lay management of schools and to replace it
with a new model of corporate decision-making.

Pressure also emerged for the internal workings of the school to be
organised in more businesslike ways; likewise, it was argued that more
emphasis should be placed upon practical and immediately useful education. The procedure for doing this proved to be effective. Schools were
unfavourably compared with business enterprises, using criteria such as
economy and efficiency. This was quickly followed by suggestions for
business and industrial practises that might be adopted by educators. By
1907 there were indications that aspects of the business ideology had
been accepted and were being applied by educators themselves.

In that year William C. Bagley, who was to be one of the leaders in
American education for the next three decades, published a textbook on
education called *Classroom Management,* which was full of business ter-
minology. Callahan notes: "Bagley stated, for example, that the problem
of classroom management was a problem of economy; it seeks to determine in what manner the working unit of the school plant may be made
to return the largest dividend upon the material investment of time, en-
ergy and money. From this point of view, classroom management was
looked upon as a 'business problem'" (1962, 7).

Bagley's declaration—that the first rule of efficient service required
unquestioned obedience from teachers—was, in his view, entirely analo-
gous with that in any other organisation or system, including great business enterprises. The new ideas spread rapidly and penetrated the
professional associations. For instance, Callahan (op. cit., 6) reports that
in 1905, at the annual meeting of the National Education Association, a
symposium was held where one of the topics included "Comparison of
Modern Business Methods and Educational Methods".

The new science promised efficiency of time and effort. After 1908
there was a heightening sense that educational measurement had ushered
in a new era with which the promise of educational efficiency could be
scientifically fulfilled. Cremin (1961, 193) notes that: "It was no surprise,
then, when the National Education Association's Department of Superin-
tendence in 1911 appointed a *Committee on Economy of Time in Education,* charging it with formulating recommendations from the systematic
removal of waste from the school curriculum". The committee made four
widely read major reports between 1915 and 1919, which argued that
economy of time would be achieved first by eliminating non-essentials

(though this clearly raised questions regarding which knowledge was essential and which was not), and secondly, by organising courses of study to conform more closely to the principles of child development. In that way, any effort expended by teachers could be maximised, thereby eliminating waste.

Teachers were vulnerable to the new science of management proposed by Taylor. Rules of thumb—or professional judgement—were discouraged. Instead it was argued that *one best way* could be determined by scientific study and used to structure a new set of practises within schools. Scientific management was embraced enthusiastically by a select group of (male) school administrators managing (primarily women) teachers using 'scientific' research conducted by (male) professors of education. In the case of school administrators, their professional survival depended upon their response to demands for efficiency. In the case of university professors, these ideas enabled the emergence of a new division within the organisation of labour legitimated by the establishment and consolidation of a new and powerful discipline within education—the science of educational administration within the academy (cf., Popkewitz 1991).

Franklin Bobbitt, an instructor in educational administration at the University of Chicago, published an influential article in 1912 on scientific management and schools. A year later he was invited to write the yearbook by the National Society for the Study of Education, where he sought to apply Taylor's economic theories to the problem of educational management. He argued that inherent in every organisation, including schools, were certain principles of management that were universally applicable. The three key principles identified by Bobbitt were: (1) standards specified by the business and industrial world, (2) scales of measurement to determine whether the "product rises to that standard", and (3) a system of independent inspection (Callahan 1962, 81–83). These, Bobbitt argued, would enable teachers to know how well they were performing in achieving that standard and then determine themselves to be either 'good', 'medium' or 'poor' teachers. A teacher who fell short of this standard was a weak teacher, while such knowledge enabled management to identify one of the major problems in schools: inefficient teachers. Though the system was dependent upon the collection of extensive records involving considerable paperwork by teachers and school administrators, it was nonetheless argued by Bobbitt that the increase in expenditure associated with this new activity more than offset rises in productivity (Callahan 1962, 87).

Bobbitt's concern with a science of education also extended to the curriculum. He was specifically interested in developing a curriculum perfectly suited to the child and the social requirements of the society. In his book published in 1924, *How to Make a Curriculum,* Bobbitt (cited in Cremin 1962, 199–200) proposed that the goal of the educational scientist—as curriculum engineer—was to identify the full range of human experience and to develop a curriculum that efficiently prepared the child for this (Cremin 1961, 199).

Taylor's model greatly appealed to the growing band of school administrators and superintendents created under Horace Mann's centralised and hierarchised system of education. This was hardly surprising, given that Taylor proposed a more active role for managers in analysing, planning and controlling the whole process, and where the judgement of the individual was to be replaced by the laws, rules and principles of the science of the job which was developed by management. More important, it facilitated the institutionalisation and consolidation of hierarchical authority, derived from the new science of administration, in schools which served to limit teachers' claim to occupational authority. The 'one best way' that underpinned this science of labour and inherent principles of efficient organisation was quickly translated into the search for the 'one best system' (Tyack 1974), a system which, in Tyack's view, ill served American society primarily because it created the conditions for increased bureaucratisation while at the same time obscuring systematic inequality. Indeed, Tyack and Hansot (1982, 107) point out that the new corporate model of schooling that emerged to replace the small central school boards often blocked the political channels by which the working class and ethnic communities had traditionally expressed their political interests in schooling. The one-room schoolhouse gave way to various experiments with the factory model of schooling, while more centralised forms of school governance enhanced the power of cosmopolitan elites whose claims to expertise and objectivity worked to disguise the political nature of education.

By the mid-1920s, the efficiency procedures had been extended to all parts of the nation, but schools were plagued by financial dilemmas which manifested themselves in continuing battles over class sizes and teachers' salaries. A burgeoning and highly politicised research literature emerged on class size and student learning. However, teachers rarely transformed this knowledge into direct political action. Urban argues that it is highly likely that this was a result of the decline of the American Federation of Teachers in the early 1920s following the anti-union push within American society (1989, 195). The social radicalism of teachers during the pre-war years, which had resulted in some gains for teachers (e.g., a victory over wage parity), was eclipsed by a bohemian radicalism and its concern with 'progressive' ideas such as the romanticisation of the child, the naturalism of science and a rebellion against formalism (Clifford 1975, 138).

> Just as prewar progressivism had given rise to a new educational out-
> look, one that cast the school as a lever of social reform, so the postwar
> protest developed its own characteristic argument: the notion that each
> individual has creative potentialities and that a school in which chil-
> dren are encouraged freely to develop these potentialities is the best
> guarantee of a larger society devoted to human work and excellence
> (Cremin 1961, 201–202).

Teachers' low union profile during the 1920s was increased by the public's nervousness about communism. An already conservative NEA retreated in its advocacy of teachers' issues (Urban 1989, 196). As a result, teachers were unable to head off the organisational changes that took place so that by the mid-1920s schools were firmly controlled by their administrators while teachers were incorporated into the lower echelons of the organisation.

Though the depression years of the early 1930s brought teachers, along with school administrators, back into public view as they publicly demonstrated against severe budget cuts imposed by school boards, it was chiefly an uphill battle against powerful business interests and reluctant education authorities. Urban observes: "Their success was at best marginal, but their efforts indicated that teachers were unwilling to submit passively while powerful economic interests tried to control the schools and those who worked in them" (1989, 196). Thus, by the early 1930s, key elements of the settlement for teachers in the United States— that is, relatively low wages, minimal levels of occupational authority resulting from the erosion of control over assessment and the curriculum, and the inability to mobilise collective forms of representation because of restrictions on striking—were embedded in the new institutional structures and practises which were left intact despite the introduction of new Keynesian ideas at the end of the 1930s (Salant 1989; Weir 1989).

Teachers—largely women—now worked in organisations shaped by the science of management and the science of human development: centralised planning, standardised school sizes, workloads and class sizes.

They had lost considerable ground to the new school administrators and superintendents who now planned and inspected their work. At the same time their expertise—or cultural assets—were derived from the various residues of the Progressive movement, manifested as the conventional wisdom on the science of the child and the science of education. Textbooks and school board reports alike referred to 'the whole child', 'intrinsic motivation' and 'adjusting the child to the school', while a child's performance and progress through school was shaped by the new science of efficiency. What were the effects of these developments on teachers' work and their labouring with students during this period? It could be argued that child-centredness concentrated teachers' political efforts not on wider social and political objectives but rather on reproducing the individualism of American society. It might also be argued that because teachers' expertise was linked to a progressive child-centred pedagogy, they were vulnerable to attack from 'experts' within the community who viewed the progressive curriculum as little more than structured play.

At the same time teachers worked in organisational settings that were far more routinised, standardised, specialised and task-oriented. As Tyack and Hansot observe:

> Under the corporate model of urban school governance, some rough parallels appeared between the structure of business enterprise and the organisations of large city schools: a large growth in the staff of the central office (where once only the superintendent and perhaps two or three assistants or clerks held sway); diversification of the structure of the schools into functional divisions such as vocational schools, guidance departments, attendance services, building and maintenance, and special schools for the handicapped; and the creation of research and planning departments to provide evidence on operations and data for forecasting. Forms multiplied and files bulged. New corps of specialists appeared. Indeed, so complex became the subdivisions that large cities sometimes required intermediate layers of supervisors of specialists so that the total number of administrators reporting to the superintendent would not be too great for effective span of control (1982, 159).

Looking back on this period from the vantage point of almost a century later, Linda Darling-Hammond observes:

> Like manufacturing industries, schools were developed as specialized organizations run by carefully prescribed procedures engineered to

yield standard products. Based on faith in rationalistic management, in the power of rules to determine human behavior, and in the ability of administrators to discover and implement common procedures to produce desired outcomes, twentieth century education policy has assumed that continually improving the *design specifications* for schoolwork—required courses, textbooks, testing instruments, and management systems—will lead to student learning. Knowledgeable teachers were not part of the equation because the bureaucratic model assumed that important decisions would be made by others in the hierarchy and handed down in the form of rules and curriculum packages based upon carefully prescribed procedures engineered to yield standard products [my emphasis] (1997, 16–17).

However, despite the transformation of the organisation of schooling and teachers' work that took place, enabling the state to *design the specifications* of teachers' curriculum (what) and assessment (how well) practises and where teachers' power and authority was largely derived from their position in the institutional hierarchy (under what conditions), Tyack and Hansot (1982) note that "talk of business" could not remove three main problems: (1) the output of education was far more difficult to measure than the product of a factory, (2) the goals of schooling were more ambiguous than profit and loss in a factory, and (3) the relationship between goals and outputs are not clear. It was also the case that teachers had some control over their pedagogical practises arising to a large extent from their commitment to progressive child-centred pedagogy. This gave teachers some room for discretion and therefore control over certain aspects of their work. However, these margins were never as wide as those negotiated by English teachers, as the following analysis reveals.

MANAGING TEACHER DISCONTENT IN ENGLAND

In England, as in the United States, the period 1910 to the mid-1920s was also significant in determining the broad features of teachers' work in the Keynesian welfare state settlement. However, whereas in the United States education and teachers' work were closely shaped by the economy/efficiency movement, in England teachers' strategic alignment with organised labour and left-wing public intellectuals unnerved the state and led to considerably more occupational authority being conceded by the state as a means of governing them. As the years wore on, teachers' public discontent with poor wages and working conditions was increasingly viewed by the state as politically dangerous—not only because committed teachers and an efficient education system were central to the reconstruction of society, but because teachers' socialist inclinations would favour Labour as the natural party to lead. Hence, if the defining phrase in America during this period would be 'an inefficient teacher is a national danger', then in England it most certainly was 'a discontented teacher is a national danger'. Though in the end what this meant for English teachers was a form of 'indirect' control over their work managed through the notion of an appropriate 'professional demeanour', teachers could—within this framework—establish their occupational authority, which gave them a considerable degree of autonomy, economic security and social status.

This is not to suggest that matters of efficiency in education were of little concern to either local taxpayers or politicians in England at the time. Indeed, the question of the most economic form of education for the children of the working class, together with the concern that exposure to education might encourage the working class to forget their labour market destination and their place in society, continued to preoccupy key decision makers (cf., Tropp 1957, 162; Simon 1974, 61). This concern was applied as much to working-class elementary teachers as to the working-class children they taught. As Gerald Grace (1987, 200) notes, during the period 1902–1911, Robert Morant, the permanent secretary to the Board of Education, held the very strong and public view that "the pretensions of the elementary schoolteachers needed to be cut back and that their relative power and independence needed to be transformed and constrained". However, in large measure these questions and concerns were translated into cost cutting, rather than—as in the United States—the implementation of particular types of management and pedagogical practises in the classroom. Thus, while the mandate for education increasingly reflected the view that education was central to the reconstruction of the society and the development of its human capital, the concern with efficiency and economy in English education was also tied to the ongoing question of class.

What were the changed conditions that produced such a high level of nervousness over the political consequences of discontented teachers during the first two and a half decades of the 20th century? On numerous occasions prior to this, teachers had expressed their unhappiness about aspects of their work, particularly in relation to the Revised Code (1870), which derided teachers' commitment to certification as unnecessary and proposed a system of payment by results (Tropp 1957, 91, 96). Regarding this, elementary teachers had certainly demonstrated their potential to be active educational campaigners. However, until the 1900s, much of their discontent had taken the form of deputations to local boards over the continuing practise of employing large numbers of cheaper, uncertified (typically female) teachers. These practises inevitably diluted the occupational authority of teachers, largely as teachers were unable to claim specialised expertise. This practise also divided teachers amongst themselves: certified male teachers resented the dilution of their craft and the depressed salaries that followed employing uncertified female teachers, while expensive teachers protested against their dismissal in favour of cheaper teachers, especially during periods of economic recession. At the turn of the 20th century, and like their United States colleagues, English teachers were an occupational group divided by social class, geography, pay, qualifications and gender.

These divisions between teachers changed, however, in quite dramatic and specific ways in the transition years leading to the Keynesian welfare state settlement. Two important developments occurred which created a new set of structuring conditions: the growing centralisation of state power and control over educational policy making, and increased pressure from activists and intellectuals for social and political change within the society. In relation to the centralisation of state power, the establishment of the Board of Education in 1899 enabled the state to direct the educational system centrally through a new set of legislative and administrative practises. This was followed in 1902 with the Education Act, where local school boards were replaced with local education authorities, based on regional or county boroughs. This effectively distanced teachers from localised politics (Grace 1987, 201). The second development, the rising tide of pressure for social and political change in England, gathered momentum, buoyed by the influence of leftist intellectuals and socialist writers such as Sydney and Beatrice Webb, R. H. Tawney, H. G. Wells and A. S. Neill. Campaigners turned their attention to better urban planning and housing, the expansion of welfare provision for children and a new educational mandate centred around the idea of a secondary education for all—including the working class.

A series of critical disputes radically altered teachers' relationship to the state. This began with the West Ham dispute in 1907, between the council and the teachers' union over the new salary system (Tropp 1957, 204). Rising unemployment and the drive for new economies had pressured local authorities into reconsidering teachers' salary rates. However, the NUT and other labour organisations mobilised in support of teachers, providing assistance to teachers if dismissed. This created a new dilemma for the council as the striking teachers were not wholly dependent upon their salary for survival. Though the dispute was settled after months of protracted discussion, the West Ham Strike was, in Lawn's view (1987, 34), a visible demonstration to a new generation of teachers that occupational association built around principles of unity rather than division, collectivism rather than individualism, was essential if teachers were to change their conditions of work.

A further series of events demonstrated the power of teachers in the political arena. We have already noted the contempt for and hostility toward teachers by the secretary of the Board of Education, Robert Morant. However, such public derision of teachers and their class pretensions turned out to be a matter of serious political misjudgement by Morant. In 1911, the NUT was able to mobilise the full force of the civil service along with other political interests to bring pressure to bear upon the Board of Education, forcing the resignation of its president and of Morant.

This event was followed in 1912 by a new wave of industrial unrest arising from the increased cost of living. Teachers, along with other workers, refused to capitulate to the new economy measures; as Tropp observes: "Attempts to economize at the expense of the teacher were giving place to agitation on the part of teachers to secure more adequate salaries and better increments" (1957, 204). Challenges also came from rural teachers protesting their poor teaching conditions (Lawn 1987, 37). In particular, the Herefordshire Case in 1914 was notable in that it was the first occasion when the NUT resorted to large-scale strike action and where it was increasingly acknowledged that the union had become a powerful political force. These strikes energised rural as well as urban teachers, and fostered a growing link with organised labour and the Independent Labour Party (ILP).

World War I (1914–1918) disrupted the work of teachers, primarily through the withdrawal of large numbers of male and many female teachers, which accentuated the problems of teacher supply. It also heightened teachers' demands for increased wages, especially when it was observed that throughout the war wages had gone up in almost every occupation except teaching (Tropp 1957, 210). Between 1917 and 1919 teacher unrest increased and a wave of strikes followed. A strike in Rhondda, the home of the new Miners Federation of Great Britain and the heart of new socialist industrial unionism, unnerved the state. The success of the Rhondda strikers in doubling their salaries sent an important signal to the state: that they would have to secure a salary scale both to manage teachers' salary demands systematically and to head off teacher discontent. "Of grave concern to Fisher [president of the Board of Education] was the significance of the unrest among teachers and the increased militancy of the profession" (Tropp 1957, 211). Lawn observes:

> The significance of the Rhonnda strike in the development of the National Union of Teachers, and all elementary school teachers lies in the fact that for the first time, the Union's recommended salary scale was achieved, not just talked about, and secondly, that to achieve a successful strike and a major pay advance, teachers worked closely with many of the young socialist miners in the Rhondda labour movement. The result of the strike and the labour alliance was to radically change the leadership of the NUT and to reorganise it fundamentally (1987, 49).

The events at Rhondda were aided by the close links between the new industrial unionists, key socialist activists and the teachers within the community. Teachers increasingly took a leading role and acted as the new focus for the left in the union while the Rhondda class teachers overcame the divisions of gender and qualification that had plagued teachers to date. Membership was extended to uncertified teachers. This created a sense of solidarity among teachers, certified or not. Funding, untrained labour and increased workloads were all on the agenda. More important, these events altered teachers' view of unionism as an appropriate political strategy. It moved teachers away from the more conservative and patriarchal craft union policy which had dominated the unions since the 1870s toward an industrial union structure which combined solidarity with their previous exclusionary strategy to secure occupational closure. In so doing, they created what Lawn describes as "a labour outlook" (Lawn 1987, 55–57).

This emerging situation among teachers was sufficient to worry the Conservative government, not only because this new service class threatened post-war reconstruction and economic development, but because they feared that teachers' discontent and their socialist affiliations would open the way for a new social order under the leadership of the Labour Party. There were two further factors that alarmed the government. One was the potential for discontented working-class teachers to use their privileged position to influence the minds of young school children with socialist principles. The second was wider than this. Teachers' views were seen as a litmus of popular sentiments, and therefore, as Simon notes, to be taken notice of by the state:

> The teaching profession could be regarded as a sensitive barometer not only to feeling within the educational world, but owing to close contact with the working and middle classes, to feelings among wide sections of the electorate. To this extent the general outlook among teachers could serve as a touchstone to popular attitudes (1974, 71).

The state's growing concern over the restlessness and resentfulness of teachers (and potentially the general populace) (Tropp 1957, 211) pressed them toward a national salary scale. In 1917 the president of the Board of Education, Mr. H.A.L. Fisher, appointed the Standing Joint Committee on a Provisional Minimum Scale of Salaries for Teachers in Elementary Schools, to look into the principles that might determine the construction of salary scales for elementary teachers. It was chaired by Lord Burnham, who in November 1919 presented the committee's proposal of a scale (Tropp 1957, 212). Fisher also responded by seeking to assist local education authorities with teacher salaries and to create a non-contributory pension scheme (Simon 1974, 15–16). In exchange, teachers were expected to act in a more 'professional' manner befitting one of the more liberal professions, including management through a Teacher Registration Council: "Now that the state *guaranteed* the fair treatment of the teacher, it expected new results" (Lawn 1987, 67). However, the urgent appeal by the Board of Education to teachers to join the council in the spirit of neutrality, professional responsibility and vocation, though supported by some within the NUT (Tropp 1957, 267), was also opposed by an equally determined number of teachers. The Teacher Registration Council never succeeded in achieving its aims and finally collapsed in 1949.

No sooner was a national pay scale in place than the wave of progress that had marked the decade for teachers was under threat both from within and without. The most serious of these came from within the NUT and centred on the NUT's lack of commitment to the question of equal pay for women (Tropp 1957, 216). Though this thorny issue threatened teachers' unity, there was still considerable reluctance within the NUT to support the "foolish feminists" (Kean 1989, 151). In the end it caused the secession of the National Federation of Women Teachers from the NUT, considerably weakening the NUT. Other divisions within the NUT emerged over the militancy of a new generation of union activists (Tropp 1957, 216). These divisions shook the NUT and it set about committing itself to an occupational ideology for the purposes of cohesion (Grace 1987, 208). The threats from without were both economic and political. By 1921, local education authorities began to argue, with the support of the Board of Education, that the economic downturn and ensuing economic hardship had created new problems in paying teachers by the new national scale. In 1921, 1922 and 1923 there was a series of moves by local authorities and the state to reduce teachers' salaries and to change their working conditions. These developments, though clearly a response to the economic conditions, were also centrally about class politics; in particular, an attack on the working class, its rising unionism and demands for greater pay. However, throughout this period the NUT refused to relinquish its role as advocate and continued its fight for salary adjustments, aggrieved by what it saw as the harsh treatment of teachers as compared with other workers.

It was during this period, in response to nervousness over teachers' move toward Labour and its explicit socialist project, that the new president of the Board of Education, Lord Eustace Percy, sought to impose what Lawn argues was a new form of rule—indirect rule—over teachers (1987, 120). Rather than impose on teachers a tight set of curricular requirements that a Labour Party in government might use for its own 'socialist' purposes, Percy sought to develop a strategy that enabled the state to regulate teachers from a distance. This new approach to the governance of education and control over teachers' work gained momentum with the defeat of the Conservative Party in 1923; from then on, Simon (1974, 71) argues, conservatives were convinced that teachers must be taken into account in election votes. This softer approach resulted in huge benefits to teachers; they were largely spared the horrors of the depression during the 1930s. It also created the sense of a new partnership between the state and teachers which later defined and structured their relationship during the Keynesian welfare state settlement.

The new partnership between teachers and the state involved promoting professionalism with 'autonomy' and praising professional common sense, at the same time attempting to block the more radical teachers at various points in their teaching career: for instance, at appointment, inspection and promotion (Lawn 1987, 133). Thus, the 1920s proved to be a decisive turning point for English teachers. They were able to use the state's obvious nervousness over teachers' ability to mobilise social assets such as labour affiliation, and their potential to influence a generation of working-class students, to claim economic assets in the form of a guaranteed wage scale, the protection of cultural assets in the form of state support for teacher certification and registration, and organisational assets in the form of occupational authority. It was through this period that we see, compared with the United States, a very different model of governance emerge for the coordination of education and teachers' labour. In effect, it created significantly more room for English teachers to manoeuvre, though always under the watchful eye of a state concerned with control of teachers' political activities through more indirect means.

KEYNESIAN IDEAS AND THE CONSOLIDATION OF THE NEW SOCIAL SETTLEMENT

I now want to examine the rise of Keynesian ideas during the 1930s and their consolidation in the new social settlement in the thirty golden years that followed the years of crisis and transition since 1900. In particular, I focus attention upon the nature of teachers' work during this settlement. I have already shown in this chapter that the settlement itself cannot be understood as separate from the struggles between teachers, the state and civil society during those crisis and transition years. Indeed, the argument advanced so far is that the architecture of the social settlement as well as teachers' outlook within that settlement can best be understood through an analysis of those transition and crisis years. However, the Keynesian welfare state settlement itself is important for locating and understanding the rise of teachers as state welfare professionals, though it must be noted that the rhetoric of professionalism was no guarantee either of teacher autonomy or of continuous support by the state for teachers' professional project. Rather, the rhetoric of professionalism often existed to guarantee teachers' commitment to servicing the welfare of others for the state, despite poor pay and working conditions.

The most important point to be made about the Keynesian welfare state settlement is that the new institutional arrangements provided an important regulatory framework for the Fordist regime of accumulation. The welfare state symbolised a new deal or post-war settlement not only between capital and labour but between capitalist democracy and its citizens around broad guarantees and rights from the state. As Ramesh Mishra (1990, 19) notes:

The severe depression and mass unemployment of the 1930s, the breakdown of democracy and rise of fascism, the Second World War, and the growing 'threat' of the spread of communism together formed the historical context of the post-war welfare state.

These social and political upheavals shook the faith of the economists in the self-regulating/self-adjusting economy and created a climate of receptiveness to new ideas and new theories. It was not, however, the depression alone that caused a change in the direction of state policy making. The emergence of the working class as a central political actor, particularly in countries such as England, Australia and Canada, along with the brief flirtation in the United States with socialism in the post World War I period, was an important backdrop to understanding the eventual adoption of Keynesianism as economic orthodoxy (Weir 1989, 53). Keynesian state welfarism thus describes a period of state interventionism in "social policy, programmes, standards and regulations in order to mitigate class conflict and to provide for, answer or accommodate certain social needs for which the capitalist mode of production in itself has no solution or makes no provision" (Teeple 1995, 15).

'Keynesianism' is derived from the new economic ideas that appeared during the 1930s in the work of John Maynard Keynes. However, the term refers more generally to the regulatory framework that includes both social and economic policy making and more specifically to a particular type of compromise between capital, labour and the state in the post-war period. Despite differences (in some cases significant) between countries, this was, as Lipietz (1989, 7) notes, composed of the following:

1. Social legislation covering minimum wage levels and a generalised collective agreement
2. A welfare state, meaning some form of advanced system of social security which meant that both wage earners and non-wage earners remained consumers
3. Credit issued by private banks but controlled by central banks as the economy demanded

Three key ideas of the new Keynesian economics underpinned the new 'golden years' settlement. First, Keynesianism broke with laissez-faire economics to argue that the state had a responsibility to intervene in the operation of the economy in order to stabilise regular fluctuations and to manage conflict between capital and organised labour. Second, Keynes proposed that the state could best deal with depression by raising the level of aggregate demand for goods. This could be done, for example, by injecting funds into the economy, thereby increasing and multiplying the purchasing power of consumers. In this way the state could manage aggregate demand. Third, Keynes rejected the idea that governments should have a balanced budget. Instead, he promoted the idea of counter-cyclical demand management; that is, that governments should engage in deficit spending during periods of recession and that this would be countered by surpluses during periods of growth. The momentum of these ideas was greatly assisted on the one hand by the development of new quantitative techniques for estimating national income and expenditure and, on the other, by the usefulness of Keynesian ideas in war planning.

Keynes's ideas were neither enthusiastically embraced everywhere nor equally influential across all economic and social policy domains (Hall 1989). The very different history of Keynesianism in England and the United States (cf., Salant 1989; Weir 1989) is an important case in point and one that I will elaborate briefly to help understand the particular nature of the sectoral settlement for teachers in each of these different social formations.

Keynes's ideas took hold in the United States in the late 1930s following what was one of the sharpest declines in economic productivity in 1937–1938. Keynes's ideas were influential among the young economists and popular economic writers, many of whom became prominent in positions within the Treasury, the Budget Bureau and the Department of Commerce (Weir 1989, 56). During the years of war planning and immediately after, these economists moved into key strategic positions within the state, including the National Strategic Planning Board, which was charged with getting the post-war planning underway (ibid., 56). However, Keynesian ideas were neither long-lasting nor deeply embedded in the social institutions in the United States as the settlement progressed. Weir argues that this had as much to do with the ideology of individualism arising from small producer capitalism and the structure of the political and social system of the United States as it did with the disorganised state of U. S. labour. Specifically, she points to the fragmented nature of the U. S. bureaucracy and the fact that expertise was very often brought in from outside the civil service. This meant that policy making was influenced more by political parties than by the commitments of civil servants. This was compounded by the disorganised state of labour within the United States, which faced not only numerous political setbacks in the post-war years, but internal disagreements within the movement itself. This was potently demonstrated in the disagreement between the American Federation of Labor (AFL) and the Congress of Industrial Organizations (CIO) over the cornerstone of a Keynesian welfare state—the Full Employment Bill of 1946. There was also violent opposition from business and farm groups to the bill which, when added to the perception that Keynesianism was a form of interventionist state planning, created the conditions for a limited state commitment to Keynesianism as an ongoing and embedded institutional and regulatory framework within the realm of social policy. There remained a superficial commitment to public sector spending, particularly in the social welfare areas, but the commitment to Keynesian ideas remained focused upon economic growth and outputs rather than worker welfare and employment. It could be argued that the historic compromise between organised capital, a semi-organised state, disorganised labour and an unorganised civil society was structured by an explicit commitment to accumulation and social control expressed through nation-building.

In England, in contrast, Keynes's ideas were slow to take hold in the 1930s and their advocates were unable to make headway until 1945. From then onward, these ideas became more central in the consolidation of the institutional structures that framed Keynesian welfare state settlement in Britain. Why was this the case? It can be argued that in Britain, these differences arose from processes in policy making, the specific nature of institutional arrangements and array of policy alternatives, all of which affected the possibilities for the acceptance and consolidation of Keynesian ideas. Weir (1989) argues that, in contrast to the United States, England had an increasingly centralised state with a powerful Treasury which, as has been shown earlier in this chapter, resisted calls for increased public spending. She also points out that right up until the end of World War II, a powerful labour movement and Labour Party resisted the compromise with capital implicit in Keynesianism and reaffirmed its commitment to a socialist agenda, including its centerpiece: nationalisation. However, as the war proceeded and Keynesian ideas became critical in the war-planning machinery, a powerful civil service dominated by the Treasury endorsed the new economic ideas supported by a united trade union movement. Keynesian ideas were thus now viewed by the labour movement and civil society as an adjunct to social programs, and by conservatives as an alternative to a more interventionist state. It was an historic compromise between organised capital, organised labour and an organised state which was, at the same time, dependent upon particular conceptions of the family, family responsibilities and citizenship entitlements.

The crucial point for my purpose in this chapter is that Keynesian ideas, while their implementation varied across nation-states, created the conditions for a more or less general willingness to accept some public sector financing of public works and social programs. This occurred around what Hay (1996, 50–51) calls "an edifice of consensus" and which Hall (1989, 6) describes as "a more general set of symbolic ideas which became a component of a class coalition and political compromise that structured the political economy of the post-world war years". Hall goes on:

> . . . although Keynes was by no means responsible for the expansion of the welfare state that is sometimes linked to his name, his theories placed increasing responsibility for economic performance on the government's shoulders and his attacks on the priority which classical economics attached to a balanced budget helped to loosen a fiscal constraint which stood in the way of more generous social programmes (1989, 4).

This edifice of consensus was erected on six pillars: full employment, the 'mixed' economy, active government, social welfare provision, the conciliation of the trade unions and the cult of expertise (Hay 1996, 51–57). Though these pillars varied in their overall appearance and solidity, they nonetheless arose from and combined with the institutional architecture established during the crisis and transition years, giving substance to the idea of a settlement.

Though all of these pillars are important, I want to single out one for particular comment—the 'cult of expertise'—largely because it relates not only to teachers' professional project during the Keynesian welfare state settlement but also to the changing role of education during this period. The idea of expertise came to characterise the post-war mind-set, which infused politicians and bureaucrats alike and which, as Hay (1996, 57) observes:

> . . . became encapsulated in the image of a scientifically managed virtuous circle of economic growth and a neutral bureaucratic rationality free from vested interest. Its development was tied to the spirit of post-war optimism, the technological revolution, the initial post-war economic boom and the emergence of the new science of the economy— Keynesianism.

The rise of expertise was also built upon the rise of the social sciences of individuals, communities and society. The educational bureaucracy became the site for a new type of expertise. In England they were the 'public servants'—a self-proclaimed and self-righteous "composite of all of the virtues of humane, service-oriented, Fabian influenced bureaucracy" as Ozga and Gewirtz (1994, 131) note in recounting interviews with the education policy elite of this period. This elite took the view that it was they who knew what was best for society and how to attain it. The educational enterprise itself became a vehicle both for producing and legitimating the new scientific knowledge. Education was also an increasingly important mechanism for sifting and sorting, selecting and stratifying within society, particularly for the new professional and service class, as well as for promoting the knowledge and skills for the Fordist regime of accumulation. The proliferation of professional expertise during this period was linked, on the one hand, to the accumulation regime underpinned by military industrial capitalism (engineers, scientists) and, on the other hand, to those institutions and knowledge forms that defined the welfare state (social welfare workers, teachers, social scientists, psychologists and so on). Not surprisingly, teachers sought to define their own expertise (though not always successfully) within the educational and social enterprise around two key elements: a notion of technical expertise based upon the new science of education (curriculum, assessment and pedagogy), and a new moral claim—social trusteeship. These two elements—the power of expertise and the goodness or social trusteeship for all classes—were in uneasy and paradoxical tension with each other, their inherently contradictory nature creating both the ammunition for outside attack and the conditions for its eventual demise. Teachers' claim to expertise during the Keynesian welfare state settlement was based on the notion of trust as well as state support for professional closure; a claim I argue in Chapter 8 is questioned by the state as producing a set of circumstances where teachers have a captive clientele of students (referred to as provider capture) and the conditions for opportunism.

TEACHERS AND THE FORDIST KEYNESIAN
WELFARE STATE SETTLEMENT

The Keynesian welfare state settlement has been regarded as providing the conditions that enabled the consolidation of the new professional or service class around what Brint (1994) has described as occupational professionalism. Brint's thesis is that the complexion of the professions changed during the course of the late 19th century and early decades of the 20th century, a move he characterises as a shift from status professionalism to occupational professionalism. One way of understanding what Brint means by this is to relate it to Lockwood's framework, discussed in Chapters 1 and 2. This framework specifies the consequences of teachers' struggles over assets under particular conditions in terms of their market, work and status situations. The professional project of occupational groups such as teachers can, in broad terms, be seen as moving from a predominant concern with status situations to one focused on work situations. For teachers, this means a preoccupation with control over varied aspects of their labour: specifically, pedagogy (how teachers teach), curriculum (what they teach), and assessment (how well they teach).

We have argued that teachers' differential ability as an occupational group to capitalise on the new conditions within the Keynesian welfare state settlement within each nation was forged during the crisis and transition years 1900–1945. These differences can well be glossed over if one were to accept, first, the transnational nature of the Keynesian welfare state settlement too uncritically, and second, the outward appearance of teaching and teachers' occupational outlook without being attentive to questions of what teachers labour on, how, under what conditions and with what outcome. I have noted the different implementation of Keynesian ideas in different nations, focusing again upon the United States and England as cases in point. These differences, captured in the historically specific accumulation/institution relation which defines a social settlement, clearly had particular consequences for key institutional sites like education and for teachers' social relations and practises

Much of the evidence assembled in our analysis of teachers' work in England and the United States suggests that, indeed, teachers were preoccupied with establishing their status situations largely through realising the value of their cultural assets—the particular expertise or technical competency which defined the labour of teachers not only as different from other workers but as one that could only be legitimatised in a particular way. We have seen how the professional project of teachers in these nations took different paths, largely as a result of their different conditions and capacities to mobilise particular types of social assets. In England, teachers were eventually successful in mobilising collective unionisation in the face of growing nervousness by the state about the rising tide of unrest within the society and teachers' potential political affiliation to the socialist movement. This enabled teachers, at least for a time, to change their market situation through salary increases as well as to shape how those were negotiated and resourced. It also enabled teachers to change the conditions under which they worked. This required a commitment by the state: namely, that it would guarantee occupational closure through the provision of credentialled activities such as training and the enforcement of regulations.

However, in the United States, teachers during those transition years lost considerable ground to the state following the close control over their work by, on the one hand, a hierarchy of managers and, on the other hand, control over the curriculum and forms of assessment. The source of teachers' control in this case did not derive from occupational authority as it did for English teachers but from their position within the organisational hierarchy within the school. This clearly limited their ability to control their work. In a Taylorist sense, teachers were task workers within a hierarchy of authority where the detail and nature of the task was controlled through a complex process of what I have already called, following Tyack and Hansot (1984), the *design specification of schoolwork.*

The Market, Work and Status Situation of American Teachers in the Keynesian Welfare State Settlement

It is now time to review the consequences for teachers in the two case studies we have been following—England and the United States—during the Keynesian welfare state settlement in terms of their market, work and status situations. In the period 1950–1970 in the United States, Clifford (1975, 166) argues that despite considerable rhetoric of professionalism at the time, teachers saw their conditions of work erode rather than be enhanced under Roosevelt's New Deal and the new Keynesian ideas. Indeed the New Deal was widely construed as a "Raw Deal for Public Schools" (Tyack, Lowe and Hansot 1984, 111). In the post-war period there was a constant shortage of teachers, and the various local and state education systems spent little money on adequate teacher training and professional development. There were a number of conditions which contributed to this poor state of affairs. Low birth rates during the depression and the casualties of war reduced the number of potential trainees for the teaching force. This was compounded by the new ideology in favour of family and motherhood, which reduced the number of female workers available for the workplace. The shortages were also a result of growing opportunities in other areas: those who had served in World War II were able to use their GI benefits afterward to prepare for other professions while the overall expansion of the post-war economy also created new opportunities for employment. The problem was escalated by the rapid expansion of the population, resulting from a sharp rise in the birth rate and the steady flow of immigrants into the United States followed by the post-war relocation and reconstruction programme.

School boards responded to this new set of conditions by hiring 'unqualified' teachers, using teacher substitutes, increasing class sizes, curtailing various programmes, and using whatever physical resources and spaces might be available in order to teach. Though the problem of the shortage of teachers lessened overall throughout the 1950s and 1960s, there were still major shortfalls in areas such as mathematics and science following the post-Sputnik pressure to upgrade the so-called hard sciences in the Cold War competition with the Soviet Union (Clifford 1975, 167). Throughout this period, teachers' market, status and work situations did not improve. Indeed, their situation deteriorated, if anything, aided in no small measure by the stance of the National Education Association (NEA) and the American Federation of Teachers (AFT). In the case of the NEA, it opposed the unionisation of teachers, believing it would reduce the extent to which teaching was considered a profession. Indeed the NEA, like common schools campaigner Catherine Beecher more than a century before (Fraser 1989, 121), took the view that teachers should commit themselves to the high ideals of service rather than pecuniary gain (Cole 1969, 3–5). This position was endorsed by the AFT which, from its inception, not only opposed the use of strikes by teachers (the NEA did not oppose strikes but it was largely unthinkable during this period) but it was the only national labour union to have a no-strike policy (Cole 1969, 6; Urban 1989, 198). By failing to mobilise social assets—in the desire to improve their status situation—teachers contributed not only to the continuation of poor working conditions and salaries but an overall decline in educational provision for the whole of America.

The Keynesian welfare state settlement, I would argue, can hardly be construed as the golden age for American teachers as state welfare professionals. The significant loss of control by teachers over the curriculum and assessment in the transition years before the settlement, combined with the limited commitment by the state to a broad programme of public sector spending on services—such as education and social welfare—created a different set of conditions for American teachers from their English counterparts. Their pedagogical activity was constrained both by the failure to prepare adequately large numbers of teachers for classroom life and by the poor organisational conditions under which their pedagogical activity took place. The very real power of teachers to pressure the state for occupational closure was mitigated by teachers' particular construction of their professional project (Urban 1989, 198–199). This project entailed an apolitical stance and an ethic of morality and service—a continuation of the notion of the classless profession promulgated by the first generation of schoolmen more than a century before (Mattingly 1975). Teachers' commitment to an ethic of service, limited unionisation, and no-strike action, in the hope that this would transform their status situation, merely limited their ability to realise their claims.

By the early 1960s the conditions shaping both the teaching profession and the wider society changed quite dramatically. The previous shortage of teachers had turned into an oversupply, while widespread teacher strikes became a new reality:

> The bench mark in this movement was probably the one-day strike of twenty-two thousand New York City teachers, more than half the city's teaching force, in April 1961. The strike was successful on several counts: its demands forced additional expenditures for teacher salaries; the state law banning strikes by public employees . . . was shown [to be] unenforceable; and the mobilizing effects of the strike were large and long-lasting, as the union that called the strike increased its membership and solidified its position as the teachers' bargaining agent (Clifford 1975, 171).

Stephen Cole's (1969) study of the unionisation of teachers during this period tied the militancy of the United Federation of Teachers (UFT)—the group that led the 1960s strike—to its mostly male and junior high school membership, their militancy arising from the general economic conditions plaguing teachers and from being forced to be remunerated on the same salary scale as female elementary school teachers.

As teachers' militancy increased, buoyed by the level of successful industrial action within the wider economy (Urban 1989, 200), so did the level of union membership. Teachers' politicisation coincided with the rising tide of dissent within America. Demands for civil rights, along with other protest movements committed to equality and equal opportunity, stimulated a crisis within public education which refused to go away:

> Teachers became more militant and well organised and won collective bargaining rights that preempted many traditional powers of school boards and superintendents. Although there was much talk about

"community control" and some actual attempts to decentralize school governance in large cities, in fact much decision making migrated upward from the local district to the state and federal legislatures and other authorities (Tyack and Hansot 1982, 215).

It was, as Tyack and Hansot (ibid.) note, a case of whether the cup was half full or half empty, depending upon which way particular interested parties looked at the situation. Reformers faced criticism from radicals and conservatives alike, while reforms were seen as either too fast or too slow. Most notably, Urban (1989, 202) observes that "the 1968 teachers' strike in New York City resulted in teachers being confronted by angry black parents who spearheaded a thrust for more community control over education, threatening the job security and other work rule provision that teachers had long fought for". As the settlement moved into crisis in the early 1970s, so too did the status of public education and teachers generating new concerns about public spending, public programmes and public accountability (Apple 1993; Carlson 1992).

The Market, Work and Status Situations of English Teachers in Keynesian Welfare Statism

Teachers' relationship to the state in England during the Keynesian welfare state settlement continued the partnership relationship that had emerged in the 1930s as a resolution to the problems of social control within the transition and crisis years. While it was not always evident where the balance of power lay between the various parties to the partnership between teachers, the central state and the local state, it was nonetheless the case that teachers were incorporated into the state's policy making machinery. Grace (1987, 209) notes that organised teachers in the NUT had a strong feeling that they were an important part of the educational enterprise and a project of social reconstruction. This involved teachers who were part of the reconstruction of the schooling system in order to realise a better future.

> In the wider social, economic and political context of Britain in the 1940s and 1950s, education was perceived to be central to national regeneration. This was the period in which the social democratic consensus about the socio-political and economic potential of education in nation life was formed. Modern schooling was seen to have the capac-

ity to strengthen democracy through citizenship education, to reduce
class divisiveness and promote social harmony and equal educational
opportunity and to contribute to economic modernisation and growth
through the more efficient cultivation of the reserves of talent in the nation (Grace 1987, 209).

Whatever the political party in power, state policy education continued to reflect this commitment to the potential transformation of society
through education—a commitment that reached its high point in the
Plowden Report (1967), where education was seen as creating the conditions of growth for the child, even overriding matters of social class and
cultural differences (Bernstein and Davies 1969). Did this new commitment by the state to the socially transformative potential of education
imply a change in teachers' status and market situations in English society? Teachers clearly had this expectation. However, such changes were
not forthcoming—an event which continued to frustrate and disillusion
teachers.

It must be noted, however, that teachers had gained and retained
considerable control within their organisations. This enabled teachers,
individually and collectively, to retain control over key aspects of their
labour: curriculum, assessment and pedagogy. It was also the case that
they were able to exercise some power as an occupational group. As in
America, there were considerable labour shortages in the post-war period which were often covered through a programme of recruiting uncertified teachers. However, Tropp (1957, 255) observes that the NUT played
an important part in the planning and execution of the scheme and that the
scheme was to be viewed as a 'short-term' policy under emergency conditions while the state expanded its training programmes in training colleges and university departments. While we might see this as an example
of the incorporation of teachers into the state (a phenomenon evident in
more recent state restructuring in countries such as Australia [see Robertson and Woock 1991] and Mexico [see Torres 1991]) it can also be seen as
the state's recognition of the political clout of teachers. There is clear evidence that teacher power had declined within the settlement. For instance,
the discontent among teachers that had so greatly concerned the state during the inter-war years could be largely ignored in the 1950s:

The agencies of the state in education in the 1950s found themselves
able to deny the teachers the sort of salary increases which they expected

and the greater professional self-government which they requested without any sense that a crisis situation would ensure. In the economic sector of teacher-state relations the power differential was in favour of the state and this applied whether the state in education was constituted by Labour or Conservative politicians. Although the teacher unions were able to secure equal pay in 1961, the relative position of teachers' salaries compared with those of skilled manual workers continued to decline in the 1960s (Grace 1987, 210).

By the late 1960s, against a background of general political and industrial unrest, the stance of teachers changed and a period of vigorous militancy ensued. This added to the sense of crisis that pervaded education from the 1970s onward. The sharp decline in economic productivity within the global economy—and perhaps more exaggerated for England, which was increasingly having to adjust to the disappearance of its former empire (and the greater competition for pursuing a neocolonial strategy—competition from the United States, in particular) created new challenges for teachers, education systems and nations as the Fordist-Keynesian welfare state settlement found itself in crisis.

CONCLUSION

The struggle over economic, cultural, organisational and social assets was not uniformly realised by teachers in the two nations that have been analysed—the United States and England. Nor did these struggles take place unhindered by the legacies of past battles or powerful ideologies that continued to shape the nature of teachers' work in each of these contexts. In this chapter I have shown, on the one hand, how the nature and organisation of teachers' work in the United States had already been influenced by Taylorist forms of scientific management, which embedded themselves into the very institutional arrangements and practises that shaped much of American education in the post-World War II period. On the other hand, teachers in England had, by the early 1920s, managed to consolidate their links with the wider labour movement and indeed had become far more political in their outlook and activities than their American counterparts. This led to a different relationship between the state and teachers, a relationship that Lawn (1996, 21) argues was a form of "indirect rule" based on the British system of colonial rule. Such a strategy sought to dampen—or at least deflect—them from engaging in socialist politics at a time when teachers' allegiance and therefore teacher control were viewed by the government of the day as very problematic. Though indirect rule was clearly effective at one level, it nonetheless provided a context in which teachers were able to negotiate greater degrees of freedom over their work than their American colleagues.

PART III

Contemporary Change

CHAPTER 5

The New Politics of 'Fast Capitalism': From Body to Soul

*FAST: Firmly fixed or attached;
rapid, quick moving, producing or
allowing quick motion;
showing too advanced time;
immoral, dissipated.*
—CONCISE OXFORD DICTIONARY 1976, 378

'FAST Capitalism'

In this chapter I examine aspects of the changing conditions for teachers and their work arising from processes of globalisation and regionalisation and which I have called, following Ben Agger (1991), 'fast capitalism'. These new dynamics have had profound consequences for how teachers' work is conceptualised and organised in schools in a range of nations—the United States, England, Canada, Australia and New Zealand, among others. In broad terms, the social relations between teachers, the state, the economy and society have been transformed.

In this chapter I use the term 'fast capitalism' as a descriptive and metaphoric category to point to a number of different but related aspects of the changed social relations of capitalist production and consumption that are part of the new social settlement. I have sought to capture aspects of these shifts in the variety of meanings given to 'fast'—as firmly fixed, rapid and quick-moving motion, advanced time, and moral dissipation. Separately and in combination, these different discursive conceptions of 'fast' are a heuristic for prying open and attempting to understand aspects of the new politics of global competitiveness and its underlying social relations of production and consumption.

FAST: Firmly Fixed or Attached

'Fast capitalism' describes what Frederic Jameson (1984) and David Harvey (1990) have called an "intensification of capitalist social relations" rather than their diminution, dilution or disappearance. Despite Francis Fukuyama's (1989) pronouncement of the end of history in the face of the collapse of the communist bloc and the rise of liberalism, or Peter Drucker's (*Post Capitalist Society,* 1993) and Piore and Sabel's (*The Second Industrial Divide,* 1984) claims that both the new technologies and an emphasis on knowledge open up the possibility for a reconstitution of labour relations and production systems, I want to suggest that capitalist social relations in the 1990s—to quote Marx's famous words—appear to be 'fast-frozen' (Marx 1932, 324).

In most advanced Western economies, the restructuring of the public and private sectors appears to have created few opportunities for previously marginalised groups within the new economy. Rather, there is growing concern that the restructuring has led to little more than the redistribution of greater wealth and opportunity for those at the top and increased poverty and marginality for those at the bottom. As Robert Reich (1997, 163) notes: "National borders no longer define our economic fates. We are now in different boats, one sinking rapidly, one sinking more slowly, and the third rising steadily". So, who is in which boat? According to Reich (op. cit.), in an advanced economy like that of the United States of America, the boat that is sinking most rapidly is the one carrying routine workers, as production continues to move to where labour is cheapest and most accessible, and as lower- and middle-level management workers whose jobs as section supervisors have been lost due to plant closings. The steadily rising boat is the new managers of production and consumption: the management consultants, public relations managers, bankers, lawyers and accountants who now operate in the regional and global economy, unhindered by national borders.

The new wealth has trickled upward, not down. In 1960, for example, the richest 20 percent of people in the world had an income thirty times greater than that of the poorest 20 percent; by 1991, this ratio had doubled to sixty times. In other words, during this period, the richest 20 percent had increased their share of world income from 70 percent to 85 percent, while the poorest 20 percent saw their income shrink from 2.3 percent to only 1.4 percent (ICEM 1996, 9). Similar patterns can be seen in many of the advanced economies, where income for the top 10 or 20 percent has increased while income for the bottom 20 or 40 percent has decreased (ICEM 1996, 12). In many of these instances, though an increasing number of males have been affected by the restructuring because of their position in high-volume manufacturing, the poorest are still women and ethnic minorities (Reich 1997, 166). The restructuring of the state and labour market resulted in a residualised social welfare system, and along with it came the feminisation of poverty, the casualisation of the labour market, and the decline in union power and membership (teachers are one of the few exceptions to the last result).

The overall decline in wages for the working and middle classes (Reich 1997), together with the overall decline in funding public sector activity—such as education and health—has resulted in significant erosions of standards of living and greater hardship for many ordinary citizens. Teachers now teach in a more polarised schooling system, where the effects of a decade of restructuring and the implementation of a variety of forms of marketisation within the health, employment, housing and educational sectors has produced unequal educational chances, endemic unemployment, poverty and third-world disease (cf., Thrupp 1999). The massive programme of privatisation of state assets over the past decade has seen the gradual depletion of state resources, largely as a growing number of privately run corporations provide public goods but where provision is shaped by the need to minimise expenditure and maximise profits. These developments can be contrasted with the increase in tax advantages, stock options and salaries to a small elite, justified as performance incentives. By contrast, the wages of public sector workers, including teachers in many Organisation for Economic and Co-operative Development (OECD) countries, has not kept pace with average wage levels (Organisation for Economic and Co-operative Development 1996, 55–65). The economic assets derived from public sector teaching have been seen increasingly as far less attractive than other types of private service occupations.

FAST: Rapid, Quick Moving, Producing or Allowing Quick Motion

A second feature of 'fast capitalism' refers to the increasingly rapid movement of capital in search of profit. The rise of finance capital, in particular, aided by the deregulation of the financial markets within nation states, is an important aspect of transnationalisation in the global economy (Hobsbawm 1994). Fast capitalism describes the switch from accumulation within the productive sphere to accumulation within the sphere of circulation—particularly money capital. In other words, the source of profit comes from speculative activity within capital markets.[1] The rapid flow of money around the globe as entrepreneurs search for profits or investment returns and/or income on unearned income has been assisted by new electronic technologies. Helleiner (1996, 193) notes that the daily volume of trading in the world's major foreign exchange and futures commodity markets reached almost $1 trillion in 1990, a figure close to forty times the value of international trade.

According to Cerny (1995, 226), financial globalisation has become irreversible, with states losing further control over their own domestic financial systems. This makes it more difficult for states to follow an autonomous path driven by domestic rather than international economic goals. Referring to the current form of financial globalisation as the new "embedded financial orthodoxy", Cerny (1995) argues that economic production and exchange will be shaped first and foremost by financial and monetary considerations leading to unstable cycles of boom and bust. Clearly this will reverberate into the political arena and civil society as fluctuations of austerity and overheating (the boom-bust cycle) take hold. Without the buffer of Keynesian state interventionism to prevent external shocks setting off domestic chain reactions, governments now have few levers to manipulate the conditions for accumulation and legitimation.

'Fast capitalism' is not confined to the operation of finance capital. It also describes social relations within the productive sector. Heightened competition among corporations tends to make the technological competitive edge obsolete within a short period of time. The use value in the process of capital valorisation is short; ephemeral, one might say. We can observe two related elements of this problem. New computer technologies now enable rapid and efficient responses to perceived market niches and manufactured tastes through short-batch production runs of goods directed toward, in some cases, individual consumers. This form of fast capitalism has come to be known as "flexible specialisation" (Piore and Sabel 1984; Boyer 1990; Coriot 1995). The term 'flexible specialisation' has been coined

> . . . to signify the potential not only to meet shifting market niches but
> also to do so through a chain of economic organisation which poten-
> tially involves cooperative relations between small firms in industrial

---

[1]At the same time, capital must diversify between productive and financial markets; it is only in the productive sphere that value can be created.

districts (pooling technology and market functions, for example), job enrichment (or, alternatively intensification) through multiple skilling and task switching, subcontracting between producers and consumers, new forms of work organisation, and just in time delivery of inputs to economise on inventories and to conform to the capacity to change product composition and quality (Fine 1995, 136).

New technologies have also facilitated the rapid internationalisation of production, enabling an unprecedented level of economic expansion. As a result, transnational capital has been able to access the productive resources and markets for distribution of the globe as a whole. Clothing and footwear can be made for a fraction of the price in low-wage periphery countries such as Malaysia, China and Indonesia. For the core countries (such as the United States, the United Kingdom, Germany and France) and their workers, this has meant a radical displacement of key segments of the productive apparatus. For example, textile production in the older industrialised countries has declined, while major gainers of export share have been selective East Asian countries, such as South Korea and Hong Kong (Dicken 1992). The effect of this shift in core countries has been to increase unemployment significantly as industrial sectors—such as automobile production, clothing and footwear—have been relocated to low-wage East Asian and Central American countries. Productive displacements also work to the disadvantage of the new host countries. For example, catering for the continual satiation of consumer taste in the core countries (such as the year-round supply of exotic vegetables) can often mean a shift away from the supply of staples for the local population. It may also mean, in the absence of protective local or national labour laws, that the production of these items for Western consumption rests on the small shoulders of exploited child labourers. The child labour conventions adopted by the International Labour Organisation (ILO) appear to have little influence on this form of transnationalised production unless enforced by organised consumer boycotts.

FAST: Showing Too Advanced Time

A further aspect of fast capitalism describes an era where adjustment to change as well as exposure to ideas and information flows is so constant that it appears to compress time and collapse our common-sense notions of space. It feels as though time is pressing hard on us, while space is diminishing in size. These developments highlight the fact that when the material practises and processes of social reproduction change, then the objective qualities, as well meanings of space and time, also change (Harvey 1990, 204).

The compression of time and space can be felt in a multiplicity of ways. With the quick flow of information around the globe, the boundaries we have come to know between the self and others are eroded. For example, new communications technologies connect and disconnect individuals across the world through a web of 'chattering' sites. Our experience of community is no longer rooted only in the material, but also in the virtual world. These erosions collapse our sense of self as a geographically bounded entity. In the same way, too, the lines between the inner and outer world are fractured and blurred as a new range of technologies—technological innovations as well as technologies of power— enable the outside world to intrude into previously protected or private spaces. For example, modems link homes and schools to the outside world, as do fax systems, the use of cellular telephones, new audit procedures, codes of social responsibility imposed by the state on its citizens and so on.

The intensification of exposure to ideas and the flow of information means that ideas are packaged in small consumable bites, within smaller and smaller time frames, into more and more spaces. Advertisers talk about the need to fill up empty or 'dead' space wherever they find it, by which they mean space not yet put to commercial use. One sphere where this is visible is the public sector transportation system. In subways and on buses, inside and outside vehicles, are all incorporated into the advertisers' world. Buses are painted to resemble packages of M & Ms in places as far from each other as Shanghai in the People's Republic of China and Pittsburgh in the United States of America. In the same way, schoolrooms are now viewed as dead space waiting for the imprint of the advertisers' hand. School corridors, for example, are now used as video billboards by Channel One (sold by Chris Whittle to K–III in 1994) (Barber 1995, 63). CommuniMed Inc., a Montreal-based firm, has also begun work on similar sorts of posters for twelve- to seventeen-year-olds in Canadian schools. The posters are located in high-traffic areas and changed regularly for greatest impact (Ontario Secondary School Teachers' Federation [OSSTF] 1995, 12). No space is exempt; rather, all space is viewed as commodifiable. This includes infomercials and the children's and other television programmes that are basically designed around some toy or other product that is sold as we watch the 'story' being told. Even Schools' Boards of Governors, for example, have been encouraged to sell advertising space on school buses while corporate logos find their way onto students' worksheets and children's uniforms, school prizes and computers in the classroom. Whether Kellogg's coupons, Kraft recipes or Kentucky Fried Chicken curriculum materials, all are evidence of the rapid growth in the activity of (transnational and local) corporations within educational institutions.

Increasingly, the assumption that the future will resemble the past no longer holds true. The knowledge and practises that provided a guide to solutions in the past are no longer seen as relevant in a world where rapid change is the norm. It is also increasingly argued that it no longer makes sense for teachers to talk about 'a career' with the same degree of certainty they did a decade ago. Security of tenure and 'a career' for teachers are giving ground to so-called flexible employment practises that specify a term of employment and a level of performance expected in the delivery of the services. Similarly, teachers are no longer able to use the touchstone of 'planning for the future' and the carrot of a 'good job' (or career) to facilitate either cooperative behaviour in classrooms or a sense that an educational credential is something worth having. Rather, it is expected that future workers will have 'a career' of disconnected and changing experiences as they move in and out of organisations, including work. This sort of future scenario ought to be enough to set most of us back on our collective heels when we contemplate the social 'craziness' of a system that deepens the divisions between those who produce and consume and those who don't. However, according to the 'fast capitalist texts' of writers like Tom Peters (1994): "If you don't feel *crazy,* you're not in touch with the times . . ." [my emphasis].

These diverse (and by no means exhaustive) elements combine in such a way that they qualitatively alter our experiences of time and space, and therefore our identities. Things seem to happen too fast and change seems to be more and more rapid. What are the effects of such intrusions? One is the rapid intensification of social experience and of labour—despite the promise that technology is labour-saving. Having time simply to relax at home, or reflect 'on the job' is increasingly limited. A second effect is that it "speeds up the mind so much that imagination takes too long" (Agger 1991, 69). Agger's point here is particularly pertinent. He argues that "fast capitalism is distinguished by the way in which the line between the textual and the material world is blurred to the point of being indistinguishable, hence making it difficult to decipher the texts of ideology which enmesh us in their thoughtlessness" (Agger 1991, 69). These two effects combine to limit the space available for speculation, mediation and reconstruction, thereby encouraging us to attend only to the local and immediate rather than the medium-term and long-term. Actions are thus always reactive and disconnected rather than strategic and connected to historical processes and projects. This can be seen particularly in the state's constant restructuring activity, as if to create a moving target that does not allow the political realities of the economic and political elites' interests and power to settle for too long. This is the new space for creating system legitimacy—an endless cycle of restructuring.

FAST: Immoral, Dissipated

Fast capitalism aptly captures Holloway's (1994, 52) insight that "capitalism is a restless mode of domination". Holloway goes on:

> The history of capital is the history of the constant flight forward, a constant flight from the inadequacy of the existing relations of exploitation, from the inadequacy of its own domination of the power of labour on which it depends. . . . The restlessness of capital is epitomised in its existence as money. In its existence as money, capital is free, free to flow globally in pursuit of obtaining maximum benefit from the exploitation of labour in pursuit of profit. Capital, of course, does not exist only as money: it flows constantly through its different functional forms, existing now as money, now as productive capital embodied in means of production and labour power, now as commodities (1994, 53).

There are three points to be made here. First, capital flows into whatever form offers the largest profit. Profit itself arises from the inherently exploitative labour relations of capitalism; relations that Marx described as immoral. Second, the search for profit means identifying new markets and reservoirs of untapped captive consumers while at the same time shaping buying behaviour in order to increase profitability. In essence, it results in the increasing colonisation of 'empty' spaces by commercial enterprise. Tapping the school market is one such example. Third, the emergence of neoliberal ideology as a justification for unfettered accumulation in the 1990s can only be described as 'unfair' in that it privileges a culture of individualism and economic consumption over the social and communitarian principles committed to responsibility for collective public goods. As I will elaborate later on, teachers and their students in schools in the 1990s have, in a variety of ways, been increasingly exposed to the excesses of fast capitalism. As a result, schools can no longer be considered relatively safe havens.

FROM BODY TO SOUL—THE NEW POLITICS OF CONSUMPTION

Unlike Fordism, where the emphasis is upon the regulation of the body and workplace production, the new social relations of post-Fordist competitiveness emphasise the manufacture and shaping of desire and need into patterns of consumption linked to identity construction. The lines that were drawn between goods and services within the Fordist economy have increasingly been blurred. According to Barber (1995, 59), goods are now "associated with or defined by symbolic interactions that belong to the service sector in its postmodern, virtual economy manifestations". The traditional relationship between production and consumption, where goods that were manufactured for profit and sold, is being reversed. Within the competitive post-Fordist economy, production now follows 'desire'. The identification of niches, advertising, 'spin' and packaging are all crucial within the post-Fordist economy. Market edge is gained through rapidly refining and responding to potential desire in much the same way that teachers are encouraged to put a 'spin' on programmes within schools to meet the desires of anxious parents in a market-based system of schooling.

In seeking to understand the nature of a commodity and, in broader terms, a political economy of consumption, it is helpful to look more closely at the properties of commodities. To begin, commodities have *social* and *physical* aspects (Fine 1995, 144). Take, for example, a pair of jeans. On the one hand, its physical aspect is as a pair of pants. On the other hand, the social aspect of a pair of jeans is connected to image: informality, chic and tough-mindedness. Purchasing a pair of jeans, therefore, is not simply a matter of acquiring a commodity for its physical properties. Rather, it is increasingly a matter of displaying material wealth and cultural capital around carefully crafted media images that knit together a fear of social alienation with a way of belonging. In the same way, too, educational credentials represent a combination of physical and social properties: the qualification *per se* (for example, a history degree from Oxford or a business degree from Harvard) and the social value it embodies, giving potential access to material and cultural resources. I will take up these issues in some depth in Chapter 6.

Additionally, "consumption is dependent upon a continuing and shifting relationship between the physical and social properties of commodities" (Fine 1995, 144). In other words, market edge is gained by paying particular attention to the relationship between the physical and the social properties of a commodity. The social properties of a commodity, as portrayed through image, may become passé or simply socially unacceptable. Alternatively, the physical properties of a commodity may come to be known as dangerous, as is the case with cigarettes. The challenge is how to alter either or both properties in order to maintain market share. The Marlboro Man, whose image was crucial to selling a brand of cigarettes for decades, has been successfully transferred to defining a new range of clothing (after the model died of lung cancer) (Barber 1995).

The critical point to be made concerning a political economy of consumption is that within the new social settlement, it is increasingly the social rather than the physical property of a commodity that determines patterns of consumption. As a result, the marketing challenge is to commodify and sell desire and need itself. Name and trademark, such as Pepsi, Coke, Converse, Nike, Esprit or Benneton attach youth, chic and vigour to for-profit merchandising. The rise of Nike as a $4 billion enterprise is not about selling shoes; rather, it is concerned with selling a name that represents a lifestyle choice—*sport*—and the images (such as Michael Jordan) associated with those choices (sex, victory, money, energy and attitude) (cf., Barber 1995). Nike sells not only shoes but a whole range of 'sport' products to 'lifestyle choosers' around the globe. In much the same way, too, schools in the competitive marketplace are encouraged to sell particular images of desired schooling in order to compete successfully in the parental choice marketplace around the globe (cf., Gewirtz et al. 1995; Dale and Robertson 1996).

The important question to be addressed, therefore, is what this shift means to the shaping of human subjects; that is, the structuring of identity and wider social relations. According to Barber (1995, 58–59), the shift from producer to consumer can be understood as a shift from the production of goods aimed at the *body* to the selling of services aimed at the *soul*. He goes on:

> Whereas the old economy, mirroring hard power, dealt in hard goods
> aimed at the body, the new economy, mirroring self power, depends on

soft services aimed at the mind and spirit (or aimed at undoing the mind and spirit). This wedding of telecommunications technologies with information and entertainment software can be called for short the infotainment telesector. The goods sector is captured by the infotainment telesector whose object is nothing less than the human soul.

Mechandising in all of its forms, according to Barber, is therefore "as much about symbols as about goods and sells not only life's necessities but lifestyles—which is the modern pathway that takes us from the body to the soul" (1995, 60). While Barber is clearly overstating the case, largely as he gives little ground to modes of resistance and in some case widespread opposition to the new politics of consumption, his analysis nonetheless is meant to highlight the highly political nature of the new forms of consumption and with it the ability to form radically new identities.

Whether Levi's jeans, Nike shoes or an educational credential from a 'high tech' school, these commodities are taken to reflect our choice of lifestyle, lifestyles that nonetheless either create social bonds or signal social distinctions. Furthermore, given that our freedom to choose is constrained by a material reality, the discursive construction of 'choice' as a lifestyle option works to position choice as an individual act of freedom. In doing so, it makes invisible the immorality of a system which economically and politically privileges particular groups over others. Thus, while Nike markets itself in the global marketplace on the backs of its tough urban youth image, these same tough urban (black?) youth—or indeed the labour in peripheral countries like Malaysia that produced the shoes in the first place—do not have the legitimately acquired income to buy either the product or the lifestyle. Unfortunately, these sorts of contradictions are not always readily apparent.

TEACHERS AND THE NEW POLITICS OF PRODUCTION AND CONSUMPTION

What does this mean for teachers in schools? As we have already seen in previous chapters, the changing relations between the state and the economy result in periodic crises and transformations in the nature of schooling and teaching. In countries where the new financial orthodoxy is more deeply embedded—such as New Zealand, the United Kingdom and the United States—it is already apparent that the context and conditions of teachers' work have altered. For example, these governments have reduced their commitment to funding education, aspects of provision have been privatised (e.g., psychological services, custodial services) and there have been increased pressures for labour flexibility within teaching. The OECD (1996), for example, notes that given the size of the teaching salary bill as a component of the overall spending on education, redirecting educational spending or pruning it back is made difficult by the fact that it appears much like a fixed cost. Pressure to increase teacher wage flexibility has been accompanied by new forms of regulation: the market, the state and the community. These have resulted from the introduction of schooling markets and new audit and accounting procedures, and through community control (for example, the media and school-based governance structures).

Given teachers' crucial role in the reproduction of labour power, changes in the productive sphere are likely to result in changes to how teachers' work is conceptualised and practised. For example, entrepreneurialism is an important personal demeanour for workers within the new flexible economy. Entrepreneurialism is also an increasingly valued teacher competency in the flexible and 'fast' school. Added to this is the 'reframing' of the school, discursively and practically, as an enterprise. Such changes to conceptions of teachers' work should be viewed not only as institutional responses to shifts within the productive sphere arising from economic flexibility, but as necessary conditions for the establishment of the new regime of accumulation and mode of regulation. Successful teachers and schools will be those that respond quickly and creatively to market signals so that they might either maintain or enhance their position (and status) within the marketplace. In essence, this means greater flexibility in the nature of teachers' conditions of employment and employment contracts; for example, tenure and the regulations governing employment.

Schools are seen as potential captive consumers in this race to gain a marketing edge and in order to shape a commitment to one brand of 'lifestyle' over another. "Children are a critical marketing concern" an Ontario Kidpower Conference Brochure states, adding: "As marketers you need to realise the profit potential you gain by effectively marketing to this increasingly powerful and influential group of people" (OSSTF 1995, 20). Little wonder, too, that huge brand-name consumer-item-producing corporations, such as Coca-Cola, Pepsi, McDonald's and Kentucky Fried Chicken, have staked out exclusive deals with local cash-strapped schools in education systems in Canada, Australia, the

United States and New Zealand. It has all the elements of a Faustian bargain.

The strategy is both clever and multi-pronged. Aside from the direct profitability of directly selling products in schools, such as magazines (for example, *Chickadee, Owl, Classroom Edition*) or food and drink products (such as Pepsi), the mailing lists obtained from students taking corporate-sponsored competitions (an example here is the 'Pepsi Challenge') in schools can be used to target children directly, while corporate sponsorship of course curriculum materials (as in Coca-Cola's Business Studies Resource Kit for Canadian Schools) promotes a particular version of the world outside and the place of business within it. All combine to provide a powerful and barely hidden message within the school curriculum; that success in enterprise in an era of 'fast capitalism' requires enterprising individuals who know how to get the commercial message across through challenging and changing the boundaries between what is regarded as socially and morally acceptable and what is not.

Corporate intrusion does not stop with students. Teachers and school administrators are offered myriad quick solutions to their restructuring problems. Through clever strategies for organising 'smart work', teachers are offered a new vision of how organisations might be managed to their advantage in the 'pacy' and 'racy' 1990s. Management guru Tom Peters promises liberation management, while well-known organisational analysts Deal and Jenkins (1994) offer a toolkit of tricks for "empowering your behind-the-scenes employees". Many principals of schools have donned their 1990s hats as the new corporate managers of schools, armed with the latest techniques for mobilising 'synergy' in an increasingly demoralised workforce. Gee and Lankshear (1995) claim that the educational system has been inundated with the latest management 'texts' stemming from the business world that emphasise an emerging new or 'fast capitalism'. This new fast capitalism, Gee (1994) notes, rests on workers proactively buying into the values and vision of the organisations for which they work in such a way that they locate authority and responsibility within themselves and not in external hierarchies. Like the blurring of the distinctions between goods and services noted earlier, fast capitalist texts blur the traditional identities of workers and managers—not to mention ignoring the category of owners as well as unpaid workers and unemployed—and celebrate change, pace, diversity, the compression of time and space, the absence of borders and the undermining of overt authority. As Gee (1994) also notes, with regard to the

United States, work on 'educational reform' has progressively converged with these business texts in its goal to produce students and reduce the costs of social reproduction suited for the 'fast capitalist' world.

DISPLACEMENTS . . . UP, OUT AND DOWN . . .

'Fast capitalism' signifies a new phase in the global economy. Our conceptions of time and space, along with patterns of production and consumption, that once hinged around a particular model of economic development—economies of scale—have been disrupted and replaced by a new economy of scope. Jessop (1993) notes that this has resulted in an uneven three-way process of 'hollowing out' in such a way that there is considerable blurring of traditional boundaries as displacements of power occur upward, outward and downward. As I have argued in this chapter, however, it would be wrong to assume that the displacements of power signal an erosion of capitalism as a dominant form of economic organisation, though this thesis does have its proponents. Rather, I contend that the displacements of power create a very different context for states as they respond to the long-term structural changes within the global economy. In the following chapter I examine what these displacements of power mean for teachers and their work in the 1990s and suggest that a state's responses are concerned as much with a re-articulation of the state's political capacities as they are with how the state might respond to the changing balance of forces within the global economy.

CHAPTER 6

Post-Fordist Discourses and Teachers' Work

*The new methods of work are inseparable from
a specific mode of living and of thinking and
feeling life*

—GRAMSCI 1971, 302

INTRODUCTION

As the restructuring of education and teachers' work proceeded through-out the 1980s and 1990s, a number of discourses emerged that sought to understand and in some cases reshape the nature of teachers' work and their workplaces. These have not by any means been a unitary discourse. Nor are they necessarily identifiable as specific practises within schools. My intention in this chapter is to highlight specific discourses that have the potential to shape not only actual events but also the underlying so-cial relations between teachers, the state, economy and civil society. These discourses offer very different analyses of society and project very different futures (cf., Watkins 1994, 1). I do not want to provide a de-tailed account of the various ideological strands within the debate, as this has already been competently undertaken by Peter Watkins (1994). Rather, for the purposes of my argument, I have schematised these per-spectives on the basis of their assumptions about the nature of society, the site for change and relations of power. These will then be used to sit-uate theoretically the post-Fordist discourses that have emerged within education. I propose to locate the key discourses into three broad per-spectives or categories: (1) new organisational principles, (2) new social visions, and (3) critical social perspectives. What differentiates each of these perspectives is the *extent* to which they critically focus upon the structure and organisation of power within the workplace and the wider society.

TOOLKITS—THE NEW ORGANISATIONAL PRINCIPLES

The new organisational principles perspective is focused on techniques for the reorganisation of the workplace. These discourses are primarily managerial in their orientation, despite the fact that they are often presented as concerned with issues of worker empowerment. Their discussions centre upon new methods for organising work to minimise managerial problems and to enhance worker productivity.

For the purpose of illuminating this perspective further, I want to draw attention to two particularly influential approaches on the current restructuring discourse: the ideas of the flexible firm (Atkinson 1988), and the Japanese models of workplace organisation (Kenney and Florida 1988). In both cases, new work and organisational principles are identified; for example, quality circles, the just-in-time system and team work. These approaches, it is argued, offer significant advantages over Taylorist and bureaucratic approaches.

Central to these two approaches is the issue of flexibility (Brunhes 1989, 12). To be competitive, firms must develop multiple forms of flexibility (Atkinson 1988). In the past, firms concentrated upon external forms of flexibility; for example, access to skills which may not have been available within the firm, or the replacement of workers who were away temporarily. However, in the new competitive economic environment, external flexibility is used to enable the transfer of *risk* outside of the enterprise. School boards, contracting out cleaning services or the creation of Charter Schools (cf., Robertson et al. 1995) are examples of this 'risk transfer'.

A second form of flexibility is internal. Internal flexibility can be differentiated as *functional, numerical* and *financial*. Functional flexibility refers to the deployment of multi-skilled staff to other sites within the workplace. Instead of down time at some workstations, and then hiring additional casual staff at another, multi-skilled workers can be moved within the factory to a new workstation to ease the pressure. In that way, costs can be minimised and productivity can be maintained. Numerical flexibility refers to the firm's option of taking on and discarding core, contract and contingency labour, dependent upon need. The number of hours worked can be modified without necessarily altering the overall number of workers. Financial flexibility allows the firm to pay incentives to particular staff, dependent upon their performance and on market demand. The flexible firm, by linking segmented labour markets to flexible strategies which minimise costs and increase strategic worker incentives, is able to maximise its productivity and competitive position. As I will show in this chapter, it is a model increasingly attractive to advocates of the restructuring of teachers' work (cf., Gerstner 1994; Hargreaves 1994).

The emergence of flexibility at this time is not coincidental. Capital was able to push flexibility forward as an organisational strategy for increased productivity—despite its inherent insecurity for workers—because of the high level of unemployment and the weakened state of trade unions. In the face of job losses and the (potential and real) flight of capital, many trade unions and government officials feel they have had few alternatives but to embrace these new flexibility strategies. More important, with unemployment no longer at the levels it was in the early 1980s, the institutionalisation of flexibility strategies is now particularly important because of the fact that labour costs might well be increased.

Since the 1980s, the Japanese factory and educational institutions have caught the eye of organisational analysts and educational reformers. Many have reported on aspects of work organisation under the names of Japanese companies; for example, Fujitsuism and Toyotaism (Doshe et al. 1985; Holloway 1987). Work in these companies is organised around work teams, job rotation, learning by doing, flexible approaches to production and a system of *just in time*. The purpose is to maximise skill, knowledge and plant usage and therefore competitiveness and productivity. Group- or team-oriented strategies overcome the problems of alienation inherent in Taylorist forms of labour organisation. Since workers learn a range of skills, from the point of view of management, surplus labour can be relocated to areas within the workplace that require additional assistance. A particular advantage is that workers with multiple skills can understand and respond to the requirements of the workplace in different locations. They therefore have a holistic sense of the product and the organisation. This promotes company loyalty as well as generating solutions to production problems. Of particular interest to researchers has been the way in which workers in teams become self-regulating. That is, the group becomes a means for the regulation of worker behaviour and performance, as opposed to regulation through hierarchical forms of supervision. However, rather than offering a new way of conceptualising relations of power between worker and manager, Doshe et al. (1985) show graphically in their research how the new organisational principles not only produce worker compliance, docility and diligence but are also able to push worker production beyond the limits set for maximum performance. This represents a further intensification of labour, but along different lines to those developed by Taylor

(1911). Because these new organisational principles are only adjustments in the technical relations of work—or in other words, choices made about which technique might be used to enhance productivity—they are little more than more sophisticated means of worker control.

An underlying theme of the new organisation principles is that while there is an explicit recognition that Taylorism has created worker dissatisfaction and alienation, there is no sense that this alienation stems from the structural relations embedded within capitalism itself. In the same vein, worker empowerment is conceived of by those in political circles (including unions) as offering greater opportunities for workers to have a say over the technical problems encountered in the workplace and in being able to choose more flexible types of work arrangements (such as flexi-time). These positions draw from the functional paradigm, deeply rooted in positivist science and regulative sociology. The existing social relations of the workplace are not contested. Rather, the division of labour is viewed as an immutable 'social fact'. Not surprisingly, these discourses have been favoured by the state and others directly involved in the restructuring of the workplace, precisely because they do not offer a critique of capitalist relations.

NEW SOCIAL VISIONS

The perspective of the new social vision theorists (Piore and Sabel 1984) is not directly concerned with the principles of work organisation on the shop floor. Instead, these theorists direct their attention to understanding the changing nature of social relationships as a result of transformations in the cultural or economic spheres. Individual agents, either as workers or consumers, have redefined the basis of existing power relationships. While a number of different positions can be discerned within this perspective, for the purposes of this discussion, they share the view that in some way—either as a result of post-modernity or the dominance of markets—the relations of late capitalism can be or have been transformed.

Advancing the "disorganised capitalism thesis", Lash and Urry (1987) argue that while modernity can be described as a period of organised capitalism, the collapse of large unions and the deindustrialisation of industry to peripheral or developing countries along with plant closures in core countries mark out a new period called 'disorganised capitalism'. They suggest that disorganised capitalism is a manifestation of post-modernity, where traditional class struggles have been replaced by the struggles of special interest groups and social movements. These pressures have disorganised capitalism, signalling a shift to new forms of social organisation.

Following the 'disorganised capitalism' debate outlined above is the work of the 'new times' theorists. This debate is most clearly evidenced in the work of Stuart Hall (1988). Hall's view is not inconsistent with that of Lash and Urry (1987), that post-Fordism has emerged from a set of broader social and cultural—and not only economic—changes. Hall suggests there is evidence of a greater degree of fragmentation and a weakening of collective identities, giving way to the emergence of new identities. Key to this new identity, suggests Hall, is the maximization of choice through personal consumption. This raises the centrality of markets in responding to the diversity of tastes and demands in these new post-modern times.

The changing nature of markets is also at the heart of Piore and Sabel's (1984) book, *The Second Industrial Divide*. They believe that for the first time, the necessary conditions exist for capital and workers to equalise their relationship by being consumers who direct their choices in the marketplace. In contrast to the 'first industrial divide'—where Taylorist/Fordist ideas (see Chapter 3) came to dominate based upon the mass production of goods and a system of state organisation of welfare, the 'second industrial divide' is centred on the principles of small-batch flexible production. This shift raises the distinct possibility of an era where production can be developed along small-site craft-oriented lines. For Piore and Sabel, the impetus toward flexible specialisation—a system of permanent innovation requiring constant change—is the result of the demands from more unpredictable markets and consumer tastes. In order to service these markets, production—using new 'chip' technology and the principle of 'just in time'—is increasingly directed toward market niches. At the same time, marketing and advertising strategies increase and diversify consumers' desires and accelerate the turnover of fashion and taste. The key proposition of Piore and Sabel (1984) is that flexible specialisation makes possible the re-emergence of the craft tradition, broken under Fordism and Taylorism. In other words, groups of independent craft workers will be linked together by a dependence on each other's skills and through craft associations. This new craft tradition, they argue, will force a unique collaboration between capital and labour, as each realises the importance of the other in meeting the demands of the market.

Piore and Sabel's social vision is consensual in its orientation. It is built on the view that the relationship between capital and labour is not necessarily exploitative. Rather, they envision an age when economic success can emerge, based upon the recovery of craft skills lost through Taylorism. In many respects, despite their connections to the socialist tradition of French philosopher Proudhon, Piore and Sabel's views on the division of labour are more consistent with those advanced by sociologist Emile Durkheim. Taylorism, as a forced division of labour, can be conceived of as a social aberration which has produced an anomic division of labour (Giddens 1972, 180–181). Workers, unable to use their skills, become frustrated and thwarted. The return to a craft tradition restores social balance, providing the necessary conditions for cooperation and consensus between workers and capital. As can be imagined, there are many criticisms of this position. Despite their popularity in policy-making circles, Piore and Sabel are regarded by more socially critical writers as failing to take account of the structural nature of the relationship between labour and capital and, of concern to us here, teachers and the state.

CRITICAL SOCIAL PERSPECTIVES

A number of critical *social perspectives* have emerged to take account of the transition from Fordism/Keynesian. For the purposes of this chapter, the work of the regulation theorists Jessop (1989; 1993), Hirsch (1991), Lipietz (1992), Boyer (1990); of David Harvey (1990); on postmodernity; and sociologist George Ritzer's (1993) account of 'McDonaldization' provide a sense of the diversity of the social critique.

Regulation theorists look backward rather than forward in developing a critical social perspective on post-Fordism. Regulationists do not provide a social vision of a post-Fordist society of the kind described by Piore and Sabel (1984) or even Hall (1988). Rather, they tentatively map out the shape of the new post-Fordist arrangements they believe are emerging, such as workplace arrangements based upon the use of core and flexible labour, work teams, new technologies, a re-articulated set of state powers, and new institutional strategies and structures (such as the devolution of responsibility to the site level) (Harvey 1990; Jessop 1993). Far from being liberating for workers, they argue that these changes further disempower and alienate workers. The further erosion of worker control can be seen in the increased intensification of work, greater managerial control, the abandonment of the social wage and supportive labour policies, increased segmentation (especially along gender lines) and management-driven flexibility. These are illustrative of the exploitative and socially corrosive effects of post-Fordist arrangements on workers. Rather than post-Fordism marking a transition beyond the social relations of capitalism, these more critical perspectives suggest a return to a purer, or 'hyper-liberal' form of late capitalism (Panitch 1994).

A somewhat different account of the new post-Fordist directions is presented by Ritzer (1993) in his book, *The McDonaldization of Society*. Ritzer provides an account of a set of principles—derived from the fast-food restaurant McDonald's—which he argues has come to dominate more and more sectors of society, including schools. In many respects, this view runs counter to those presented above. McDonaldization, after all, is a system of mass production centred around four principles: efficiency, predictability, calculability and control. For Ritzer (1993), efficiency is the search for the optimum means to an end as found in the emergence of televised shopping or computerised teaching packages. Calculability, on the other hand, refers to the emphasis upon quantity to the detriment of quality and where quantity becomes a substitute (redefinition) for quality, such as the provision of large lectures to students as opposed to smaller discussion groups. Predictability is centred upon creating conditions whereby the consumer knows what to expect at all times; for example, when products displayed in a particular national or international food chain are located in the same place, the provision of a national curriculum or commercially produced curricular packages, so that employers and parents can expect to access essentially the same product regardless of where they live geographically. Finally, Ritzer argues, these new techniques of power—efficiency, calculability, predictability and control—along with the technologies that make it possible, provides a new means for control over workers.

These logics are not confined to the organisation of profitable organisations, but can be seen in the non-profit sector as well. The post-Fordist dimensions of Ritzer's analysis lies both in highlighting the demeanour of flexibility essential to the casual and peripheral workforce, and in suggesting that mass production—underpinned by a more flexible labour force—will be key to the organisation of workplaces. This stands in stark contrast to the position taken by Piore and Sabel, but is consistent with Harvey (1990), who argues that flexible accumulation is precisely that: a configuration of accumulation strategies—including mass production—which are centred upon principles of more flexible labour usage.

Overall, the differences between these post-Fordist perspectives or discourses arise as a result of competing accounts of the organising dynamics within societies. The roots of worker alienation and the potential for autonomy are conceptualised differently. For example, Piore and Sabel (1984) see the possibility for a consensus between the new craft workers and the owners of capital arising as a result of a transformation in the technology which underpinned the first industrial divide and which took the form of mass production. On the other hand, regulation theorists such as Jessop (1990) and Lipietz (1992) regard the social relations that derive from capitalist forms of organisation as inherently conflicting. Far from moving away from capitalist social relations, this period of transition reasserts the primacy of the economic and the commodity form over other spheres of social life. Alternatively, Stuart Hall (1988) draws his insights from postmodernist theory, focusing our attention to the way our subjective realities and identities are socially constructed.

POST-FORDIST DISCOURSES ON RESTRUCTURING TEACHERS' LABOUR

> *Unfortunately schools are not organized to*
> *work "smart"; it is not called mass education*
> *for nothing. Schools teach by brute force; they*
> *are based on an explicit factory model, with the*
> *teacher as the worker and the student as the*
> *product. Mass production is the objective. . . .*
> *Schools must reinvent themselves in order to*
> *survive. The "discipline of the market" holds*
> *the key.*
> —Gerstner et al. 1994, 19, 231

Few would argue with the tenor of IBM chief Lew Gerstner and colleagues in their assessment of the problems posed by post-war mass schooling. Where the differences arise, however, is what to do about it. Either way, almost all solutions—largely from the right—propose a set of actions which radically alter teachers' workplaces.

Two dominant perspectives are evident. On the one hand, a body of writing has emerged (cf., Ashenden 1992; Schools' Council 1992; Hargreaves 1994; Caldwell 1995) which draws almost exclusively on the new organisation principles discussed earlier. A somewhat different set of discourses has presented a new vision for teacher empowerment (cf., Mathews et al. 1988; Chubb and Moe 1990; Romanish 1991; Gerstner et al. 1994). A final set of discourses have arisen as a critique of the hegemonic post-Fordist perspectives (cf., Ball 1990; Watkins 1994; Robertson 1994,

1995). These analysts point to the problematic nature of post-Fordist developments for teachers, particularly as the restructuring of teachers' work has been built upon the deregulation of their existing conditions and the establishment of a new set of market- and management-oriented principles.

TOOLS FOR MANAGING—NEW PRINCIPLES FOR REORGANISING

According to analysts such as Ashenden (1992), if teachers were to develop a new set of work practises, not only would they reinstate their tarnished professional image, but teaching would become a more rewarding occupation. Three commonly shared assumptions are evident within this perspective. To begin, change is viewed as the logical working out of the system's dynamics. Education theorist Brian Caldwell (1995), for example, identifies a set of 'mega-trends' which he suggests will inevitably shape education and teachers' work into the next millenium: self-managing schools, accountability, quality education for each individual and computer technology. Rising above the politics of the left or the right, these 'inevitable' trends appear to be the result of a global teleology. For example, in Caldwell's view, the self-management of schools "is long overdue; is consistent with developments elsewhere in the public and the private sectors, in education and in other fields of endeavour; and is probably irreversible" (1995, 2). By holding back changes, schools have limited the possibilities for their own self-renewal (Gerstner et al. 1994). These views fail to acknowledge that not only is system change often highly problematic, but as I have argued earlier, is also the result of particular vested interests being pursued. Mega-trends, far from being objective features of the educational landscape, represent a particular set of interests: the interests of the ruling class and transnational capital.

A second assumption is the belief that teachers' difficulties arise because of the organisation of their workplaces. This creates a disequilibrium which disturbs their optimal functioning. The factors include the codification of industrial gains, an increase in the number of tasks within the school, and the lack of a hierarchical structure for teachers. Restructuring provides an opportunity for teachers to create new roles to overcome this disequilibrium and as a result experience greater job satisfaction. Ashenden (1992) argues that during the Keynesian welfare state settlement, Australian teachers codified their industrial gains. For example, teachers negotiated with the state regarding who did what sort of work, who had access to the teaching profession, the hours over which the work was performed, the length and number of periods teachers spent teaching, and above all, the size and nature of the standardised educational group. This locked into place a particular definition of teachers' work, a "dominant way of doing work, a labour process for both education workers and for students, and a particular pattern of working relationship between teachers and students" (Ashenden 1992, 62–63). In Ashenden's mind, these definitions of teachers' work are largely counterproductive, as they create problems of inflexibility for teachers and interfere in their capacity to achieve quality learning outcomes.

Teacher unions are pointed to as one of the culprits in creating this state of affairs. Further, it is argued that the poor standing of teachers has much to do with the public perception that claims for more resources by the unions is not necessarily likely to deliver quality provision of education (Ashenden 1992). A similar position is taken by the Royal Commission on Learning in their report to the Government in Ontario, Canada, in 1994. The commission poses this question in their deliberations on restructuring: "Has the orientation toward collective bargaining issues occurred at the expense of the development of teaching as a profession?" (Royal Commission on Learning 1994, Volume III, 8). The report points out that the promotion of teaching as a profession and the need to address broad-ranging issues facing teachers as workers have been undermined by the 'contractual imperatives' of the various unions. By implication, new approaches to the organisation and regulation of teachers' work, including the establishment of a College of Teachers to oversee teachers' professional concerns, will result in the restoration of public confidence as well as "keep pace with the needs of individual teachers and with changing policies and practices" (1994, 11). In essence, these proposals call for either the abolition of teacher unions or at least a reduction in their powers, and the establishment of a professional body (following the Piore and Sabel model) to regulate teacher practise.

A third assumption is that teachers' dissatisfaction with their jobs has arisen not as a result of the loss of control over important aspects of their work, the decline in salaries, or the withdrawal of public support, but rather as a result of the fact that teachers are asked to undertake multiple tasks, many of which are trivial and could be performed by someone else on a lower wage. Ashenden (1992, 57) cites the handling of complaints about student behaviour from other teachers, making phone calls or writing letters to parents, and parent interviews as examples. This leads to a forced and therefore anomic division of labour; anomic because the tasks assigned do not coincide with the aptitudes of the worker—in this case the teacher—which then leads to dissatisfaction.

For Ashenden, like Durkheim, this is not a necessary characteristic of the division of labour. Rather, it can be resolved through a reallocation of tasks and a further division of labour involving a range of 'education workers' (Ashenden 1992; Hargreaves 1994; Caldwell 1995). These education workers would range, in both their levels of training, credentials and conditions of employment, from a fully certified and registered teacher employed full time, to a variety of hourly rate and short-term 'education workers' employed to undertake specific 'non-teaching' or 'low-level' teaching tasks.

Teachers' dissatisfaction with their jobs also results from the conflicting nature of the student teacher relationship. There is no doubt that many teachers would agree with Ashenden (1992) on this point. However, his failure to situate teachers' conflicts with students within the wider power relations which shape schools—in particular class, race and gender relations—means that proposals for the restructuring of the classroom simply produce the same inequities and the same conflicts. In short, they fail to address the underlying tensions which exist in the classroom between teachers and students and the material structural conditions—including class size—in which these relations get constructed.

These three assumptions form the basis for a specific set of proposals for restructuring teachers' work. In essence, they are managerial strategies. Teachers must learn to manage their time and their tasks better. One way of going about this is to 'reinvent' education. Teachers can also gain inspiration from a new set of industry metaphors, such as 'high tech' hospitals (Hargreaves 1994) or crash-conscious aircraft industries (Caldwell 1995). However, the value of these metaphors for the equitable reorganisation of schools appears to be limited when one considers these sectors more closely. For instance, while there may well be private 'high tech' hospitals, the public health sector has faced an increase in patient waiting lists.

In order to facilitate the better management of teachers' workplaces, proponents draw from the grab bag of literature on the Japanese workplace, the flexible firm and new managerial strategies. Transformational leadership, quality circles, work teams, flexible deployment of labour, paraprofessionals, site-based management, systems work units, business-school partnerships, new technology, weaker boundaries between the public and the private sector, self-directed student learning centres and many more are identified in order to "liberate teachers from the expectations that they cannot satisfy" (Caldwell 1995, 5). The organising principle for teachers is flexibility. *Labour flexibility* can be achieved through the stratification of teachers' work. *Skill flexibility* can be accomplished by using computing technology in the classroom, managing a range of groups of different ages and sizes, or employing more diverse approaches to teaching and managing. *Fiscal flexibility* can be accrued through business partnerships, cheaper staff, larger classes and fewer teachers.

A key notion is that "workplaces would produce more for all concerned, not because people were working harder or investing more, but because they were working differently" (Ashenden 1992, 65). In Ashenden and Caldwell's proposals, working differently means working with up to one-third fewer professionally trained teaching colleagues; supervising the work of others, including parents, other paraprofessionals and trainee teachers; doing more 'real' teaching; taking larger classes and using more computers. These propositions seem to require two shifts. One, the reconstruction of our own social expectations regarding work; in this regard Caldwell (1995) notes that teachers should no longer expect to be employed in a job long term. Two, that the current forms of teacher regulation, such as unionisation, be abandoned as this impedes the opportunity to 'de-codify' current work practises and reduces the potential for site-based flexibility. These two challenges are at the heart of Alberta Education's 1994 proposals for teacher licensing every five years and ending the requirement for teachers to belong to a union in order to work.

Absent from these troubling discourses is any discussion about the differential power of teachers and their employer—the state. More particularly, these proponents ignore the capacity for individual teachers to negotiate a set of work conditions that meet their needs within the new deregulated environment. Nor do they consider the effect of increased stratification on teachers and their workplace relations. Romanish (1991) reports on the difficulties teacher stratification posed for one highly regarded and innovative school in Minnesota which drew a visit from President Bush in May 1991. According to Romanish, Bush's visit "rekindled difficulties amongst the teaching staff as only the four special category, highest paid, teachers were included in the meeting with Bush" (1991, 100). The divisions among these teachers stemmed from the fact that there were two classifications of teachers in the school: one group of regular teachers on twelve-month contracts while the other were full-time tenured ('core') workers on a higher rate of pay. Disputes within the school had centred on who performed which teaching tasks, and it was reported that resolving these issues required the services of a mediating consultant over the course of the school year. Paradoxically, despite the potential for the escalation of conflict within the school, it is assumed that these modes of organisation will enhance a collegial and team-oriented approach to administration and pedagogy.

A further troubling aspect is that teachers are presented as free to make choices about whether they would prefer to belong to the expanded and less well-paid contract and contingency labour market, or to accept greater responsibility and higher pay and enter the core labour market for teachers. Clearly there are teachers who, for a variety of reasons, 'choose' not to work full time. However, in an era of high unemployment and insecurity, surplus teachers will not only have few choices as to which segment of the labour market they enter but also what rate of pay they receive. There are few protections in a deregulated labour market.

On the other hand, core workers, while receiving a higher rate of pay as an incentive to shoulder responsibility and work with the new organisational principles, will find little space for a more critical pedagogical practise. Teaching is likely to be further intensified by a combination of increased managerial tasks, reduced 'down time' on tasks not construed as real teaching, and more entrepreneurial activity, all legitimized as the work of the new professional teacher. The parallels to Ford's $5.00 a day and Taylor's pig-iron handler of more than seventy years ago (see Chapter 4) provide some clues as to how the transition of workers to new forms of work organisation is being managed.

SOCIAL VISIONS, MARKETS AND
TEACHER EMPOWERMENT

A second set of discourses carries a particular social vision for the reconstruction and 'reinvention' of education and of teachers' work based largely on the debureaucratisation of education and the regulation of markets. These discourses are distinguished from those addressed in the previous section by their attention to schools as institutions in wider social settings.

In *Empowering Teachers: Restructuring Schools for the 21st Century* (1991), Bruce Romanish argues that while the provision of public education needs to shift in new directions, it should not lose sight of its democratic function within society. Like Ashenden and Caldwell, Romanish maintains that the empowerment of teachers must be at the centre of the reforms. He also agrees that the factory model for the organisation of schools is dysfunctional. However, Romanish (1991, 99–100) is highly critical of the new organising principles (such as quality circles, site-based management, the flexible deployment of labour) that have typified the proposed changes to teachers' work. Rather, in his view, genuine teacher empowerment will only arise when teachers are able to practise their 'craft' under more enabling conditions within schools. These enabling conditions, such as teachers being responsible for: (1) the appointment of other teachers, (2) determination of curriculum and instruction and (3) management of their own organisational practises, do not bear the stamp of the industrial bureaucratic model. Instead, this social vision of the debureacratisation of schooling and a return to the craft model would, according to Romanish (1991), generate an environment of trust and a new professionalism for teachers.

While this vision is laudable and important aspects of Romanish's proposals need to be pursued, he fails to situate the school and its attendant social relations within a cultural *and* economic context. By focusing upon the bureaucratic and ignoring the social relations of production, Romanish offers a proposal for the empowerment of teachers as the new craft workers unhindered by the economic sphere. In doing so he ignores not only teachers' pursuit of their own interests in the state's legitimation work but also the centrality of teachers to that work. The paradoxical failure to see the material relations that structure schooling, at a time when these relations are even more evident and more constraining, leads Romanish into the same difficulties encountered by Piore and Sabel (1984), which I have outlined earlier.

A somewhat different view on the over-bureaucratisation of schooling and teachers' work is offered by public choice theorists Chubb and Moe (1990). They conclude that the bureaucratic characteristics of public schools, and in particular the level of external control by governing agencies, make the prospects for successful and democratic education unlikely. Chubb points particularly to at least four factors that have shaped American public schools: (1) consolidation of schools with little room for flexibility, (2) standardisation of curriculum/pedagogy, (3) centralisation of bureaucratic control, and (4) routinisation of schooling experiences (1990, 230). According to their analysis, layers of bureaucracy—in the name of democracy—grow over time, stifling one of the most important elements in effective schools: autonomy (Chubb and Moe, 1990). Chubb and Moe argue that turning to the *market* as an instrument to arbitrate choice will lead to autonomy. Markets promote autonomy by enabling all participants to make decisions for themselves. By implication, teachers would have the capacity to act more autonomously in those schools shaped by the principles of the market.

In this type of market framework, notes Ranson, the view is that:

markets will sift and sort, if schools are to be successful, they need to find a niche—a specialised segment of the market to which they can appeal and attract support: targeting particular values and learning-discipline, religion, socio-economic and ethnic make-up of students (1993, 333) .

Central to the market-based social vision of Chubb and Moe (1990), and expressed in various ways in the United Kingdom, New Zealand, Canada and the United States, is the democratisation of institutional settings and the creation of market settings entailing decentralisation, competition, autonomy, choice, clarity of mission, strong leadership, teachers profes-sionalism and team cooperation.

The lack of a market mode of organising schools is crucial to the analysis advanced by IBM executive Gerstner and his colleagues in their book *Reinventing Education* (1994). In a scathing attack on public schools, they argue:

> Schools are not organized to be productive or inefficient, even by assembly-line standards, and certainly not by the standards of modern high performance organizations. Indeed, looking at them leaves one inescapable conclusion: schools are organized to be inefficient. Grossly inefficient. Schools are low tech, labor organizations with poorly articulated goals, low standards, and next to nonexistent measures of performance. If someone—as in a case study done by a business school, for example—set out to design as inefficient an organization as could be conceived, it would be modern public schools (Gerstner et al. 1994, 234).

Gerstner et al. argue that schools, by operating outside of the market, have been insulated from the necessity for change. Through deregulating schools, fostering choice and employing risk-taking teachers, schools can be reinvented. Following the work team model, teachers should be encouraged to work in small groups with students as coaches, counsellors, learning managers, leaders, learners and future innovators; to accept differential salaries for performance; and to monitor their students' behaviour. In this equation, teachers are 'learner managers' armed with the latest technology, while the students are the learners.

The vision of democracy delivered by the market is deeply problematic. As Levin (1990, 248) points out, the introduction of markets and consumer choice into the organisation of schooling is far from simple. For example, there is a tension between the provision of common schools for the reinforcement of democratic institutions in society, and the provision of individual and family choice to meet narrower parochial and private goals. In some respects Chubb and Moe's position, with its focus on consumption, choice and markets, is not unlike Stuart Hall's (1988). These seem strange bedfellows, but the two are drawn together by the logic of choice and the conflation of the market economy with autonomous subjects. In the case of Chubb and Moe, however, their assumptions about choice are based on the rationality of the chooser, the plurality of power and the neutrality of the market.

But the market is a political creation, designed for political purposes (Ranson 1993, 338). In this regard, public choice theorists ignore the way in which markets themselves shape and constrain choices—including future choices (Cerny 1990, 57). The paradox is that consumer choice empowers the producers as schools begin to differentiate themselves to fit specific niches in the educational market. As a result, "the intention of increasing choice results not only in the product being altered but choice itself being reduced or eliminated. This paradox does not emerge by chance but from the principles which emerge to govern interaction in the market" (Ranson 1993, 336). The market can thus be seen as working to constrain choice. More particularly, it seeks to redistribute power and redirect society away from elements of social democracy which found expression in the latter stages of the Keynesian-Fordist settlement, toward a neoliberal order.

The market, as an organiser of teachers' work, reconstructs and redefines the meaning and purpose of teaching. Teachers are expected to work within a new value context as 'risk entrepreneurs' and the shapers of tastes (Gerstner et al. 1994), where "image and impression management are now more important than the educational process, [where] elements of control have been shifted from the producer (teachers) to the consumer (parents) via open enrollments, parental choice and per capita funding" (Ball 1993, 108). With all the shades of a Faustian bargain, the onus is on schools and teachers to attract clients, maximise income, put "shrewdness before principles" (Ball 1993, 109), and ignore the confusion of social relations with exchange relationships.

A different social vision for the restructuring of teachers' labour, which critiques the heavy hand of bureaucracy, challenges the privileging of bourgeois knowledge within faculties of education, and questions the capacity of the private sector to deliver democratic options, can be seen in the positions taken by Mathews (1989) and Carmichael (1989) in Australia. Drawing upon the work of Piore and Sabel (1984), union sec-

retary Laurie Carmichael and activist John Mathews argued that the transition offered a unique opportunity for unions to negotiate and arrive at a
consensus as to the changes taking place in the workplace. Using the
structure of the Accord—a tripartite agreement between the federal state,
transnational capital and peak unions—to push forward a consensus on
workplace change, Carmichael affirms the view that the Taylorist-based
division of labour in schools must be replaced by a new pattern of organisation. According to Carmichael, for Australia to be economically competitive, it must embrace the new technological revolution and develop a
"more highly skilled workforce . . . with a greater sophistication and in-
teractiveness of functions and work processes . . . [with] an ever increasing level of [worker] participation in decision-making" (1989, 26). To
enable this process, the federally funded National Schools Project, under
the auspices of the Accord partners, has created the conditions that
would enable schools to pilot new patterns of work organisation for
teachers. Despite the latitude in challenging existing school regulations
(such as teacher supervision of playgrounds, or class sizes), participating
schools have worked within a tightly prescribed framework: for example, they must be outcome-oriented, focus upon student workplace competencies, and explore approaches to teamwork. Carmichael and others
also insisted that project schools work unhindered by teacher education
faculties. That is, they should seek solutions either from within their own
ranks or from industry. Some observers have interpreted this as a railing
against bourgeois intellectuals who have perpetuated the hegemony of
liberal meritocracy on the working class (Seddon 1993). That may well
be the case. However, the highly prescriptive nature of the new work
framework for teachers—with its focus upon skills, outcomes and worker
control—merely replaces one ideology with the more powerful neoliberal agenda.

CRITICAL SOCIAL PERSPECTIVES ON TEACHERS' WORK

A number of socially critical researchers have focused their attention on
the changing work context for teachers. Stephen Ball's (1993) work on
teachers offers an insightful analysis of the shifting forms of control that
now define teaching and teachers' work. Ball identifies a matrix of power
relations which are currently shaping the reconstruction of teachers'
work. These he delineates as the curriculum, management and the market. Drawing upon research on teachers in secondary schools (1993,

106), Ball notes that curriculum changes (such as the national curriculum, testing and so on) have increased the technical elements of teachers' work and reduced the professional elements. In other words, the spaces available for professional autonomy are reduced as a result of the imposition of standardisation and normalisation processes—measurement, hierarchy and regulation—on classroom practise. The emergence of the market within education, on the other hand, positions teachers within a new value context. As Ball says, the new relations of 'producer' (teacher) and 'consumer' (student) focus the work of teachers in a new light; that is, the relationship between teachers and students is given a commodity exchange value. It would seem that what is different in this new social formation is that the hidden curriculum of schooling, at least in Bourdieu's and Passeron's (1977) terms as cultural/social/symbolic capital exchange, is no longer hidden. Rather, it is an explicit focus within the new post-Fordist context.

As Ball notes (1993, 109), "The market leaves little alternative but to engage in individualistic, competitive activity, even though by doing so this must result in a worsened educational experience for some children". Intimately linked to the market is the role of management, a mechanism which, according to Ball, provides for a 'no-hands' state steering of teachers' work at a distance. With coercion replaced by self- and site-based steering, self-monitoring and individual accountability, the new post-Fordist arrangements provide no means for protest or complaint against the system, at the same time decreasing the need for overt control.

> The individualization of consciousness oriented toward performativity, constitutes a more subtle, yet more totalizing form of control of teachers than is available in the top-down prescriptive steering of state Fordism. Resisters in this context threaten the survival of colleagues rather than policies. Values and interests are thoroughly conflated. And in the use of discretionary payments, loyalty and commitment become criteria for preferment alongside aspects of 'performance' (Ball 1993, 111).

It is a point also made by Codd (1993) in the New Zealand context. By devolving bulk funding for teachers' salaries to the local level and placing teachers on individual employment contracts linked to a system of merit pay for performance, the old institutional structures—such as teachers' unions—are no longer able to apply political pressure for changes to the conditions under which teachers work (such as class sizes, professional support).

Drawing upon the post-Fordist literature, Watkins (1993, 137) has described the devolution of management to teachers and the local community as "vertical disintegration"; this process involves a powerful central governing body that feeds off smaller units which are satellites, subsidiaries or subcontractors to the powerful central unit. Charter schools, of the type to be found in fledgling form in Alberta, Canada, are an example of this. It is only through smaller units operating at the local level that market relations can operate effectively. In this sense, teachers in self-managed schools, employed within different segments of the labour market of teaching, can be encouraged to compete with each other for clients and funds.

The notion of a 'systems work unit'—a group of teachers who work (collegially) together to deliver a predetermined outcome, a notion that has been central to the National Schools Project in Australia—is a further example of vertical disintegration. By locating power within the centre through tightened controls, and streamlining the functional lines of responsibility downwards, administrators and teachers are given the task of implementing the new global agenda, at the same time determining and managing the 'riot threshold' crucial to successful implementation. This is referred to by Doshe et al. as management by stress (1985). The smaller units act as 'shock absorbers' by deflecting major local, social, fiscal and industrial crises away from the state (Watkins 1993, 141). The creation of scope for technical innovation within a structured field of action controls the political outcomes while pressing for solutions, much like the workers in Toyota's factory (Price 1994, 83). Drawing upon a significant body of Japanese research, Price (1994, 83) notes that quality circles, work teams and job rotation nonetheless led to "constant rationalisation, expanding job tasks, routinisation of standard work movement, and long work hours", where workers were put under severe stress. Price's observations on Japanisation are consistent with accounts of teachers' work in the new era (cf., Sparkes and Bloomer 1993; Robertson 1994; Muschamp et al. 1995).

In this respect, too, Smyth (1991, 2) addresses the rekindled interest in teacher work teams and collegiality, arguing that "it is part of a broader strategy (deliberate or otherwise), to harness teachers more effectively to the work of economic reconstruction". Far from collegiality being a desirable teacher-to-teacher relationship, it is a mandatory policy

option for voluntary involvement providing "collegial on-the-job forms
of professional development for teachers in a context in which the steer-
age and policy directions are unquestionably being framed from outside
schools, with teachers being incorporated (or coopted?) to work out the
implementation details" (Smyth 1991, 8).

In several cases writers, including myself (cf., Robertson 1994,
1995; Soucek 1994), have built upon the work of the French regulation
theorists, arguing that the shifts toward a more flexible regime of accumulation have been paralleled by significant transformations in the
institutional structure of education, in the modes of regulation (individual/
institutional) that shape individual teacher behaviour, as well as the organisation of their labour in schools. Soucek (1994) examines the way in
which the new educational competency movement has shaped the terrain
on which teachers' work in Australia is now situated. This in turn has
provided for a telescoping of general and vocational education in order
that they correspond to the labour market demands of post-Fordism. In
my own work, I have shown that teachers' work in Australia is increasingly shaped by very different institutional dynamics: entrepreneurialism, flexibility, managerialism and competitivism (Robertson 1994;
1995). These dynamics are framed within a structured field of action
which works to constrain teachers' actions.

How far and in which ways these developments might constrain
teacher action is at the heart of Dale's (1994) critical review of Ritzer's
analysis of 'McDonaldization' presented earlier. While at one level, accepting that there are broad parallels between recent changes to education systems and the principles of McDonaldization, Dale argues that in
order to understand these issues more clearly we need to focus on both
the structures and processes, the institutions and discourses through
which education policy is constituted, and how the agenda for education
is set. In other words, what we need to look at is the effect of these
changes, rather than what is being proposed. These 'effects' are mediated
by the pattern of schooling, or the resources with which it takes place, as
well as the "irreducible minimum of the pedagogic transaction" (Dale
1994, 254–255). What might be termed the 'irreducible minimum', or
IM, is "what remains when all politically and technically feasible means
of monitoring, evaluation, appraisal and inspection of teachers has been
exhausted and the fundamental requirements of the job have not". Given
that there are elements of the work of teachers that cannot be reduced
to the demands of efficiency, predictability, calculability and control,
despite the fact that they might be shaped by the various regulatory

mechanisms in place, this means that there can never be complete control of teachers. Furthermore, it provides the fundamental basis for the professional culture on which teacher resistance is rooted. Thus, despite concerted efforts at the control of teachers, either through the move from teacher licensing to teacher regulation, incentives, subcontracting work, competency-based teacher education, more narrow definitions of teachers' jobs, the radical restructuring of teacher education, inspections, all of which limit the ways in which teachers work, Dale argues that given schools are social institutions which do not encourage or enable predictability, calculability, control and efficiency (1994, 261). These insights help us understand the modalities of teachers' workplaces—modalities of uncertainty which underpin the pedagogical relationship and which provide the basis for both individual mediation and organised action. It is to these issues that I wish finally to turn.

CONCLUSION

While some writers might rightly quibble over whether the transformation is toward a post-Fordist economy or not, clearly the Fordist Keynesian welfare state settlement of the post-World War II years has collapsed and we are in a transition to something. And as Harvey (1990, 121) has argued, "if there is some kind of transformation in the political economy of late twentieth century capitalism, then it behoves us to establish how deep and fundamental the transformation might be". In this chapter I have highlighted the different post-Fordist discourses that have emerged following the breakdown of the Fordist/Keynesian settlement and the class compromise which characterised it. The contradictions and problems generated within the Fordist system of regulation created the necessity for a new social settlement, based upon a reassertion of class rule through a new set of strategies developed by capital (national and global) both intellectually and in political practise. According to Rustin, the post-Fordist hypothesis—despite its problems—is "the nearest thing we have to a paradigm which can link widespread changes in forms of production to changes in class relations, state forms and individual identities" (1989, 56). This fact can be seen not only in the reorganisation of teachers' work and the changing relationship between teachers and the state but in the way in which the emergence of the market has offered a new social vision—a new set of values—around which that might be performed.

CHAPTER 7

Ratcheting Up the Marketness Factor: Managing Compliance to the Competitive State Project

BRINGING THE STATE-MARKET RELATION INTO VIEW

It has become commonplace to conceptualise the state and market as antagonistic forces, each with its interests to protect with neither giving ground to the other. However, the increased 'marketness' factor—that is, the tendency for exchange relations to be driven almost exclusively by price and economic considerations—in the reorganisation of teachers' work, which is itself an outcome of the state's actions, seems to be curi ously disregarded in these analyses. In this chapter I want to bring the relationship between teachers, the state and the economy into sharp focus and examine the ways in which this rhetorical juxtaposition of 'state' and 'market'—as fundamentally opposed sites—works to maintain an ideological separation of the political from the economic spheres. The outcome of this strategic separation conceals the state's real interest: that is, the important role for the state in creating a regulatory framework for the organisation of teachers' labour.

I have argued throughout this book that teachers are central to the state's work (accumulation, legitimation, control). However, teachers as a large occupational group represent a significant drain on state resources—largely in fixed salaries—at a time when the state must redirect its resources into policies and programmes aimed at promoting the conditions for a competitive advantage within the global and regional economy. The state must therefore explore new ways to create the conditions for teachers to contribute directly and indirectly to the 'competitive state project' under a set of terms and conditions that are sympathetic to the state's hegemonic project and not teachers' existing professional project. In this chapter I examine the way in which neoliberal states have deliberately pursued a strategy of "ratcheting up the marketness factor" in teachers' work. The market mode of regulating teachers, I suggest, challenges the basis of teachers' claim to professionalism during the Keynesian welfare state settlement in quite fundamental ways. The professionalism of the service class through the post-war period was based upon two interconnected claims: one moral, centred upon the notion of social trusteeship of the welfare of others; and the other technical, centred on pedagogical expertise (cf., Brint 1994). Neo-liberals promoting the market challenges this claim as self-interested 'provider capture' open to teacher opportunism. However, the question arises as to whether the neoliberal of the state pursued through both the market and tighter state auditing of teachers' work rather than minimising opportunism, *create* the conditions for it because of their commitment to individualism and self-interest rather than the interests of the collective, service, goodwill and trust.

ECONOMIC MARKETS AND THEIR RELATIONSHIP TO THE STATE

In order to understand better both sides of the duo—'state' and 'market'—in the 1990s and the relationship between the two, I want to begin by examining closely the nature of economic markets and their relationship to the state. This is important if we are to understand the way in which the 'marketness factor' has been strategically used by the state to dislocate existing tacit norms in which contracts between the welfare state and teachers were embedded. In this chapter I use to notion of 'embeddedness' to describe the way in which the motivations of actors are assumed to be shaped by social factors other than just economic and instrumental ones.

'Eulogising' and 'Demonising' in the State–Market Binary

Claims that contrast the state and market as opposing sites or opposite sides of the same coin, which foster zero-sum assumptions that where the market does not exist, the state does, and which see the state as good and the market as bad (or vice versa), lean heavily on a highly ideological reading of both markets and the state. This ideological eulogising and demonising cannot be sheeted home only to neoliberal or 'new right' proponents seeking to glorify the market and damn the state with the view that greater market freedom will increase economic efficiency. The political left is equally polemical. As analysts such as Block (1996) and Sayer (1995) point out, the problem for the left is the tendency to conflate capitalism with markets, to see all of the ills of capitalism as arising from markets (and implicitly to reglorify the state), and to assume that all market relations are the same. In his book, *The Vampire State,* Block (1996, 43) observes:

> . . . the idea of condemning the state because political power is sometimes abused is comparable to condemning markets in general because human greed sometimes produces horrible consequences. The reality is that both markets and political power are necessary components of any complex human society, and that these societies have to find ways to protect themselves from the excesses caused by those who recklessly pursue both political power and economic wealth.

Block's observations are particularly pertinent here. Market-based economic exchanges and some form of state are necessary components of any complex society. For instance, markets can and do exist in socialist economies, though this is not to suggest that marketisation processes in countries such as the People's Republic of China or Vietnam are necessarily or completely in line with socialist principles. Peasants may sell a particular percentage of their produce in the local marketplace while non-essential or 'luxury' items such as perfumes may be available in specialised outlets as items for exchange at market-based values.

Though the political left either demonises or demystifies markets, it is hard to deny that certain types of economic exchanges might in some respects be better coordinated by the market (Sayer 1995). Leaving aside the not unimportant issue of whether families might not have sufficient resources to purchase items within the marketplace (because their labour activity does not generate sufficient income), or that consumers' preferences are often manipulated by advertisers in particular ways, we might argue that a footware manufacturer is likely to operate more efficiently if responding to market cues (such as preferred sizing, styles, colour and so on) rather than a state-defined formula for production as we might have found in some socialist economies. In the same way, a restaurateur will quickly learn to change the menu, charge lower prices, relocate or employ a different cook if trade is flagging rather than go out of business. However, arguing that all exchanges be managed by the market mode, including those goods and services we can argue are public and social goods, such as education, is clearly another matter. We need to be clear about what goods and services are best provided by the state as a social good, and what goods and services are best coordinated through the market mode.

It is clear, then, that despite the neoliberal eulogizing of markets as free, spontaneous and unregulated by the state, markets are complex sets of relationships regulated by the state. This is largely because, as Offe and Ronge (1984, 122) explain, the "key problem for capitalist societies is the fact that the dynamics of capitalist development seem to exhibit a constant tendency to *paralyse* the commodity form of value". In other words, leaving the system of production and exchange unregulated creates the conditions for both economic and political instability. Businesses may collapse because of the tendency toward monopolisation leading to a lack of competitiveness and efficiency. Alternatively, transnational companies may be hesitant about investing in a country's economy because of labour instability (as is the case with parts of Eastern Europe and Asia), or the lack of a public infrastructure, such as education, training, communication and transport systems. Thus, as Andrew Sayer observes, while the state is frequently and unceremoniously cast by neoliberal proponents as distorting economic and political transactions and therefore an unnecessary interference, this is largely ideological chain rattling for other political purposes. Rather, "the state is a normal feature of real markets, as a precondition of their existence. Markets depend on the state for regulation, protection of property rights and the currency" (Sayer 1996, 87).

Far from the state and market being antithetical to each other, they are necessary pre-conditions for each other, though the form that each takes is dependent on the nature of the social settlement (for example, Keynesian welfare statism). On the one hand, markets depend on the state for establishing the political conditions for private accumulation, for instance through regulation and protection. On the other hand, the state, for its own power and continued existence, depends on the efficient workings of the market as part of the system of economic production and exchange. This relationship of mutual dependence, however, is fraught with contradictions and is, therefore, an unstable one. In order to stabilise the relationship between the political and the economic, the state must put into place policies that institutionalise, routinise and regulate market exchange relationships, though clearly what is important here is how, and in whose interests, the state acts.

The routinisation of markets and their regulation by the state has been central to the development of organised capitalism. That is, there has historically been an attempt to *reduce* the 'marketness' of the economy, which I have already defined earlier as the tendency for exchanges of any kind to be driven only by price and economic considerations. For example, large firms and organisations—and here I include powerful professions—have used their resources to reduce price competition and to create a monopoly environment, including gaining state support for this through protections and various forms of registration. The move away from those markets where each exchange is characterised by price only (and which are therefore inherently unstable) to explicit and implicit contracts, promises increased organisational stability and growth and greater extraction of surplus value (in the form of efficiencies) in exchange for employee loyalty, job security and mobility.

However, routinisation and regulation can also lead to inefficiencies of other kinds in industries. For instance, when firms are protected by the state from outside competitors (such as the car industry in Australia during the 1950s and 1960s), they are under no great pressure to keep up with new technological developments or to look for efficiencies in their work practises in order to make a profit and stay in business. While there may well be good reasons for the state to offer these sorts of protections to key industries, such as in Japan, where rice farmers are heavily subsidised by the state because it is regarded as crucial that Japan is not dependent on foreign markets for its staples, it is also the case that state subsidisation limits the possibility of market failure.

The regulation of markets within the economic substructure is dependent upon a complex state infrastructure, though the nature of that infrastructure is clearly changing. However, this infrastructure has included a judicial system; for example, to referee competition among capitals; a state regulatory system, for example, systems of state arbitration to manage disputes and wage claims between capital and labour, various primary production boards—such as marketing boards—to guarantee a stable annual return in the face of instabilities arising from natural disasters like floods or draughts; or state-funded education and training systems whose purpose it is to produce workers with the necessary basic knowledge and skills that enable them to enter various labour markets and to function as avid, if not effective, consumers.

The state's regulatory infrastructure, while necessary, is expensive largely as it absorbs labour and revenue. For instance, teachers' salaries in countries such as Australia and New Zealand absorb approximately

5 percent of GDP. Given, too, that the state is a site shaped by the politics of democratic legitimation, changing the 'mix' of state provision, funding and regulation is always tricky for governing political parties—not only because parties in power are motivated by the desire to stay in power, but because restructuring can expose the state's material interests and sources of power leading to greater politicisation and therefore destabilisation and subversion. For instance, during election campaigns, teacher unions in Western Australia (Robertson and Chadbourne 1996), Ontario, Canada (Martell 1995) and New Zealand (Jesson 1994) have been able to point to savage cuts to public sector schooling, job losses within the teaching profession and a decline in teachers' salaries while tax rates for corporations have been slashed and executive salaries increased. While it is not always clear what consequences teachers' organised protests or campaigns might have for electoral results—or indeed for teachers and their workplaces following elections—there is little doubt that political parties seeking election would rather have teachers on their side than opposed to them.

Stability is a central feature of social settlements. It is therefore not surprising that the state's regulatory infrastructure tends toward routinisation and rigidification. In the case of the welfare state settlement, routinisation was shaped by factors such as the application of the principles of universalisation arising from the state's democratic legitimation needs. That is, there are tendencies for institutions—once established—to protect their own interests and to make the necessary changes to accommodate external conditions (March and Olsen 1996).

State regulatory activity, while on the one hand leading to stability, on the other hand limits the flexibility and therefore the steering capacity of the state. This is particularly problematic during periods of social and economic transformation when the embedded norms and institutional practises (for instance of Keynesianism) are likely to be contradictory to the new policy strategies (inspired by a variety of neoliberalisms) being pursued by particular interests within the state. Ratcheting up the 'marketness factor' during periods of economic and social transformation is a mechanism enabling the state to put into place policies crucial to ongoing capital accumulation in the face of the movement of capital and workplaces to a range of sites globally and of potential worker subversion and struggle from workers. This is particularly likely to be the case with those members of the service class whose professional projects were once hinged to state welfarism but must now be entrusted by the new competitive contractual state to make judgements on the basis of what is now regarded as an 'inadequate' and 'morally hazardous' set of professional norms and institutional practises (cf., Robertson et al. 1997).

THE INSTITUTIONAL NATURE OF
STATE–MARKET RELATIONS

We are now in a position to draw together the argument so far by making three main observations about economic markets and the state. First, economic markets are sets of institutional arrangements regulated by national states international agreements or treaties (for example, EU, NAFTA, ASEAN) or organisations (for example, WTO). Hodgson (1988) provides a useful elaboration of the first point that markets are sets of institutional arrangements, when he notes that markets can be conceptualised as a set of institutions in which a large number of exchanges of a specific type regularly take place and which, to a large extent, are facilitated by those institutions. That is, in order to understand particular market relations, we need to understand the practises and settings that enable such exchanges to be made in a regular and organised way. For instance, discussion of markets must take account of the legal and institutional framing of the contexts in which these exchanges take place. In the case of public sector teachers, given the state's varying roles as employer, funder, provider and/or regulator of compulsory and post-compulsory education, we must focus attention on various institutions within the state apparatus and community (including teacher education programmes, registration bodies and so on) that form, limit and shape the 'education market'. Because of the specificity of the political order of schooling (Connell 1995), the teachers' labour market is likely to differ in substantial ways from that of other public sector workers.

Second, formal rules are never sufficient to determine every output of the operation of markets. They necessarily assume a range of implicit/tacit social arrangements. I will refer to these non-formal but essential aspects as 'embedded'. This does not mean that they are left to the decisions and practises of participants. Rather, they are always subject to regulation by the state, the only institution that is able to legislate. As I have argued above, markets are always framed by a set of settlement-specific political rights (in the case of labour markets, for example, the right to belong to a union or the right to strike) which are negotiated between workers and their employers, or, in the case of public sector teachers, between teachers and the state. However, in the final instance, only the state (in its local, national or sometimes international forms) can legally enforce those aspects that have been codified, such as the number of teaching contact hours, levels of wages, qualifications or certification to teach. It may, however, rule indirectly and protect teachers' claim for a licensed professionalism and closure in exchange for commitment from teachers to the state's political project.

Third, the institutional framing and accompanying tacit social arrangements of markets are fraught with contradictions and are therefore occasions for and sites of struggle. As a result, the precise nature of the relationship between teachers, the state, markets and community changes over time, as the state must manage the instabilities arising not only from the accumulation process itself but from the contradictions in the state's own policy-making activities. These contradictions may, finally, result in a crisis of legitimacy for the state unless it takes steps to deflect or mediate the crisis in some way through generating new political and economic projects as solutions (Habermas 1979). It is precisely at this point that the state must seek new policy options; for example, reducing the size and cost of its labour force, getting rid of some programs and implementing others, or maximizing the returns on revenues spent (efficiencies and effectiveness). Alternatively, downsizing the labour force may be managed through redundancies, the failure to hire or early retirements.

FURTHER DIMENSIONS OF MARKET RELATIONS— 'MARKETNESS' AND 'EMBEDDEDNESS'

A further important aspect of market relations in relation to workers is encapsulated in the notion of 'embeddedness' and 'marketness'. These ideas are really important for understanding the range of motivations of workers in particular types of settings. As I have noted earlier in the chapter, 'embeddedness' refers to the way in which the "marketness factor" has been reduced and that the motivations of actors are assumed to be shaped by social factors other than just economic and instrumental ones. A school board, for example, may decide that the spiritual values, expertise, trust, experience and the personal pedagogical style of an applicant should also be taken into account when making a decision about who to appoint to the available position within the school.

The 'marketness factor', on the other hand, describes the extent of dominance of price and *economic instrumentalism* in exchanges. For instance, when faced with a decision about hiring a teacher, a school board, motivated only by price, would decide to offer the teaching position to the applicant prepared to accept the lowest level of renumeration (pay and other work-related benefits). Of course, this is not always likely to be the case, though increasingly we might see education departments and school boards considering this option in the face of diminishing fiscal resources. Alternatively, a science teacher might argue for a higher salary than other teachers within the school because of the importance assigned by the state to science as a school subject.

According to Block (1990), professionalisation has been a social means to reduce opportunism in markets, especially where information inequalities are particularly significant; for example, not being aware of the precise nature or quality of the service prior to the contract. In this regard, professionalism is a means of socialising an individual into a code of ethics and institutionally based social practises and therefore a mechanism for indirect control exercised by the state. We should also note, however, that as Lawn (1988) and others point out (cf., Lawn and Grace 1987; Ozga 1988) and which I detailed in Chapter 4, professionalism has been a double-edged sword which teachers also use to carve out strategic space for individual and collective autonomous action. These strategic negotiations center around 'trust' and 'expertise'; trust that the professional will make expert decisions within a framework which has been sanctioned by the state in exchange for the state's guarantee of the profession's monopoly of the labour market. The modern capitalist state has tended to rely on occupational groups that are committed to a notion of service (rather than opportunistic self-interest), because of the significant investment of skill in such workers, the need to have a high level of predictability of service and loyalty (recognised as life-long employment and promotion by seniority), and the significance of such professional groups to the state's ideological work. In exchange for licensed autonomy, professions within the welfare state, such as teachers, were given the promise of continuity, security and job mobility. At the same time, teachers have used the ideology of professionalism as part of an attempt to define the circumstances under which their own labour power is transformed into labour. The notion of professionalism, involving a monopolised expertise, an ethic of service and a less than wholly commodified relationship with both client and employer, gave teachers a protected labour market and discretion over aspects of both the process and product of their work. Paradoxically, however, neoliberal proponents argue in the opposite direction to the analysis presented by Block (1990) above: that the professionalism of the post-war period, to the extent that trust and closure limited scrutiny from outsiders and therefore public accountability, was rife with opportunism. This is primarily as teachers are viewed like any other economic agent—self-interested and self-maximising.While aspects of this claim might be true, that teachers are self-interested and self-maximising, there is considerable evidence of teachers' significant commitments to teaching beyond a narrow economic contract.

Until the late 1970s, a paradigm of professionalism and within it a conception of teacher professionalism underlay decisions about the nature of the economic exchange between teachers and the state. Elements of both the service to be provided and of the reasons for it, remained tacit—though consciously so. That is, 'they were known', even if not stated. The very existence of these tacit features bore witness to, and reinforced, the particular notion of professionalism which defined the precise nature of the sectoral settlement between teachers and the state within a given historical-political context. The important point to be made here, too, is that 'embeddedness' refers not to individuals but to the particular ideologies and social practises of individuals and institutions, such as professional codes of conduct, family considerations, or commitment to ethical, moral or spiritual values involved in the exchange. The exchange of goodwill between teachers as an occupational group and the state, for example in the form of voluntary labour, is a case in point (cf., Robertson and Chadbourne 1998). Embeddedness and marketness, as dimensions of market relations, highlight the 'trust' versus 'contract' binary which is implied in the institutional framing of professional labour versus blue-collar occupations in the Keynesian welfare state period.

MANAGING TEACHERS' COMMITMENT TO THE NEW SETTLEMENT

I now want to examine more closely the four forms that policy directed toward restructuring teachers' work has taken. These I identified as *commodification, management, control* and *codification*. While I have separated these policy stances into four broad categories for the sake of argument and for the purposes of clarity, they should not be viewed as discrete or mutually exclusive categories. Rather, their combined effect is to change contexts and conditions under which teachers work in the 1990s.

Commodifying Labour

Until the 1980s, public sector teachers worked in that sector of the economy not directly controlled by the market mechanism. It was also the case that while teachers laboured, they did not produce commodities for profit in the marketplace. Rather, teachers were involved in producing what Offe and Ronge (1984, 127) have described as "use values"—skills and knowledge that place future workers in a position to sell their labour. By the 1990s, however, this was changing. I have already noted that teachers are important in the system of state regulation. They have an involvement in developing, on the one hand, the appropriate knowledge, skills and attitudes in future labour power; and on the other hand, a commitment from citizens to the norms and practises essential to capitalist expansion (for example, self-betterment, the distribution of credentials on the basis of merit, and possessive individualism). Productive workers and conforming citizens are central to the unhindered process of capital accumulation. The tendency for state agencies, such as education, to expand as a response to the requirements of democratic legitimation and capital accumulation, means the expansion of the human labour power and material resources required to operate those agencies. State revenues come from taxes, revenues that are not then directly available for the creation of surplus values, for profit, and therefore the accumulation process. Teachers' labour power and the revenues necessary to operate teachers' workplaces are 'units of value' and are, therefore, not *directly* controlled by the market mode. Indeed, part of teachers' labour goes into what might be seen as the distraction of the liberal humanist project. Those units of value (like a teacher) that do not *directly and completely* contribute to the capital accumulation process and are not directly controlled by the market mode exist in 'decommodified form'. The commodification of teachers' labour refers to the process where aspects of teachers' work are either returned to the market and therefore directly controlled by the market, or where *marketlike* mechanisms are introduced which redirect teachers' labour more resolutely toward the requirements of capital accumulation.

There are a number of ways in which we can see teachers' labour being commodified. One way is through the direct 'downsizing' of the teaching labour force as whole categories of teachers are retrenched, to be funded by private means if necessary. An example here includes the cuts to kindergarten services in Alberta, Canada, in 1994. In this instance, Albertan parents who sought to purchase services which they had previously been entitled to—a kindergarten programme for their child— were required to pay directly for the programme themselves. As a consequence of the state's diminished role in funding and providing early childhood education (though nonetheless regulating the conditions for provision) and parents' increased responsibility, parents are directly engaged in a market relationship with the school.

A further instance of commodification working through the downsizing mechanism can be evidenced in, under the rubric of corporate managerialism and a flatter, more efficient post-Fordist bureaucratic structure, the 'pruning' of the central administration. Previously centralised services to teachers, such as curriculum development and research activities, have in a number of instances been privatised. These services are then 'purchased' back on the basis of competitive tenders to private consultants. The application of the principles of the marketplace, where previous 'providers' of various services (as in the bureaucracy) are now 'sellers', is viewed as necessary to providing a more efficient and cost-effective service. Consultants' services, as we know, can also be controlled and regulated more easily; they can be given the brief and told to get on with it. Consultants can also just as easily be ignored or disregarded if the service they provide is viewed as less than adequate. Consultants are flexible; that is, they can be discarded by an organisation or firm at the conclusion of a contract. They may also be a cheaper option on a salary bill, especially when additional and hidden costs of employing labour power, such as holiday pay, sick pay, union time, superannuation, operation costs and so on, are taken into account. Consultants, as I will show later on, provide the perfect opportunity for the state as employer, to convert potential labour power fully into actual labour.

Second, following significantly reduced revenues to schools, schools have pursued a number of strategies resulting in the increased commodification of teachers' work. One strategy has been to look to teachers within the school to engage directly in revenue-making activity, such as in selling education services to foreign full-fee-paying students, as in the case of New Zealand public secondary and primary schools, or selling a range of secretarial, computing, automotive or catering services within the community. These are all aspects of the commercialisation of schools I discuss in Chapter 8. A further strategy pursued by schools is the

'privatisation' and 'peripheralisation' of some aspects of the school programme and to 'essentialise' the rest as a *de facto* core. What this means is
that the introduction of marketlike tools, such as 'user-pays', make available some aspects of the school's formerly essential curriculum to those
who are interested and who can afford to pay for the service being provided. Activities that might once have been part of a more extensive and
state-funded programme but with no apparent direct use value, such as art
classes (pottery, painting), languages (e.g., Spanish in New Zealand or
Australia, where Asian languages are seen as essential to economic competitiveness), or outdoor education, are available at a price to interested
customers (parents). These programmes operate on marketlike principles:
if the customers are happy, they will come back for more and recommend
the programme to their friends. In theory, if the customers are not happy
(the price is too high, the outcomes not apparent, or the teacher inadequate), the service will fold. What is left as part of the school's state-
funded programme is then, by definition, the essential educational
entitlement to be offered to all students within the school, unaffected by a
market mode of exchange.

Third, teachers' work is commodified to the extent that their labour
and their workplace are drawn into the economic-productive sphere. The
increased commercial activity in schools takes many and varied forms.
For instance, teachers' work environments offer legitimacy to commercial products such as breakfast cereals or magazines (Robertson 1994)
and are increasingly targeted by marketing experts. The combined effect
of these three forms of commodification is to reduce the cost of education to the state, while at the same time exposing teachers to marketlike
mechanisms. Teachers can no longer hide behind their somewhat neutral
and decommodified relationship. Rather, they are *directly* and *indirectly*
caught up in selling products and services for profit as part of the state's
new political project.

Managing for More

The second major set of policies are directed at the closer management
of teachers; in particular, the *management* of those circumstances which
improve the conversion of teachers' labour power into productive labour.
In other words, given that teachers' labour power is only *potential* labour
power available to the state, the job of management is to establish and
manage those conditions which enable the employer to maximise the
conversion of labour power into labour. There are a number of ways

in which the state has managed to do this. First, under the rubric of a 'renewed professionalism', the state has implemented a series of policies, such as the devolution of management to schools, performance appraisal for teachers, the development of teaching councils (displacement of teacher unions) and new 'professional' career paths such as the institution of Advanced Skills Teachers. These policies establish the conditions whereby the state, through an ideology of professionalism, can manage more closely the extraction of labour from teachers' labour power. Not only are teachers allocated a wider range of tasks to perform within the school, such as making management decisions about aspects of a schools budget or programme, but they are monitored more closely and placed in a position where they account to their peers and superiors for the work they do in the school. Efficiency and effectiveness are important organising touchstones in this renewed professionalism.

A further way in which the conversion of teachers' labour power into labour works occurs is through processes such as contracting, tendering and privatising aspects of teachers' work in schools. The privatisation of large areas of work for teachers, such as particular areas of research, curriculum development and professional development, to be bought back by schools in the form of contractualised consultant services, results in schools and the central administration being able to impose a set of conditions for working and reporting that reduces the margins for discretion on the part of these specialised teachers. The means for management is the introduction of contractualised (and therefore legal) agreements which specify nature and length of service, type of output, forms of reporting and so on.

Controlling Use Values

New mechanisms have also emerged to *control* more directly the process and product of teachers' labour. Increased marketness promotes teachers' commitment to the production of a new set of 'use values' (knowledge and skills) in students necessary for participation as workers and consumers (and less so as citizens) in the global economy. At one level, the precise nature of the use value is varied, dependent on the potential nature of the labour to be performed. It is hardly surprising, then, that the state has increasingly funded programmes for gifted and talented children within schools, in some cases diverting resources away from programmes such as special education. In other cases, the state has created the opportunity through the workings of the market, for some schools to identify themselves as premier schools, adept at promoting potential use values within the global labour market. At another level, the competitive contractual state has to promote—through a range of activities such as international testing regimes, mathematics and science competitions—the values of the new settlement: individualism, competitivism, self-interest and entrepreneurialism among both students and teachers.

Codification

A central feature of the service classes' relationship to the welfare state, including professionals employed by the state, was an implicit and embedded contract that was symbolised above all in the notion of goodwill. This was exchanged for both security of tenure, status, an adequate income and state support for professional closure. In the main, teachers were in control of aspects of the exchange partly as teachers determined these to be 'goodwill' and therefore outside of the state's managerial purview. Embeddedness, however, enables the profession to exercise greater control over crucial aspects of their work and at the same time widens the space for judgement. While these margins for determination might well be useful to the state—for instance, as a form of licensed autonomy (Dale 1982) when the outcomes are both predictable and at least not disruptive to the state's agenda, it is also the case that during periods of transition and transformation that the state will seek to regulate more closely the work of teachers in order to promote a new professional ethic in line with the new social settlement. The introduction of market-based principles, where competition among schools (school markets, league tables) as well as competition between teachers (such as performance payment, differential salaries) is promoted for the purposes of greater control and extraction of use values, teachers' work is more likely to be driven by explicitly instrumental and monetarist concerns rather than the embedded norms of the Keynesian welfare state period of service, goodwill and care. In order to make comparisons between competing units, the nature of the tasks to be compared, and the levels of performance of those tasks, must be identified and codified to make them visible.

CONCLUSION

Playing up the 'marketness factor' in teachers' work enables interests within the state to shape a new relationship with teachers as public sector workers. The increased 'marketness' of teachers' work must therefore be viewed as a political act—creating the conditions for extracting more use value from teachers (intensification of labour) while managing the conditions under which the exchange value of teachers' work can be maximised. The marketness factor has taken four forms: the *commodification* of aspects of teachers labour; new forms of *management* aimed especially at improving the conversion of teachers' labour power into productive labour; new mechanisms to *control* the process and product of teachers' labour more directly; and the *codification* of the implicit norms in which the contracts had been embedded, symbolised above all in the notion of teachers' goodwill.

The outcome of these policies for teachers is that they are now more instrumentally focused on externally controlled definitions of process and product regulated by a combination of community, market and state modes. Given that at the same time teachers are increasingly assigned different subject and performance values and rewards in the marketplace, they have become more politically and socially divided as an occupational group. The combined effect of these policies is that the margin for discretion over pedagogic transactions is more likely to be curtailed and realigned and teacher alienation increased. Further, stripping away the embedded norms of teachers' labour explicit in the Keynesian welfare state settlement (an ethic of respect, care, trust, solidarity, service, loyalty) leaves a new morality that legitimates *economic self-interest* and a politics of self-regulation as an entrepreneurial accumulating unit rather than a self with social interests and responsibilities. In Alvin Gouldner's (1979) terms, it means severing and reworking the contradictory relationship between the goodness-power paradox which had come to define the work of teachers as state professionals in the post-war period so that it is transformed into a new technical expertise more closely aligned with managerial expertise within the service class and the morality of the competitive contractual settlement (Robertson and Dale 1998). This is little more than thinly disguised opportunism and a betrayal of democracy (Lasch 1995). While recasting the ideological and structural contexts and meanings of teachers' work and the way in which it is valued and rewarded places serious limitations on teachers' capacities to participate in a political and collective social project, many teachers have also had a remarkable capacity historically—together with other human beings—to continue, individually and collectively, to struggle to retain a focus upon dignity, decency and solidarity in their labour, despite structural and ideological changes (cf., Ginsburg 1995; Robertson and Smaller 1996; Apple and Beane 1999).

CHAPTER 8

Fast Schools and the New Politics of Production and Consumption

INTRODUCTION

Looking at teachers' workplaces in countries such as England, the United States, Canada, Australia and New Zealand in an era of 'fast capitalism', both the traditional *distinctions* and the *divisions* between schools and the economy have all but collapsed. Schools are increasingly in danger of losing their distinctiveness from the economy as institutional sites committed to the contradictory imperatives of capitalist accumulation and democratic politics (Carnoy and Levin 1985). In this chapter I examine the ways in which, at the end of the 20th century, schools and their teachers have been hitched—not always successfully—to the accumulation project as small competitive units within the national and global economy. Similarly, the divisions between schools and the economic sphere have considerably weakened with the penetration of corporate capital into hitherto inaccessible aspects of the workings of the school. In short, I argue that many schools have—in some cases reluctantly and in other cases willingly—increasingly become transformed into 'fast schools'. The fact that such conflations and intrusions are no longer viewed by many teachers as unusual may well be regarded as evidence enough that a new sectoral settlement in education is on the way.

THE SOCIAL RELATIONS OF PRODUCTION AND CONSUMPTION

Before elaborating on the ways in which the transformations arising from fast capitalism are evident in schools, I want to draw a distinction between production and consumption relations within schools and to comment on the importance of both in understanding the social relations of schooling within the new settlement. By production relations, I am referring to the social relations of capitalist production which arise from the relationship between the owners of the means of production and the actual producers of goods and services; a relationship I have noted in Chapter 1 that is essentially antagonistic and exploitative. In this relationship, capital is dependent upon labour while labour is dependent upon capital. Schools are bearers of capitalist social relations, largely because of their centrality both in producing labour and in reproducing the social relations of capitalism. Moreover, even within schools, teachers labour with students under particular exploitative conditions. Having said this, I do not want to infer some form of crude theory of correspondence. Schools cannot be reduced to being sites for the production of labour and the reproduction of the social relations of capital. As Livingstone (1995, 67) rightly points out, schools are also "structured ensembles of social relations mediating a wide array of contending political demands" such as race and gender; they are clearly very important for the state in dealing with its core problems—those of accumulation, legitimation and control (Dale 1982).

Production relations can be seen in three broad ways:

- Schooling aligned with the 'competitive state' project;
- Reorganisation of social and administrative relationships within schools based upon concepts of flexible organisation;
- Fostering school/corporate sector relations directed toward product development.

Consumption relations, in contrast, refer to modes of consumption that both produce and reproduce patterns of inequality. It is 'a mode of being', a way of gaining identity, meaning and prestige in contemporary society (Sarup 1996, 105). Thus, just as class relations are determined by the (non-) ownership of the means of production, so the main division within the sphere of consumption is determined by the non-ownership of the means to fulfill consumption requirements. According to Peter Saunders (1986), the major division within the sphere of consumption is between those who can meet their consumption needs through personal ownership and those who cannot. In some of these cases, individuals and families are dependent upon the state to provide them with the means for meeting their consumption requirements. Increasingly, within 'fast capitalism' consumption is privatised rather than socialised. Some of this move to privatisation is the result of public dissatisfaction with aspects of socialised provision. However, it is clearly the case too that this dissatisfaction has arisen as a result of a very public campaign by capital to transform existing patterns of state provision in ways that facilitate new patterns of production and consumption.

In addition to production relations, consumption relations in schools can be conceptualised in three ways as follows:

- The reconceptualisation of schools as representing 'lifestyle choices' within the educational marketplace.
- The development of school/corporate sector deals directed toward product and lifestyle consumption.
- The recasting of identity as cyborg/consumer in a knowledge/ information world.

Changes in the production and consumption relationship between individuals, schools, society and the economy, separately and collectively, represent a significant change in the context and conditions of teachers' work in the 1990s. Taken together, these six broad shifts in production and consumption relations map the emerging and complex post-Fordist settlement in schools. In this new social settlement, teachers must reproduce labour power committed to an enterprise culture as well as create subjects responsive to an image conscious and individualised, commodification-consumption culture. In the rest of this chapter I look closely at each of these broad shifts and their implications for the nature of the work that teachers do.

CO-OPTING SCHOOLING TO THE COMPETITIVE STATE PROJECT

By the early 1980s, governments in a number of countries had accepted the view that the conventional remedies offered by incremental policy making in the public sector were inadequate in the face of a globalising economy. Tinkering with the existing system of education, argued new right proponents inside and outside the state, would do little to assist nation-states to meet the challenges posed by the "globalization predicament" (du Gay 1994, 31). In order to position themselves within the global economy, nation-states (in particular, those within the core and semi-periphery) have increasingly taken the view that the national interest is best served by embracing the transnational dimension in new ways. This has involved the reconceptualisation of the state within a global economy as a 'competitive state'. This creates a new set of dynamics leading to even further transnational expansion. Notes Cerny (1995), "[T]he so-called competitive state is itself obliged by the imperatives of global competition to expand transnationalisation" aided by what Wade (1996) refers to as "the market-friendly model". What Wade is seeking to describe here is the view that the market is conceived as the only efficient mechanism for the organisation of economic, political and social exchanges and relationships. An explicit dimension of the 'competitive state' and 'market-friendly' models espoused by supranational bodies such as the Trilateral Commission, World Bank and OECD is, as Marchak (1993, 105) notes, that governments must be strengthened relative to citizens' and democratic interests "so that they could better recreate the necessary conditions for the restructuring of economies in a global marketplace". Throughout the 1980s, governments of all political persuasions, whether social democratic, as in the case of Australia and New Zealand, or liberal conservatives, as in the case of the United Kingdom and the United States, were quick to embrace the market-friendly, competitive state model.

The market-friendly, competitive state model is underpinned by three key restructuring tools: deregulation, competitiveness and privatisation. *Deregulation* refers to the removal of the state in intervening aspects of public and private sector activity, through its withdrawal from aspects of funding, provision and modes of regulation, state (except as guarantor of free movement of capital and profits but not labour). *Competitiveness* is the justification for dismantling welfare states and their various apparatuses built up in the post-World War II period, the argument being that "government had undercut healthy entrepreneurship through its interference in the free market" (Marchak 1993, 93). Excessive welfare provisions, trade and labour protectionism, overactive minority group representation and a top-heavy public bureaucracy were all seen by restructuring proponents as overburdening 'democracies' and undermining their competitiveness within the global economy (Marchak 1993, 106). Finally, *privatisation* describes the sale of government businesses, agencies or services to private owners and where accountability for efficiency is to profit-oriented shareholders. The privatisation of school custodial services, or the contractualisation of education services in Baltimore to Education Alternatives Inc. are two such examples. Within this market-friendly, competitive state framework, schools are viewed as competitive units within the national and the global economy. Schools are enterprises committed discursively and practically to the competitive state project.

Restructuring the labour market, and indeed, reconceiving the division of labour along new local and global dimensions, has accompanied the reshaping of the state. In essence, many states have taken seriously the notion that developed nations should rethink the ways in which they can 'add value' to the economy by moving beyond the old industrial categories that defined the nature of work. Robert Reich (1992), advisor to Clinton in the 1992 election campaign in the United States and later appointed Clinton's Secretary of Labor, has argued that within the global economy there are now four categories of jobs: routine production services, in-person services, symbolic-analytic services and the old industrial workers and professionals (such as secretaries, farmers, teachers, miners). 'Routine production services' refer to routine mundane activities such as credit purchases, billing systems or packaging—many of which are located in what are often called free enterprise or economic development zones and which are typified by cheap labour and tax reduction provisions. In-person services, on the other hand, refer to services—many of which are routine—provided in person, such as car cleaning or personalised banking. These services are therefore provided locally, though they may very well be organised or franchised via a transnational organisation. These in-person services require a high level of personal communication skills, punctuality and reliability. The state's perception that this shift is taking place is evidenced both at the level of policy and the level of the new curriculums for schools. "Symbolic analysts", argues Reich (1992, 177), are a new breed of worker that is involved in problem solving, management, development and so on. The globe is their orbit, working in a range of ways: alone, in teams, using the World Wide Web and so on. In the final category, the industrial workers and professionals, the state and economic interests have sought to reorient the work of professionals toward services that can be sold within the global economy rather than services delivered within the local economy paid for by the state. Compulsory schooling and higher education are now profitable export industries. For teachers in schools, this sort of development has changed teachers' work in schools in often dramatic ways (Singh 1996; Dale and Robertson 1997). This is not to suggest that teachers at the chalk face are necessarily likely to directly see the benefits of additional money going into the school. Rather, the state may use these export industries as a way of increasing its own revenues, or enable schools to make up shortfalls in state funding through recruiting foreign fee paying students into state-funded and -provided schools (see Chen 1997; Dale and Robertson 1997). Successful schools in this new knowledge business are those able to direct (often scarce) resources within the school, fiscal and physical, into marketing and recruiting such students abroad. Trading in educational services has attracted a growing number of private firms keen to trade in educational credentials and the acquisition of cultural and social capital. While aspects of their trade have been regulated by the state, this has sometimes come after the failure of some of these enterprises to deliver on their contractual obligations, causing more than a ripple of consternation between governments.

What have these developments meant for how teachers' work is conceptualised in the 1990s classroom? In essence, the changes are encapsulated in what I will call the Eight Es for Successful Teachers. The Eight Es refers to a largely rhetorical though emblematic formula for conceptualising teachers' work in 'fast schools'. That is, *empowered* teachers in the 1990s successful schools are ones who are *efficient* and *effective* with the resources at hand, *entrepreneurial,* oriented to the *economic,* committed to *excellence,* and ones who embrace the values and vision of the *enterprise,* including a recasting of *equity* as equal opportunity to pursue individual self-interest rather than equity of social outcomes for collective actors. With this as the new formula, teachers' work has been extended and intensified in new ways in schools: greater involvement in school-level administration, more accountability to regulatory bodies such as school audit agencies and their definitions of excellence, and prioritising the development and teaching of workplace competencies. With their principals as managers of enterprises, teachers have been encouraged to make up the funding shortfall through implementing and be submissive to more efficient corporate-style management (Smyth 1993). To build successful school enterprises, school administrators and teachers are urged to develop a whole new range of skills, to seek lessons from the marketing experts on how to package the schooling image to 'choice' conscious parents (Ball 1994), to solicit corporate funds and build corporate partnerships (Harris 1993; Apple 1994; Barlow and Robertson 1994; Robertson 1995), to apply the latest business techniques to ensure excellence and quality (Gee 1996) and to sell their educational services in the international educational marketplace (Dale and Robertson 1996).

How have these proposals affected teachers' relationships down at 'the chalk face'? In many respects a critical literature documenting these outcomes is scarce. What we do know, however, is that for some teachers the new principles for success create further divisions within the profession and within schools (cf., Robertson 1994). Teachers compete with each other for scarce resources; meanwhile, the game rules for success mean that competitive and entrepreneurial teachers win. In the same way, too, teachers who embrace the values and visions of the enterprise are seen as committed and dedicated workers and are differentially rewarded. The costs are high for education. For some teachers, the new principles for success undermine opportunities for collegiality with colleagues (Smyth 1993), cut across their commitments to students by taking them out of the classroom (Robertson 1993), intensify their labour (Apple 1993) and lead to growing discrepancies in salaries between different categories of teachers. Not surprisingly governments have sought to head off teacher union demands for adequate levels of resourcing and better levels of pay by seeking to restructure the industrial relations frameworks which, until the 1980s, had shaped teachers' work and defined teachers' relationship to the Keynesian welfare state.

NEW PRODUCTION CONCEPTS AND
THE FLEXIBLE WORKER

As I have argued earlier in Chapter 5, fast capitalism signals a decisive shift in forms of work organisation within advanced capitalist economies following direct confrontation with the rigidities of Fordism (Harvey 1990). I also noted that the emergence of new ways of organising production systems—loosely referred to as *flexible specialisation*—have enabled the development of new sets of institutions and social and economic relationships, including the way in which labour is organised. Florida and Kenny observe:

> The hallmarks of post-war socio-economic organisation, mass production industry, pyramidal bureaucracy, vertically integrated corporations and functionally specialised work are being transformed by the rise of new technologies, new systems of work and organisation production and new social arrangements (1994, 248).

Since the early 1980s, work within the productive sphere has systematically been restructured. Enabled by the emergence of new 'just in time' technologies and as a response to the growing difficulties of coordinating industrial mass production based on the principle of 'just in case', the institutions that make up the production system (such as the corporations) have become more vertically integrated, structures have flattened, and middle management eliminated. Flexible specialisation is viewed as the cure for the sclerosis of big firms. The essential idea here is that in the context of saturated markets and customers with specific requirements in terms of choice, competitive firms must learn to be fast and flexible and to provide flexibility at low cost, with good customer service and rapid manufacturing.

Compared to mass production, flexible specialisation (or lean production) has a number of distinctive characteristics. That is, flexible specialisation involves the use of fewer resources while increasing production volume, a closer relationship with subcontractors and retailers, the development of a number of sub-processes at any one time to shorten product lead time, and the use of 'quality' processes (such as total quality management) in order to achieve flawless production (or zero defects).

Lean production and flexible specialisation is dependent on new ways of organising labour, which now exist alongside traditional patterns of Taylorized labour. These have emerged around worker and labour market flexibility. Workers must therefore learn to be innovative with ideas for products, to focus their attention on simultaneous projects or diversify their skills to encompass new ones and to manage their own work processes. Kern and Schumann (1987) have labelled these labour processes 'new production concepts', arguing that they represent a radical departure from the Taylorist patterns of work organisation. The 'new production concepts' refer to an explicit reliance on increasingly skilled labour, task integration (including management tasks) and the reprofessionalisation of occupations (including self-regulation). While Kern and Schumann document empirically important changes taking place in industry, they point out that the 'new production concepts' refer only to key industries and that they will never entirely replace mass production. Rather, as Harvey (1990) argues, flexible specialisation must be located within a broader framework called 'flexible accumulation', which would include piecework, mass production, flexible specialisation and various types of cottage industries. These various elements of flexible accumulation make up a new flexible labour market structure based on a primary core group of highly skilled workers (organised around the new production concepts and functional flexibility), a first peripheral group organised on the basis of numerical flexibility (such as longer term contracts) and a second peripheral group which provides even greater numerical flexibility (made up of workers with short-term contracts, job sharers, part-time and casual workers and public subsidy trainees) (Harvey 1990, 151).

While having noted these shifts, an important caveat must be noted: that is, that economic transformation entails social adaptation as well as technological and cultural change. New institutional arrangements do not emerge *tabula rasa* but rather reflect the legacy of old social and institutional forms and practises; institutional forms and practises which, themselves, are the outcome of particular political struggles and compromises. This is important in thinking about the precise nature and form of teachers' work and workplaces within the new post-Fordist settlement. While the market mode is increasingly dominant as a means of regulating teachers' work, the bureaucratic mode of regulation is still apparent. These competing regulatory modes create significant tensions for teachers within schools. This is because, on the one hand, schools are conceived of as publicly accountable institutions to audit bodies. As such, failure carries with it a high political price for a government. And on the other hand, the logic of the market requires that those schools and teachers which do not embrace the new definition of success may very well be faced with market failure.

Given teachers' dual role in (1) the reproduction of labour power (for flexible enterprise), and (2) the production of subjects who embody particular social dispositions and moral orientations within the social order (enterprising/flexible), when transformations take place within the economy, existing institutional arrangements and practises begin to unravel. Not surprisingly, the demands on teachers as workers also change. These demands occur in two ways. First, teachers' work and workplace alter as schools and successful teachers refashion themselves—using the Eight Es—as competitive enterprises. Second, the school curriculum alters as teachers are encouraged to teach the competencies required by workers and citizens in the new social and economic order.

Enterprise and entrepreneurialism in schools work in a number of ways. The demise of the rigid bureaucratic model within education and the rise of the enterprising, self-managing, flexible school has created spaces for individual teachers to become more entrepreneurial; the corollary of this is that entrepreneurialism is now a precondition for success for teachers (Robertson 1994). For some teachers, these new conditions create new opportunities to reorient their careers in new directions. Whether setting up partnerships with the corporate sector, developing innovative responses to requests from industry for curriculum relevance, marketing the school to the wider community, or establishing a business enterprise within the school (e.g., a catering service, word-processing services, vehicle repairs), entrepreneurial teachers have quickly learned to mobilise resources and support both within the school and outside it.

Like the economy, the schooling system has been restructured so that a powerful central body feeds off "numerous smaller units which are satellites, subsidiaries or subcontractors to the powerful central unit" (Watkins 1993, 137). In the same way, too, power is located within the educational center through tightened controls and the minimisation of the functional lines of responsibility downwards. Administrators and teachers are given the task of implementing the new enterprise agenda and, at the same time, determining and managing the 'riot threshold' central to successful implementation. This has been referred to as 'management by stress'. The riot threshold refers to determining how much pressure can be placed upon workers, or in the case of educational settings upon teachers and students, without losing control over the quality of the product while moving toward "zero defects". At least one school division in Ontario, Canada, is now offering product guarantees. Should the student 'product' turn out to be deficient, in the view of his or her employer, then retraining is guaranteed by the school (Robertson 1995, 12).

In addition, as I have argued in considerable detail already, the school curriculum—viewed in its widest sense—alters to embrace the social dispositions and moral orientations for workers and citizens in the new social and economic order. The curriculum—that is, what it is that teachers and students labour over (Connell 1995), changes as a consequence. However, access to the core labour market is determined by credentials, credentials to which *access* is increasingly allocated using the principles of 'choice' and the market (and not bureaucratic selection on the basis of apparent ability to benefit or geographic access) and credentials are *achieved* on 'merit'. Credential access and achievement now require the exercise of significant social capital. The ideology of meritocracy, central to the operation of the state-bureaucratic mode, is now linked to the ideology of choice central to the operation of the state-market mode. Greater differentiation in the labour market is now legitimated by greater responsibility in credential acquisition.

SCHOOLS AS PRODUCTION SITES

The creation of schools as production sites has eroded the traditional distinctions between schools and the economy. Schools are increasingly viewed as small production sites either operating independently or as affiliates and adjuncts to local businesses and large corporations. When schools are thought of as production sites, this redefines the scope of teachers' work; they now work as direct agents of corporate capital or as site managers of business ventures.

Bryan Palmer (1995) provides a fascinating account of how Goodyear, a transnational corporation, moved into the small town of Napanee in eastern Canada. The company sought support for the move from the local school community, including teachers and students. While there were oppositional voices within the community, Palmer notes that these voices were quickly silenced. In essence, the school became a small productive unit of the company, managed by the same workplace relations as Goodyear. Programme Think, implemented within the school, might be viewed as an oppressive system of regulation and surveillance where students were asked to regulate their own and others' behaviour as a form of self-discipline—at least from the point of view of students and teachers having to manage it's implementation. Programme Fire, on the other hand, was a system of pink-slipping students who violated the rules of the job, such as coming late to class or not getting assignments in on time. In both cases, these direct forms of worker socialisation promoted a particular ideological view of the successful worker—the capacity to follow instructions, dependability, personal presentation and constant performance. The crucial difference here is how much of it took place directly within the school. At the same time, school students became involved in resolving production difficulties for the company in their industrial physics classes, thereby increasing the company's efficiency. As Palmer notes, these kinds of projects were viewed by the company as a type of outsourcing or contracting out of the company's work. However, "the workers only received the wages of incorporation and the price of the product was paid in kind with the bestowal of gifts" (1995, 36).

LIFESTYLE CHOICES IN THE SCHOOLING 'SUPER' MARKET

The consumption relations of fast capitalism in schooling can also be seen in the reconceptualisation of schools as situated within an educational 'super' marketplace. The emergence of principles of 'choice', exercised within the educational marketplace, are significant developments shaping teachers' workplaces in the 1990s.

A range of countries, including the United States (cf., Henig 1995; Clune and Witte 1990), the United Kingdom (cf., Gewirtz, Ball and Bowe 1995), Canada (cf., Robertson et al. 1995; Delhi 1996), New Zealand (cf., Gordon 1993, 1997) and Australia (cf., Kenway 1995; Kenway and Epstein 1996) have embraced both the rhetoric of choice and/or markets. While there are considerable variations from system to system, it is nonetheless fair to suggest that some form of choice and/or markets are on the restructuring agendas of each of these countries.

Much of the choice/markets agenda has been shaped by the criticisms of schools as inefficient bureaucracies that are unresponsive either to community or individual interests. It is argued that institutional unresponsiveness and inefficiency is the result of provider capture (Chubb and Moe 1997). That is, teachers as a professional group have enjoyed the protection of the state from a discerning community of parents who, it is suggested, have a right to exercise a choice about the desirable education for their child. In short, the choice/market proponents argue that provider capture has resulted in system inefficiencies and the failure to provide any incentive to teachers for innovative and client-responsive practises.

In New Zealand, in a report written in 1987, the Treasury argued that problems of efficiency and equity in education could only be addressed through 'choice' and where family or individuals were constructed as the customers of educational services (cf., Codd, Gordon and Harker 1997; Gordon 1997). Similarly, in England and Wales, the Education Reform Act of 1988 brought about fundamental changes in the way that educational services were provided (Whitty, Power and Halpin 1998). The general aim of these reforms has been to introduce a more competitive market approach to the allocation of resources in the education system and to (ostensibly) increase the range of parental choice over children's schooling. However, in both the case of New Zealand and the United Kingdom, the size of a school's budget is linked to the number of pupils it could attract to the school.

The argument that the market should deliver public sector goods, such as education or health care services, was made on the back of orchestrated criticism of big government and the inefficiency of the state's bureaucratic apparatus—including the ways in which schools are organised—in responding to the community. Markets, according to a various assortment of public choice theorists, are (1) more *efficient* modes for the allocation of goods and services (cf., Chubb and Moe 1990; Coleman 1990); (2) more *equitable,* in that they are responsive to the needs and desires of clients (as opposed to public sector bureaucracies characterised by quasi-monopoly status and therefore provider capture); and (3) more *democratic* in that they maximise the freedom of individuals to choose intervention in their own lifestyles, unhindered by the state.

The market model of schooling operates something like a 'super' market. For example, 'boutique' schools seek to attract customers with particular types of needs, such as in an exclusive private school, a girls' single sex school or magnet schools. The 'local store' school recruits students from within the community, while a range of client-tailored 'shopping mall' schools draw in some or many of their students from outside their own immediate locale by offering a combination of 'boutique' and relatively undifferentiated streams within the school programme. In this model, schools compete within what Gewirtz, Ball and Bowe (1995) have called circuits of schooling—circuits that enable "different groups of parents to 'plug into' each of the circuits and each circuit empowers its students differently in terms of life chances" (ibid., 53). Schools within and between circuits compete to deliver most wanted services to potential consumers, or to define consumer tastes through advertising image. Circuits also operate *within* particular kinds of schools, as in the 'shopping mall' version. Even in this context, there are winners and losers (Wexler 1995). In my own research I found highly specialised programmes within a high school, such as fashion, music or cricket directed toward attracting particular types of consumers into the school from outside the local community (cf., Robertson 1994). The adjunct to this is that the majority of students in the school were located in undifferentiated programmes; many of these students had few hopes for the future. Whether buying a future job (high-tech schools), status (elite private schools), success (cosmopolitan schools) or a sense of local community (local school), potential consumers are assumed to have gathered the information and weighed the evidence of their lifestyle choice.

There are two important points to be made here about both choice and markets. First, conceptions of 'choice', 'choosing' and 'chooser' give little ground to the way in which the materiality of life and cultural resources combine to shape and limit choice. Instead, class, race and gender are conveniently ignored, except as ways of thinking about advertising angles, potential niches or future consumers. A growing research literature points to the fact that race, class and gender are crucial variables in who gets what from the 'market-friendly' model (cf., Gewirtz, Ball and Bowe 1995; Lauder 1994). This is not to suggest that 'choice', even within schooling, is an entirely new phenomenon. Private schools have, for a long time, been an alternative to public sector provision in Australia, the United States and the United Kingdom, enabling a process of social differentiation to take place. Now, however:

Well resourced choosers now have *free rein* to guarantee and reproduce, as best they can, their existing cultural, social and economic ad-

vantages in the new complex and blurred hierarchy of schools. Class
selection is revalorised by the market. [emphasis added] (Gewirtz, Ball
and Bowe 1995, 23).

Gewirtz, Ball and Bowe (1995) provide a considerable amount of
evidence as to how class selection takes place in schools in the United
Kingdom. The 'skill' of the chooser, they argue, lies not so much in
whether they are capable or efficient as choosers. Rather, it refers to a
particular set of cultural capacities that are unevenly distributed across
the population. In other words, argue Gewirtz, Ball and Bowe (1995), social judgement and taste (as theorised by Bourdieu 1997), or the possession of a cultural code, enables the consumer to decode the relative value
of the commodity to be purchased.

In this model, individuals make choices about what and how much
they will consume; they are choice maximisers. However, the choice
model makes the assumption that being an educational consumer is (or
should be) a universally valued category and that schooling is primarily
about individual consumption (for job preparation) and not about public
goals (such as the production of citizens). The exercise of choice (taste)
differentiates consumers from each other. Those who fail to exercise that
choice, or indeed choose less 'valued' programmes are pathologised as
failing to care for their children. Such a simplistic account of the relationship between schools and contemporary society deflects attention from an
economic and political system that has created a growing underclass.

Thinking about markets and schooling choice in this way is important. However, it fails to pay sufficient attention to the way in which
schools themselves choose their potential customers. Schools seek to be
selective in the sorts of students they attract to the school. This is all the
more important when confidence in the school image is more and more
critical. As I have already argued, market edge is maintained through
managing the relationship between the physical and social properties of
a commodity. This is important for schools. Schools that fail to be selective about the students they attract to the school may well find the social
property of the commodity—such as academically competitive and well-
disciplined students—is recast. In the same way, too many foreign, black
or Asian students in a school, or classes for intellectually disabled students, may be seen as tarnishing the image the school wants to project
within the marketplace. Selecting students on the basis of a higher social
class background can provide the school with some insurance against
this 'risk', although some schools may well seek a market niche for
lower working-class students. Nonetheless, whatever the basis for class

selection, all will bring with them very different sorts of resources—social, economic and cultural.

The corollary of this is that homogeneous groups of parents seeking to school their children with others like them might be seen to be seeking a pooled insurance risk for their child against the risk of marginalisation within the labour market and society. In other words, parents as consumers in the schooling marketplace, in exercising a choice, must be guaranteed that the product they purchase can potentially be exchanged for economic security, cultural recognition and preservation, and political power within society. Commodified education in the market-friendly model of schooling is thus about establishing the conditions that guarantee advantage within society in an increasingly competitive world.

Accompanying the market-friendly model of education is a booming industry in how to market education. The suggestions provided by this industry is described by Kenway (1995, 3). Schools are told that *packaging* is crucial to effective marketing:

> Packaging is partly about marketing a product and an image to those outside the institution and this, we are told, must not be haphazard or ad hoc. It requires careful planning which involves operation mission statements, a long term focus, the development of appropriate financial, organisation, personnel and technological infrastructures, the recruitment of experts if possible, market research and evaluation and the re-orientation of staff (human resources) to external relations. And further, packaging for the market is also about being strategic. It is about developing a 'product/market' mix which allows the institution to gain a 'differential advantage'. This means making decisions about 'concentration'; about which aspects of 'the product' to emphasize, resource and promote (opportunity cost) and which to discard (starve) because of their lack of marketability. Secondly, it means making decisions about which segments of the market to 'target' for research, publicity and investment. It means keeping a constant weather eye on 'the opposition' in order to assess their relative strengths and weaknesses. It also means having an eye to the future and seizing new market opportunities before others do (Kenway 1995, 3).

For secondary schools in countries such as New Zealand, Canada, Australia and the United Kingdom, developing a product-market mix in order to augment decreasing operational budgets has entailed various types of packaging directed toward different market niches. In a growing number of public secondary schools in New Zealand, this entails the identification of consumers in countries as far away as Japan, Hong Kong, Malaysia, Korea, Taiwan and Chile. Education, in these instances, is packaged as cultural and language exposure and a means of ensuring success in the global economy. For these local schools, surviving locally means surviving in the global marketplace. Indeed, local failure, as a result of the exercise of choice within the local educational marketplace, can be mediated by success within the international educational marketplace. There are, clearly, advantages in having an international student body within a school. It may very well enhance, rather than detract, the value of the school's product. Furthermore, an international body of students might be viewed as an important dimension of the school's programme. Whatever the impact that international students have on the school, they now commodified sets of social relations with potential risk and exchange value to be managed by the school.

It is not yet clear what effects this sort of market innovation has on local school populations. One distinct danger is that scarce resources are diverted into advertising, recruiting and resourcing international students at the cost of local students. Another is that the income generated by foreign students, because it is at the margins, gives the overseas consumer individual influence over the education system in another country (Dale and Robertson 1997). It is here that we can see most clearly the blurring of boundaries—geographic and political—with consequences for our conception and experience of community. The experience of *community in school* may be undermined when some parts of the school population (students and/or teachers) are treated differently than the rest. Additionally, the notion of a *school in a community* is challenged by the opening up of public schools to students who may well live in different countries. In both cases the changing nature of the relationship between school and community raises important questions for consideration: schools are sites increasingly responsive to a 'globally situated' rather than 'locally situated' community. Furthermore, what are the implications for our notions of collective responsibility and the public good when schools are viewed as sites composed of a myriad of individual economic transactions. The market conception, argue Bryk, Lee and Smith (1990, 188–189), employs a language and basic conceptualisation of schooling that is antithetical to the social foundations of schooling. They further add: "Although individual entrepreneurship may fuel economic development, it rings less true as a basic motivation for processes of human development" (ibid.). The point, however, is that in a system of schooling that privileges the individual and the economic over the social and the collective, as in 'fast capitalism', processes of human development are only of concern to teachers to the extent that they help understand individuals as economic producers and consumers, as opposed to a broader notion of what it means to be human.

PRODUCT AND LIFESTYLE CONSUMPTION

By the late 1980s and early 1990s, the state systematically set about promoting the development of partnerships between schools and the business community. It also sanctioned opening up aspects of public provision to full-scale private enterprise. The development of self-managing schools has been crucial to this enterprise. By reducing the funds available to local schools at the same time that an enterprise ideology is promoted, local schools have been encouraged to seek resources from a willing business community. Alternately, business has sought either to co-opt local schools to their productive endeavors or to enter the new schooling marketplace in search of profitable activity.

The abundant examples of the rapid intrusion of fast capital into schools illustrates my point. In Australia, Apple Macintosh computers ran a nationwide campaign in conjunction with Coles, a large grocery chain. Schools participating in the programme asked students to collect receipts from Coles. Classrooms were pitted against each other in a weekly battle to bring in the highest totals on receipts. These were then carefully collated, totalled and recorded by a teacher in the school following a precise formula. Critical totals can be exchanged for an Apple computer; technology that is highly valued because it is able to compete with neighbouring schools. These programmes have a ripple effect on schools. Teachers involved work as unpaid salesmen and saleswomen for these big corporate bodies—Coles and Apple—while small retail outlets within local communities feel the pressure of the shift in trade to the large grocery chain. What advertisers value is the extra legitimation they feel an academic environment, such as a school and teachers, that offers their products. In commenting on *What!*, a popular magazine in Canadian schools, Media Kit note that *"Kidsworld Magazine* stands out from all the other kids media because our publication is enjoyed in the non-cluttered, non-competitive and less commercial classroom environment." Like it or not, teachers' classrooms work as subtle enticements to value one product over another, while teachers also act as tacit endorsees of a range of consumer products and services.

A second example describes the intrusion of companies such as Pepsi into the schooling marketplace. A landmark deal between Pepsi and the Toronto School Board in 1993 gave Pepsi monopoly rights to advertise its products on school property (Roberts 1994, 8). For little more than a million dollars, Pepsi gained the right to install its dispensers in all schools across the city for three years and for what even the industry viewed as "a share of the gullet". Despite protests from teachers, students and health groups, board trustees believed there was little alternative available to them in the face of cost cutting. The fact that the local community is left making the decision to open the floodgates to corporate capital mediates the inevitable contradictions that confront the state. The sheer speed at which these developments are occurring bewilders some observers. In the words of one teacher commenting upon Pepsi's deal with the Toronto School Board: "If people live in an eternal present, that serves the corporate interests quite well. . . . It seems like all the direct influences are becoming more direct every day. It's like being in a room where the walls are closing in. It's almost bewildering the speed at which it is happening" (Roberts 1994, 10).

Michael Apple (1993) also writes on the explosion of deals between schools and the corporate sector, driven by a diminishing tax base available to the state as a result of tax breaks and tax reductions to minimise the flight of capital and attract new money. School communities have, as result, welcomed the exchange of 'free' technology in exchange for guaranteed audiences of Whittle news and advertising beamed in by satellite. A contract with Whittle Communication for schools can mean that a given school must be able to guarantee that "ninety percent of pupils watch ninety percent of the time . . . ten minutes of 'news' and two minutes of commercials . . . every school day for three to five years" (Apple 1993, 97). The number of schools that have signed on is staggering— over eleven and a half thousand schools under contact in the United States by 1992 (Apple 1993, 98).

CYBORGS AND CONSUMERISM IN AN INFORMATION WORLD

"Our identities", observes Madan Sarup (1996, 105) "are influenced, among other things, by what we consume, what we wear, the commodities we buy, what we see and read, how we conceive our sexuality, what we think of society and the changes we believe it is undergoing". One area where schools have increasingly sought to promote a particular pattern of consumption and identity is in the acquisition of 'high tech' computing and the ways in which this can be used to display both an eagerness to enter the world of fast capitalism and as a means of facilitating access to that world.

Schools, in searching for a competitive edge in the schooling marketplace, have willingly succumbed to what Robins and Webster (1989) describe as the technical fix. Being able to display to prospective parents and students a roomful of the latest computer equipment is clearly an advantage in the school competition stakes. However, a particular type of computer literacy as a mark of distinction in the new age is one thing; the material resources to own a computer—indeed, your own personal portable computer—is another. At one level it can be argued that a room of computers is a mode of socialised consumption, though clearly not all schools are in a position to provide the same levels of resourcing. However, some schools with evidently well-resourced parents now require that students purchase their own portable computers to be used throughout the day at school. We might call this mode of consumption 'privatised'.

Privatised consumption of access to the cyborg world not only opens up new means of accessing information—for instance, through the Internet—but at the same time, it reproduces unequal relations within society. That is, "increased access to information occurs differentially in relation to one's position in the class structure" (Poster 1990, 6). Poster goes as far as to argue that one way in which we can understand the importance of this new form of communication is to conceptualise it, as Marx did with modes of production, as a *mode of information* (ibid.). According to Poster, modes of information refers to "the way in which history may be periodised by variations in the current structure in this case of symbolic exchange, but also that the current culture gives a certain fetishistic importance to information" (Poster 1990, 6). Given that information is presented as the key to contemporary living, where society is divided between the information rich and the information poor, and that the 'informed' individual is a new social ideal, particularly for the middle and ruling classes, then it is not surprising that those schools that can have access to cyberspace have been quick to discern this new form of cultural distinction and to respond to it.

It must also be noted that students' access to a wider world of knowledge in space creates new challenges for teachers working in classrooms. On the one hand, privatised patterns of technological consumption exaggerate what is already evident in those forms of cultural capital described by Bourdieu (1996). The inequities in schooling are not mediated by new forms of consumption in that not all students are able to draw on the cultural resources (now no longer contained in socialised spaces like local community libraries, but privatised modes through the Internet). However, the identity of the student as 'knower' and the world to be known is not constrained by the traditional categories of schooling life. There is an increasingly sharp distinction between the fast, shifting and often erotic exchanges in cyberspace and the slower and often apparently more mundane exchanges in the classroom. Assumed disembodied identities in space—where gender, age, race and class are deliberately overturned—compete with the embodied identity of classroom life. The unreal and real, fleeting and heavy moments of time-space work together in often unpredictable ways to create a more fragmented sense of community and solidarity.

FAST SCHOOLS: A NEW TERRAIN FOR PROFESSIONALISM

In this chapter I have outlined key aspects of the new terrain of struggle for teachers—the challenge of the global economy and the emergence of the schooling market as a means of promoting not only the efficient production of workers and consumers but as a practical articulation of the state's political capacities. The commodification of a growing number of aspects of the public sector, including schooling, have arisen as a means of reducing the dependence by the community on the public purse yet regulated in such a way that the state is able to retain control. Teachers increasingly find themselves balancing a series of acts on high stakes wires: between the old commitment of welfare and service and the new commitment oriented toward the enterprise and entrepreneurialism. The new organisational structures of post-Fordism, with its differentiated hierarchy, less secure patterns of employment, differential rewards in terms of individually negotiated wages, where status is dependent upon the circuit of schooling, and where the new forms of social assets are dependent upon community networks rather than associations such as unions, suggest that teachers as an occupational category will be fractured and reconfigured as workers in a cascading pattern of exploitation. For the first time in more than half a century, teachers' ability to convert material, cultural, organisational and social assets into privileged access to the middle class is under pressure. These issues are taken up in the following and final chapter.

PART IV

Critical Realities Reviewed

CHAPTER 9

Critical Realities Reviewed

INTRODUCTION

Using the theoretical insights developed in the first half of this book, I want to return to the detail of the changing conditions and contexts that now frame and shape the work of teachers in the 1990s so as to make sense of the underlying shifts taking place. We can begin by noting the significance of the changes that have occurred at a number of levels. First, developments within the global economy (see Chapter 5) have combined to create new problems for nations and their governments. Second, the exhaustion of political alternatives within the Keynesian welfare state paradigm, together with the loss of confidence in the institutional frameworks of the post-war period, signal the end of an era and the beginning of a new period of political and economic turmoil. In this new environment, restructuring has entered the lexicon of both the developed and developing world (cf., Amin 1990), where terms and phrases such as 'reorganisation', 'restructuring', 'structurally adjusting' and 'structural adjustment' have become particular points along a continuum of economic and political redevelopment and reregulation at all levels of the political playing field.

Within this new framework of crisis, restructuring and change, a new set of questions in relation to teachers and their work has now emerged—questions I will address in order to draw together the various arguments developed throughout the book. What is the new educational mandate for teachers in schools? How and in what way has the new politics of fast capitalism and fast schools transformed the nature of teachers' class assets? What are the consequences of this transformation for teachers' market, work and status situations? Finally, how might we understand teachers' professional project in the 1990s? These are important questions with, as yet, little by way of detailed and conclusive answers. There is still considerable debate over the shape and meaning of the restructuring. Thus, though the contours of the settlement are increasingly visible, it remains formative rather than congealed as a set of firmly fixed social structures and social relations. It is also the case that this process has been hampered by the lack of detailed, systematic and rigorous comparative work which focuses on teachers as an occupational group, though there have been some advances in this area (see, e.g., Lawn 1985; Ginsburg and Lindsay 1995). And while there are a growing number of more detailed country studies (cf., Menter et al. 1997), it is difficult to compare them as they deploy quite different frameworks for analysis. My observations, therefore, are necessarily speculative and broad-ranging rather than focused on the specific accumulation-institution relation within and across nations and how teachers' work is structured and practised within that.

With these few comments in mind, this chapter will proceed in the following manner. I will make a number of broad comments on the changing mandate, capacity and governance of education systems in OECD countries after a decade or more of restructuring within and across nations. I will then turn to an exploration of the consequences of the reworking of state-economy-civil society relations for teachers and their class assets, and how this is reflected in their market, work and status situations. Finally I will review the nature of teachers' professional project in the 1990s and suggest that the reconceptualisation of professionalism as individual entrepreneurship and managerialism threatens to create new fissures between teachers and to fragment them as an occupational category. I will argue that this process will create new occupational identities among teachers. This is likely to reduce the cohesiveness and consciousness of teachers as a group formed around a moral project of service (goodness) and reinforced through a political strategy of solidarism (power). The new moral project of a cadre of teachers committed to managing the market and the client, in combination with a political strategy of individualism and exclusion, will contribute to the construction of very different conceptions of teacher professionalism and, as a result, privilege very different types of teachers.

A NEW EDUCATIONAL MANDATE

The new conditions of fast capitalism and the rise of the competition state have necessarily generated the need for a new educational mandate. A central principle within this new mandate is that educational systems, through creating appropriately skilled and entrepreneurial citizens and workers able to generate new and added economic values, will enable nations to be responsive to changing conditions within the international marketplace. Competitiveness is thus viewed as a social value and a social good which is applied not only to schools and students, but to teachers as well. Through educationally driven economic success, it is argued that a nation will be able to generate the level of economic prosperity that can trickle down to the whole of the community. The new educational mandate is thus shaped by the economic instrumentalism of the new social settlement and the competitive individualism of the new worker citizen.

Implementing this new mandate has posed considerable difficulty in education systems where many teachers remain not only steeped in but committed to the values of collectivism, social welfarism and social trusteeship. Further, teachers across the OECD countries have either retained or increased their membership of unions and collective forms of association, despite declines in union membership among workers overall. The politics that surround the implementation of the new educational mandate is thus shaped, on the one hand, by the state's political project (itself prone to contradictions between accumulation, legitimation and control) and, on the other hand, by teachers' own professional project aimed at increasing economic assets, securing state and community support for claims to expertise and generating conditions that enable teachers to have a degree of occupational autonomy. Not surprisingly, these two competing projects have, over the past decade or more, generated considerable conflict between teachers and the state (Lawn 1985; Robertson and Smaller 1996; Bascia 1997).

Competition states have sought to emphasise their commitment to capital accumulation by private interests through strategies such as reducing public sector expenditure in areas like education, health and housing. The state has then redirected these funds to an assortment of 'competitiveness' strategies; for instance, investment incentives, promotion of exports, 'sunrise' industries, training programmes, enterprise zones and so on. At the same time, a significant percentage of public sector activity has become vulnerable to recommodification in order to generate income. States have also argued that different administrative arrangements for the delivery of public services, such as the devolution of management decisions to local communities and the creation of more competitive arrangements between service providers, will improve worker performance and bring about a more efficient delivery of services while creating greater flexibility at the level of the organisation. Within the education sector, as in industry, competitiveness in the new market economy is increasingly based on factors such as efficiency, 'quality', product differentiation, product management and the capacity to react quickly to consumer needs, or at least those needs associated with consumers with resources, though it must be emphasised that constructions of quality are always political and are the outcome of struggle over meaning and practise. The constant pressure by the state to foster and protect capital accumulation (partly through minimal taxation and flexible labour laws) has acquired considerable legitimacy where, as has been noted elsewhere, the tension between accumulation and legitimation is eroded to the point where accumulation *is* legitimation (Dale and Robertson 1997). The legitimation burden of the state is, at least in the short term, considerably reduced by this conflation of the requirements of capitalism and democracy, though it will be interesting to see whether and how this can be sustained in the long run. In nations such as New Zealand, where public sector restructuring has been informed by hardline neoliberal proponents within and outside the state, there is growing evidence that the much vaunted trickle down effect has been propelled— with considerable state support—upward (Chatterjee 1998). Furthermore, within the schooling sector, almost a decade of school markets and parental choice has delivered growing social polarisation between social classes and communities (Lauder et al. 1995), leading to new fears of social breakdown and individual alienation.

At the same time that restructuring states have sought to limit or even reduce spending on education, teachers have argued against the erosion of the conditions of their work and for increased economic reward (Robertson 1993; Jesson 1995; Robertson and Chadbourne 1998). Teachers have also tried to limit the encroachment of the new administrative structures on their occupational authority and autonomy, as well as resist strategies by the state that would promote competition between teachers for scarce resources. Their success in doing so has been variable. Indeed, a central argument in this book is that, historically, teachers' success in securing and protecting occupational autonomy is dependent on their ability to mobilise collectively and to resist pressures from the state, market and community not only to reconceptualise the pattern and content of their labour but the individuation of teachers' employment conditions. The fact that teachers' unions are still in the state's firing line suggests that teachers will face an uphill battle in protecting their collective interests (cf., Robertson and Smaller 1996).

RESHAPING THE MODES OF GOVERNANCE

States, in order to implement the new educational mandate in the new competitive contractual settlement, have introduced far-reaching reform of the governance structure of education. Much of this agenda has ridden on the back of a constant attack on the quality of teachers and their competence (cf., Ball and Goodson 1985; Wexler 1987; Ozga 1988; Berliner and Biddle 1995; Robertson 1996). As I have already observed, there has been a considerable degree of consistency and similarity in the arguments that have been advanced across nations, in particular that teachers have prioritised their own interests and in doing so failed to respond to the voices of parents and the needs of local communities. Armed with charges of provider capture and arguments for greater community participation and efficiency through local-level management of resources, states have radically changed the modes of governance of education. All this has had a dramatic impact upon teachers and their work. States have altered the funding, provision and regulation of education and at the same time reordered the priorities of state, market and community institutions through which education is coordinated. As a consequence, in most OECD countries there has been a shift away from a variant of the Keynesian model of a state-funded, -provided and -regulated system of education to one where these activities have been dispersed by the state to include market and community institutions. These strategic displacements of power in the governance of education and teachers' work should be viewed as an attempt by states to manage their increased vulnerability to 'risk' in a turbulent and unpredictable global economy which—as can be seen with the economic crisis in Asia—is itself prone to crisis. This has led states to reassess the fiscal and political risks associated with such turbulence and relocate the management of the consequences of this risk to other sites along the state-economy-civil society triad. In summary most OECD states have sought to reduce their commitment to the funding and provision of education while reviewing and 're-scoping' important regulatory activity to now include the market (competition) and the community modes (local school boards). At the same time, states have maintained close control of the overall framing and output functions (policy, curriculum, assessment, audit) of education, putting considerable pressure on teachers' professional project. As a result, a new set of organisational forms are emerging, shaped by the complex and contradictory interplay of the state, market and community around notions of flexibility, productivity and quality and which generate the conditions for new internal organisational patterns and industrial relations regimes.

It is hardly surprising that these new initiatives have been opposed by many within the teaching profession, though there is growing evidence that the nature of the new governance structures will divide teachers as an occupational group, as is the intention. These divisions will deflect the fallout of various political struggles away from the state, either locating them within local communities, or individualising them as the consequence of choices by actors in the marketplace. I will return to this point later when I examine the nature of teachers' professional project in the 1990s. For the moment, however, I want to examine in more detail the ways in which the nature of teachers' class assets have been transformed as a result of the restructuring of education.

THE TRANSFORMATION OF ASSETS

What are the consequences of these changed conditions for the transformation of class assets for teachers? In Chapters 1 and 2 I developed a framework to enable a more complex account of teachers as class actors employed by the state. I suggested that by mapping the linkages between causes, contingent conditions and real consequences for how teachers experience the social world it was possible to plot teachers' class location across space and time. In chapters 3 and 4, and through an illustrative analysis of teachers' work in two social formations—England and the United States—and across two social settlements—laissez-faire liberalism and Keynesian welfare statism—I sought to show how teachers' capacity to realise economic, cultural organisation and social assets resulted in a particular configuration of market, work and status situations. However, the precise nature of an asset, whether economic, social, cultural or organisational, changes with new circumstances and under new conditions. What counts as a legitimate asset and how it might be converted to maximise value are the object of and outcome of struggle between teachers and their employers, and now teachers themselves. We can see this most clearly when we examine the nature of these assets in different social settlements. The new conditions associated with fast capitalism have, I suggest, challenged the legitimacy of existing forms of economic, cultural, organisational and social assets and have been the basis of their transformation.

From Trusteeship to Entrepreneurship—the 'New' Expertise

Cultural capital is a cultural asset; it has its own value and can be converted into social power. Cultural capital can take a number of forms: educational credentials, the embodiment of taste, and artifacts (Bourdieu 1984). In the case of teachers as professionals, the value of cultural assets exists in claims to socially useful knowledge or expertise and subsequent occupational authority and status. During the Keynesian welfare state settlement, teachers sought—though not always successfully—to convert their claims to expertise into social status and economic rewards. For American teachers (see Chapter 5), this tended to be through the use of exclusionary strategies such as certification and registration. However, English teachers employed, with considerable success, a dual strategy to secure social closure: (1) exclusion based upon certification and registration and (2) solidarism organised through unionism.

During the Keynesian welfare state settlement, two elements—one *technical* and the other *moral*—were central to teachers' claims to professional expertise. Teachers organised their *technical* claim around either a subject discipline or pedagogical expertise. Secondary teachers' technical expertise was largely centred upon university-derived discipline-based knowledge. However, primary teachers' claim to a subject-based discipline has been more difficult to sustain since their knowledge base is organised, in Bernstein's (1996) terms, as an integrated code rather than collection code. That is, for primary teachers, the boundaries between the knowledge disciplines are blurred rather than defined. As a result, primary teachers have sought to establish their claims to expertise around notions of pedagogy, such as child-centred enquiry and the various methods through which this pedagogy can be advanced. However, as the crisis years and restructuring have progressed, both primary and secondary teachers' technical expertise has been found fundamentally wanting by the critics. Secondary teachers, they argued, perpetuate a knowledge base and division of knowledge that is largely irrelevant to a competitive state within the economy, while primary teachers' ideological commitment to a child-centred pedagogy is viewed as creating the conditions where children fail to acquire the basic skills such as reading, writing and arithmetic.

The *moral* element of teachers' claim to expertise was, by way of contrast, constructed through and expressed as *social trusteeship*. Teachers, as members of the 'new class', sought to present their interests as universal rather than as aligned with any class, though clearly their pursuit of economic and cultural assets, objectively and subjectively set them aside from at least one of the classes they serviced—the working class. This very paradox of power and goodness that Gouldner (1979) identifies, however, was used by neoliberals to critique teachers and their interests. This exposed the soft underbelly of teachers' professional project in the post-war settlement. The force of this critique has been aided by a wave of disenchanted post-modern and post-structural social theorists committed to the politics of difference and whose criticism of expertise and grand narratives has been intended to expose and dislodge claims to social trusteeship as illegitimate. Whatever the validity of their arguments, the effect has been to weaken teachers' claims to expertise in 'socially useful' knowledge in the face of an increasingly skeptical public with highly specialised experts and their capacity to provide useful solutions to important social problems.

In the theoretical uncertainty that has followed, neoliberals have discursively attacked and claimed—with considerable certainty—the new terrain of the restructuring agenda. The sharp end of this neoliberal critique, which I might add has escalated the loss of faith in professionals, combines a number of aspects. One criticism is concerned with the ways in which the cultural capital of teachers has shored up opportunities for teachers as a self-interested class, rather than for those within the community that teachers portend to service. In other words, it is argued that education has been run in the interests of the providers rather than either the students or the community, leading to criticisms of 'provider capture'. It is argued that instead of teachers subjecting captive communities to their 'professional judgement', they should be more responsive to and governed by the preferences of the community of consumers they seek to serve. A second criticism concerns itself with the potential for opportunism built into teachers' expertise claims, particularly centred on the notion of trust and autonomy. Key government agencies within restructuring states, drawing upon the ideas of new public management theorists, have argued that in the contractual relationship between teachers and the minister, both parties are likely to withhold important information about their performance in order to protect their own interests (cf., Robertson et al. 1997). The explicit distrust of each party to a contract that underpins the new contractualism and which is increasingly used to (re-)order the state's affairs, has had an important impact on how teachers' work is conceived and monitored by the state and its agencies. This has led to the codification of important aspects of teachers' work. A third criticism by neoliberal proponents is that consumers should be allowed to choose the educational service they prefer. In order to enable this, aspects of the old centralised and bureacratised system have been deregulated, creating a market-based dynamic through which preferences and choices can be made.

As I have argued in Chapter 8, a major fallout for teachers of these different critiques is that the basis of their expertise that had sustained teachers over the welfare state settlement is now under attack. These new institutional and organisational conditions have created spaces for the emergence of a new set of teacher values and identities built around the reorganisation of schools and their reorientation to the labour market. In this environment, *teacher entrepreneurship* is increasingly valued as the new cultural asset by schools fighting for positions within the marketplace. In a very real sense, too, 'market'-oriented competencies of teachers contribute real dollar value back into the underfunded organisations in which teachers work; for example, when teachers create new privately funded scholarship-based programmes (see Robertson 1994), draw in fee-paying students (Dale and Robertson 1997) or promote corporate sponsorship schemes (Harris 1993; Apple 1993; Molnar 1996).

We can now begin to see the double movement of the inversion and reconstruction of the moral dimension of teachers' claim to expertise. *'Doing well by doing good'* is transformed to *'doing good by doing well'*. This centres the moral weight of teachers' claim upon the self rather than the other and in the process enables the establishment of a new claim: that the aggregate benefit to individuals is valued above expertise claims that seek to benefit the collective. The reconstruction of teacher morality as individualism, entrepreneurship, competitivism and outputs thus transforms the nature of cultural assets, creating the conditions for a new and very different type of teacher professional. Now teachers' goodness is no longer aligned with representing the social interests of a universal class (*doing good*) but is centred upon their own economic interests (*doing well*) which will, it is assumed, lead to the benefit of the collective. Where once all teachers benefited together, now they benefit at each other's expense. In this process, power is relocated to the individual and not the collective. However, the irony here is that the benefits to the individual, including occupational autonomy, are likely to be eroded by the diminution of the power of the collective.

Aside from matters of how teachers have used their cultural capital to further their own professional project, there is now growing pressure by the state on the 'value' of teachers' credentials. Though in some places the state is seeking to withdraw from its position as monopoly provider, for the time being it remains the dominant, if not literally the monopsonist purchaser of accredited teaching skills. Since the state manages both the supply and demand aspects of teachers' professional labour, the state has considerable power over 'teacher value'. There are a number of ways in which states have reduced the value of teachers' credentials: through increased competition between providers of teacher education training programmes, resulting in the tendency toward much shorter training periods for teachers; limiting the funding of training places, thus creating problems of supply; or locating the bulk of teacher training into schools, using a variety of models of training, including school-based teacher mentoring. Whatever the legitimate and pedagogical grounds for this latter approach, the more practical orientation in a school-based teacher-training programme contributes to the demystification of teacher training as specialist university-based expertise, reducing it to technique. The state has also diminished the value of teachers' credentials by employing non-credentialled teachers where there are acute shortages. Though it might be assumed—using the logic of market supply and demand—that shortages would force teachers' wages up, restructuring states have resisted demands for salary increases as far as possible, through employing non-credentialled labour or importing teachers from overseas (cf., Robertson 1998).

From Procedural to Market Bureaucracy—the New Organisational Form

One of the most profound changes taking place in education has occurred at the level of organisation. These shifts have transformed the nature of organisational assets for teachers. Organisational assets refer to those advantages that might be secured by particular workers as a result of an advantageous position within the organisation. This advantage might be structural (for instance, position in the organisational hierarchy) or resource-based (for instance, organisational knowledge or critical skills specific to the to the ongoing functioning of the organisation).

Coriat (1995, 133–135) describes different types of organisational forms that have been historically linked to different regimes of accumulation. Drawing on the work of Chandler, Coriat (1995, 136) describes the early form of organisation as the unitary or 'U' firm. With the introduction of Taylorism this simple unitary form (typical of the early schools; see Hamilton 1989) was transformed to a 'M' firm: a multi-divisional form within a vertical and highly hierarchical organisation. Along this continuum of complexity it is possible to plot various types of elementary and secondary schools, depending upon factors such as size, geography and philosophy. The 'M' form of organisation can best be described as a *procedural bureaucracy* (Considine 1996): a more rigid, hierarchical and rule-oriented organisation based on the principles of scientific management outlined in the earlier part of this book. Power in a procedural bureaucracy is derived from one's structural position within the hierarchy, while control is oriented by knowledge of the rules and procedures that govern the internal workings of the organisation. In this case, organisational assets can be seen as an *internally oriented* and *rule-based* and where the organisational asset is inherent in one's formally defined role within the organisation.

Few teachers would disagree that the restructuring by states has resulted in the transformation of educational organisations following a complex process of delayering, downsizing and devolution. In the old bureaucratic system teachers made the long march up the organisational ladder by leaving the classroom and acquiring managerial experience, whether in schools or the regional or central administration of the state. The days of acquiring organisational assets by virtue of loyalty and the development of administrative expertise are now largely over. I am not suggesting managerial positions have all but disappeared; rather, there are a new range of positions and career paths within the educational system and educational organisations that do not fit neatly into the old pyramidal structure.

There are a number of models that the state might have used for this purpose. A dominant model appears to be a reinvigorated or derived form of Taylorism arising from the centrality of managerialism with its emphasis upon productivity and output, and the creation of new types of organisational hierarchies. This is not to suggest that there has not been a hierarchy among teachers. However, in comparison to other bureaucratic organisations, schools have been considerably flatter in structure. One example of a new category of teacher-labour is the Advanced Skills Teacher (AST) in Australia, where teachers' classroom-based expertise is recognised and rewarded through title, what might appear to be greater occupational autonomy and additional performance incentives. The AST is quite similar to the new *teacher-manager* who is responsible for a range of other teachers and educational workers within the school (for example, teachers' assistant, school-based student teacher). Teacher-managers not only manage the work of other educational workers within the school but, like the Advanced Skills Teachers, incorporate more managerial tasks into their jobs. In both of these cases, a new 'authority' currency arises based on a combination of managerial expertise and productivity-based output registered through student performance and the 'value' of the school's output in the marketplace. Performance pay differentiates among teachers and creates a new economic hierarchy among teachers. However, increased levels of power and control for some teachers will be at the expense of their colleagues who will command less occupational authority. These developments create the potential for conflict between teachers not only subjectively as they struggle over resources but objectively in that these assets place them in a potentially exploitative relationship to their colleagues.

The reintegration of managerial and teaching activity appears, at first glance, to be a new solution to the Taylorist tendency to sever the relationship between the conception of teaching and its execution. On the surface, then, this shift has the appearance of greater autonomy, and one that teachers themselves have found appealing as it enables them to move beyond the confines of the classroom. However, I agree with Kern and Schumann's (1989) general point that these new concepts for the reorganisation of productive labour mask the way in which the tasks of professionals are highly constrained by the steering frameworks of the organisation. This most certainly applies to teachers in the 1990s, where the state's educational mandate and the new modes of governance provide a more rigid and tightly prescribed framework for controlling teachers' pedagogical, curriculum and assessment work. This can be seen particularly in the United Kingdom and New Zealand, where educational organisations are regulated not only by managerialism and the market but by the activities of auditors and evaluators. In England, school inspection is carried out by the Office for Standards in Teaching and Education (OFSTED), while in New Zealand, schools are reviewed and audited by the Education Review Office (ERO) and the Auditor General's Office. Through codifying and standardising school life and teacher practises, these create new rigidities in schools and teachers' work (Robertson et al. 1997).

The process of further stratification within organisations has gone hand in hand with flattening other aspects. For example, various component parts of educational organisations have been privatised or 'out-sourced', such as accounting, and custodial or professional development services. Why and how have these two apparently opposing tendencies occurred? The reasons for this can be found in the new political and economic environment for organisations. In order to survive in an increasingly turbulent and competitive environment, educational organisations must be more flexible regarding how and what type of labour is deployed, how education is packaged and marketed, and how they promote commitment and trust to the organisation. As I have argued in Chapter 6, there is considerable interest among policy makers in developing more flexibility in the use of teacher labour within schools. For instance, in New Zealand, bulk-funding teachers' salaries will create opportunities for schools, if they implement the scheme, to deploy labour as they see fit at the same time as enabling the school to sidestep the collective employment contract for teachers by offering individual contracts and incentives. In this situation there is considerable fear that these sorts of initiatives will reduce the number of highly skilled and more highly paid teachers, and contribute to the expansion of various types of temporary teaching in the form of short-term, contracted and consultancy-based teacher labour (Robertson 1998; Robertson 1999).

The ILO (1996, 42) reports the increasing tendency among upper-middle and high-income economies to employ teachers on temporary or limited term contracts, though at present this still represents only around 10 percent of the teaching force. This is to be distinguished from part time teaching, which is less of a financially driven form of increased flexibility and more a response to both the desires of individual teachers for different work and career choices (op. cit., 42). These are contrasted by the ILO's (op. cit., 43) exclusive versus inclusive flexibility. Exclusive temporary teachers are the consequence of a commitment by the state to limit funds to education and to increase the possibilities of reducing the teaching force or replacing the teaching force with younger, less qualified teaches if the need arises. This strategy, observes the ILO, has not resulted in raising school quality (op. cit., 43). Inclusive strategies, on the other hand, focus on increasing educational productivity by adjusting the relationship between families and work and making it possible for educational systems to employ highly qualified teachers committed to a career but limited by family obligations.

It is possible to see the pattern of exclusiveness already emerging, though this takes a number of forms. One is a pool of *temporary teachers* who have a peripheral and excluded relationship to schools and to better conditions of work. The second group of exclusive labour—*teacher bricoleur*—arises as a consequence of the state reducing its regional and central administrative functions and outsourcing these to private consultants, many of whom were previously employed by the state. They now form what Martin (1998) describes as a new middle-class group—a group I would suggest has few loyalties either to teachers as a collective or to the state. In his study of new patterns of work and careers and new orientations to the labour market in Australia, Martin (1998) develops a very interesting analysis and model of an emerging group he calls 'new middle-class bricoleurs'. This model responds to the decline of managerial expertise and the rise of new identity expectations, which do not fit easily into either managerialism or professionalism but which are at the same time oriented to problems of complexity and unpredictability. This new middle-class group of bricoleurs mobilise a new form of socially useful knowledge they connect to a particular pattern of labour market engagement. They tend to be more individualistic in their outlook, use whatever tools are at their disposal, and are driven not by a commitment to a long-term career or organisation but the completion of a task.

It is pertinent at this point to return to the distinction between cultural and organisational assets in order to assess the impact of the restructuring on organisational assets. Savage et al. (1992) argue that cultural assets (such as a credential) have a wider value than organisational assets, which are organisation-specific. As a result, the value of an organisational asset is not easily transferred outside the organisation. I concur with this view in relation to *procedural bureaucracies,* where in procedural bureaucratic settings, organisational assets are inherent in the *role* and where roles are given authority by rules and regulations. However, these orientations change with what Considine (1996) describes as a *market-bureaucratic* form of organisation. These are more flexible organisations oriented toward knowledge of the external environment—the market. In market-bureaucratic organisations, organisational assets are inherent in the *person* whose authority is derived from knowledge of key markets and social networks. Organisational assets of value move from the internal to the external environment and are located not in rules but in those persons who control *externally oriented market-based* activity. We can now begin to see how *market-bureaucratic* settings (see Considine 1996) create conditions that enable the *teacher-entrepreneur* to benefit from market-based organisational knowledge. For example, teachers with developed organisational skills, such as a network for fundraising or contacts in foreign communities to recruit students into the school, are likely to be valued and rewarded for this externally oriented knowledge.

The crucial point here is that because entrepreneurial teachers' organisational knowledge is external rather than internal, they are able to use these assets in other settings that also depend on knowledge of and networks in the external environment.

One consequence of devolution and the implementation of a market philosophy is that there is now growing differentiation within and between schools. New categories of specialised expertise have been added to descriptions of teachers' work in schools, such as 'teacher-in-charge of overseas students' or 'marketing expert' with often few clear lines of demarcation between administrative and teaching staff. However, the expansion of such categories, particularly as they relate to the schools' entrepreneurial activity, means there is considerable blurring of the lines of authority and with it occupational power. A second consequence of devolution is that Taylorist tendencies have been crosscut with other models where various types of political actors, including the state, have sought to generate new organisational forms for specific political purposes.

In Australia the federal government's funded schools in the National Schools' Project experimented with new, innovative organisational forms, though always within the framework of the new competitive Australia (Chadbourne 1992). At the same time, new social movements have been able to capture new space for their political projects. In New Zealand, the indigenous Maori population used devolutionary policy to generate a new 'Kura Kaupapa Maori' schooling movement committed to fostering and developing Maori language and conscientisation, to promote political aims (Smith 1997). Ethnic groups in Australia and Canada, such as Muslims, have successfully used the new conditions to create their own organisations committed to the production of ethnic identities. These organisations will clearly vary in their organisational form and create quite different conditions for the realisation of organisation assets.

In sum, the transformation of organisational assets offers mixed blessings for teachers. On the one hand, the demise of centralised bureaucracies with its rules and hierarchies places teachers in a subordinate position to school managers, though this is more acute for primary school than for secondary school teachers, in that the latter were able to use their discipline-based expertise to mediate the effects of management and create greater degrees of occupational autonomy. On the other hand, more flexible organisations promise not only greater differentiation of tasks to be undertaken by teachers and administrators in schools in order to respond more adequately to the new competitive environment, but the flat structure of teaching will be hierarchical so that some teachers will have considerably more organisational assets than others in the form of organisational power. Further, the new post-Fordist developments mean that individual teachers will be in a position to convert particular types of informal organisational knowledge oriented to the competitive marketplace into economic and cultural assets within their immediate organisation and elsewhere.

From Collective to Individual Association

Social assets are a form of social capital consisting of social obligations or 'connections' that enable either individuals or groups to realise certain ends that are relatively unobtainable in their absence. Social assets might be thought of as types of institutionalised social relationships, though these types vary in their formality: for instance, teacher unions, subject associations, networks, or information channels. The value of a social asset is dependent upon the ability to exclude others from that particular social relationship. For example, some of the benefits of membership in a teacher union are available only to those who are members, as in the case of a collective employment contract, while particular schools might be able to depend upon their old boys' network to access additional resources. Teacher unions have historically been a powerful form of association for teachers which, when mobilized around particular issues or agendas, brought benefits to the collective that were unobtainable by individuals.

Three distinctive tendencies, which have transformed social assets and with them the capacity for teachers to realise particular types of class assets, can be identified as arising from the new settlement. The first arises with the privileging of neoliberalism in the new settlement as an organising ideology with its emphasis upon individualism and free choice over collectivism and social responsibility. Those social assets that have been dependent upon a democratic social ideology, such as labour unions, are increasingly decentred in the struggle over ways of representing the interests of workers and their rights. Indeed, neoliberals have argued that in the modern global economy, not only have traditional forms of labour representation failed to take account of the new politics of difference, but that the notion of a working class is considered to be increasingly passé, following the demise of Fordism. This has heightened intellectual and public skepticism as to the role of labour unions in modern societies at precisely that point in time when these forms of collective representation are crucially important in the ongoing struggle between capital and labour. Although one can note problems with some labour unions, public scepticism about labour unions has also been fuelled by interests that benefit economically and politically from the demise of organised labour. A second tendency arises from the first and is related to the considerable pressure upon, and potential demise of, teachers' unions as a means of collective representation, while a third concerns the growing importance of a variety of social networks in a market-based social economy. As I have already commented at some length on the rise of a variety of neoliberalism as an ideological motor that now frames and shapes the new educational mandate and modes of governance, I want to turn my attention to the other two: (1) individual versus collective forms of representation, and (2) the growing importance of social networks.

Like unions in general, teacher unions have been in the state's firing line as the restructuring of the education sector and teachers' workplaces has progressed over the past decade and a half. Competition states view the role and place of unions within the new settlement as a set of archaic structures and self-interested practises that are products of a bygone age: Fordism and state welfarism. Where once large unions were part of a triadic relationship with mass industry and centralised state planning, the new regime of accumulation is driven by firm's responsiveness to rapidly changing market conditions within a new industrial relations framework. Though there are variations across countries, depending on the relative power of organised labour, competition states have chiefly argued consistently against teacher unionisation on grounds such as freedom to choose as an individual, economic efficiency, organisational flexibility and worker professionalism.

These stand in stark contrast to the relationship between labour and the state in the post-war period in many of the OECD countries (for example, England, Australia, New Zealand, France and Canada). During the Keynesian welfare state settlement, as I have argued elsewhere (Robertson and Chadbourne 1998), the industrial relations regimes of nations were framed by a welfare-state collectivist model underpinned by a Fordist regime of accumulation and regulated by some variation of Keynesianism committed to a social and a minimum wage. Control over labour was regulated through the incorporation of unions into the affairs of the state or through fostering a commitment to a depoliticised professionalism.

With the collapse of the Keynesian welfare state settlement, there was no doubt that the forms of labour organisation that had sustained this settlement would be found wanting. I do not intend to suggest, like neo-liberal critics of unionisation, a functionalist argument here. That is, in the new settlement, collective forms of representation are an inadequate means for presenting worker interests. Rather, it is precisely because large unions were so successful in promoting the interests of workers as a collective in the post-war period that both the state and capital have sought to restructure these modes of interest representation.

Hardly surprising, states that display capital and competition have attacked traditional labour unions in order to promote a new work order based on increased productivity through the intensification of labour and the creation of more flexible employment arrangements. This has resulted in states, in the face of variable resistance from workers, seeking to develop a more individualistic market-oriented regime of industrial relations controlled through the negotiation of individual contracts. The 'new contractualism', as it has been called by Davis et al. (1997), assumes that each party to the agreement freely consents to this exchange. However, as Margaret Wilson (1997) observes of the Employment Contracts Act in New Zealand, the notion of *free consent* is clearly deeply problematic here where in capitalist economies workers must sell their labour in order survive and where private corporations within minimal state regulation, or the state as employer, are able to regulate labour market conditions to their own advantage; for instance, by enabling labour to be imported from elsewhere.

Within the education sector, competition states have sought to challenge and change the relationship between themselves as employer and teachers as employees. During the first phase of the restructuring, states reduced expenditure on education by pruning back spending on capital works and operational costs, while at the same time attempting either to reduce (cf., Soucek and Pannu 1996) or at least hold down (Robertson 1994) teacher salary costs. It has become increasingly apparent that states face growing economic and political uncertainty as a result of their vulnerability within the global economy. This has resulted in a second phase of restructuring committed to reworking, not only the way in which teachers' labour is deployed in schools (curriculum, pedagogy, assessment), but also the way they are employed. In short, states have recognised that they must renegotiate the frameworks within which teachers are employed in order to reduce the cost of the overall teacher salary bill as well as find a means of differentiating between teachers in order to promote more competitive teacher performance.

Teachers' salaries are a major part of the overall cost of education. Any reduction in expenditures on education or intensification of work would need to take account of the ways in which teachers' salaries are negotiated and funded. In the United Kingdom, for example, the state pays out more than £11 billion in teachers' salaries—around 80 percent of the state's educational budget (Sinclair et al. 1995). The figures for other OECD countries are roughly similar—teachers' salaries make up between 60 to 80 percent of the total cost of education (OECD 1996, 56). Throughout this period, teacher salaries have remained a more or less centralised cost to government negotiated through some form of collective agreement with a bargaining agent whether a union or professional association. To date, teachers have been able to draw upon teacher unions as a crucial social asset in seeking to protect (though not always as successfully as they would want) their economic, cultural and organisational assets. Indeed, teacher unions have argued that following restructuring teachers have increased the range of tasks that make up their work and, at the same time, their levels of productivity. For teachers in Western Australian, for instance, this resulted in salary increases (Robertson 1994). For this reason, the state has viewed teacher unions, along with other forms of collective organisation, as standing in the way of negotiating important flexibilities in the employment and deployment of teacher labour in schools, including new categories of educational workers.

The dilemma for the state is how to break the welfare state collectivist model of industrial relations that has shaped teachers' relationship to the state and put in place a competitive, individualistic model that will enable greater flexibility over teachers' wages in the face of vehement pockets of organised political opposition. A competitive individualistic model of industrial relations will enable schools to negotiate individual teacher contracts which deliver numerical and fiscal flexibility to schools and the capacity to scrutinize more closely the individual performance of teachers. However, teachers and their unions, in some cases with the support of the community, have resisted the state's attempts at reform of the industrial relations regime. A further dilemma facing the state is how to maintain teachers' commitment to the state's educational mandate and to economic competitiveness when, at present, teachers have organised numerical power and the potential to flex their political muscle.

Hardly surprisingly, teacher unions have opposed early manoeuvers by the state to redefine the place of unions and the right of unions to be sole collective bargaining agent, largely as they threaten the disintegration of unions and with it a potentially powerful social asset. In some cases teachers have also been able to mobilise workers in other sites. For instance, in the United Kingdom, Sinclair et al. (1995; 1996) report that teachers have developed extensive and supportive relationships with the Local Education Authorities, school managers and other local trade unions in order to progress their cause and cases. States have also been unable to ignore the voices of teachers because, contrary to elsewhere in the labour movement, the membership of teacher unions has increased and teacher union activity has escalated. The problem of how to impose a new regime is therefore complex for the state, with no clear resolution in sight. To progress the implementation of the new educational mandate in the education sector, states need the support of teachers. However, these very reforms are viewed by teachers as having an adverse effect upon the work. Furthermore, many teachers remain committed to the values of state welfarism, though these values and their associated practises are likely to be eroded over time as a result of the transformation of cultural and organisational assets. Teacher unions and associations that have mobilised and used solidarism as a strategy have been able to secure cultural, organisational and economic assets for teachers. Their potential demise is therefore a matter of considerable significance for teachers as an occupational group and for their class location. Fragmentation and individuation is likely to reduce the potential power of teachers as an occupational group, leading to a more individualised professionalism.

A second feature of the transformation of social assets in the new competitive contractual settlement is the growing importance of various types of networks. Within the wider literature on post-Fordism and flexible production, networks in the guise of alliances or relational contracting are gaining new importance as a mode of coordination of flexible production. Networks consist of "inter-linked units exchanging information and services for mutual benefit" (Sayer 1995, 106). They are dependent upon trust in order to function effectively in the new competitive environment. I want to suggest that networks will become increasingly more important for schools and teachers as competitive units within the marketplace. Those within the network are able to access cultural and fiscal resources not available to others outside. This might operate at the level of both the school and the teacher. Schools are now more and more dependent upon their communities for a variety of resources: funds, expertise in governance, school financing, corporate sector relationships and so on. Membership of key social networks is an important social asset enabling particular schools to derive benefits not available to other schools. To the extent that individual teachers may be employed on contracts or valued because of their access to important social networks, they will derive particular benefits from these social networks. This is similar to the experience of teachers in the United States during the laissez-faire liberal settlement that I examined in Chapter 3: individual teachers were able to use their political connections within the local community in order to promote their own interests at the expense of others. The important point to be made here is that these forms of association are not transparent. Instead, as I have argued in Chapter 1, these types of social assets operate in institutional settings and contexts where power relations and the exercise of power are likely to be less visible. It is more personal, less formal and not codified, and as a result has the appearance of mystique. Contesting the rules for inclusion and exclusion is, therefore, much more difficult. Furthermore, social networks, as a form of social asset, are more likely to be dependent upon the cultural capital of individuals rather than socialised access to cultural capital through unionisation. Given that social networks are more likely to reinforce those practises that promote individualism rather than collectivism, precisely because of the informality of the principle of inclusion and exclusion, social networks will reproduce the cycle of individual economic or cultural privilege that sustains the social network in the first place.

TEACHERS' SITUATIONS IN THE NEW MILLENNIUM

What, then, can we say about teachers' situations at the dawn of the 21st century? I have suggested that the transformation of assets—economic, cultural, organisational and social—has had significant consequences for the work, market and status situations of teachers. One way we might assess this is by looking at the international statistics on teachers collected by agencies such as the Organisation for Economic and Cooperative Development (OECD); United Nations Education, Scientific and Cultural Organisation (UNESCO); and the International Labour Organisation (ILO). Following more than a decade of restructuring in both the developed and the developing world, there is considerable interest by these agencies in indicators of broad trends of these changes. The OECD, in the introduction to the 1997 *Education at a Glance* report, argues that its interest in the development of indicators to map trends in education arises from governments within the OECD community:

... seeking effective policies for enhancing economic productivity through education, employing incentives to promote the efficiency of the administration of schooling and searching for additional resources to meet increasing demands for education (p. 5).

The OECD notes that the development of indicators is intended to "provide an insight into the comparative functioning of education systems—focusing on human and financial resources invested in education and on returns to these investments" (ibid.). However, they also observe in their report, *The Teacher Today* (1990, 15), "there is no single established source of international statistics on teachers"; and where these data do exist:

... [the] value and comparability of the data is still critically dependent on the definitions, coverage and quality of the information sent by the countries from which the base is constructed. Countries differ concerning the degree to which their teacher data include various nonteaching and administrative personnel, the types and sectors of education and training that are counted in and to which teaching staff refer, and the definitions and statistical treatment of full-time and part-time teachers.

This point is reiterated in their 1997 report on educational indicators (OECD 1997, 7–8), though here the OECD argues that there has been considerable development in aspects of data gathering as a result of new definitions and debate among policy makers. While acknowledging the problems inherent in comparing country data sets on teachers, this has not prevented the OECD from making full comment on what it views as important issues and trends on teachers' work to be raised with member countries. Indeed, this is the very point I want to raise here. Given that the OECD represents the interests of powerful member states and the multi-national corporate sector, and, it can be argued convincingly, is ideologically committed to the new global competitive agenda (Marchak 1993, 54–55), it is a matter of considerable significance how it articulates the issues and trends concerning teachers. In other words, given that the OECD sets important dimensions of the reform agenda for member nations on economic and other public sector activity, the assumptions upon which this agenda are framed is very important, even if member nations choose to ignore the agenda.

Teachers' pay, conditions of work and social status are viewed as important by the OECD, if their range of publications and the focus of their reporting over the past decade or more can be used as a guide. Since the early 1980s, the OECD has released a series of reports concerned with matters such as teacher quality, educational labour market flexibility, teacher supply, teacher assessment, the role of the teacher and teacher education (cf., OECD 1990a; 1990b). By the early 1990s, the nature of their reporting changed to include detailed comparisons of teachers in various member countries. In their 1996 report, *Education at a Glance,* the OECD identifies teachers' market (pay) and work situations (teacher-student ratio) as significant issues facing states committed to using education to foster economic growth and development. This problem, described as a "high-stakes balancing act" (OECD 1996, 56), is seen to arise for states when they must manage the fiscal risks associated with the global economy; yet they make sure these policies do not undermine the conditions for successful global competitiveness—educational and economic productivity. The OECD remarks:

> Under these conditions, teachers' pay has been an important issue because:
> - Teachers are generally viewed as the key to improved education, though pay levels do not directly determine teacher performance, the rewards and conditions of teaching can influence recruitment retention and teacher morale;
> - Their salaries represent the greater part of education spending— some 60 percent in the case of primary and secondary education;
> - Teachers are generally organised into powerful collective bargaining units, often able to influence the direction of educational reform and educational costs (OECD 1996, 56).

These three elements—teachers' salaries, the salary component of education spending and teacher unions—are viewed by the OECD as critical policy elements for competitive states and are reported upon by the OECD in increasing detail in their annual reports called *Education at a Glance.* A central issue concerns the relationship between teacher salary and student-teacher ratios. While high teacher salaries and low student-teacher ratios are viewed by teachers as a highly desirable set of market and work conditions, clearly this is a risky strategy for states as this gives states very little flexibility in reducing expenditure on education if and when necessary. Larger student-teacher ratios, however, mean fewer teachers are employed, which potentially reduces the overall spending on education. The OECD reports on a range of these configurations:

- High student-teacher ratios offset by increasing teacher salaries, as in the United States and the United Kingdom;
- Low teaching hours and small class sizes adding significantly to the average cost of students, as in Austria and Italy;
- Low teacher salaries and high pupil-teacher ratios as in New Zealand—though it is observed this has contributed to a loss of teacher morale and to problems of teacher supply.

Leaving aside the (important) issue of the way in which calls for efficiency in teachers' (and others') labour are based on a system in which the benefits of production are privately and unequally accumulated (for a more detailed analysis of that point, see Chapter 5, *The New Politics of Fast Capitalism*), the OECD indicators are of interest precisely as we are able to gain some sense of the political agenda setting at the supra-national and national levels, though they are at best broad aggregations of data which, at one level, conceal more than they reveal about the *realpolitik* of teachers' work within a social formation and the different vantage points from which teachers collectively and subjectively experience those changes. We have, then, little sense of the real differences that have emerged *between* teachers as a result of the state's pursuit of flexibility. To what extent do differences in the basis of teachers' economic assets—of whether they are salaried, waged or work for a fee, for example—shape the outlook and therefore the class consciousness of these different categories of teachers? Furthermore, to what extent do the different conditions of employment within organisations implemented in order to create greater flexibility produce different perceptions of the social world? As Lockwood (1958, 15) observed of the black-coated worker when compared to the manual worker—both of whom might be called proletarian—"it is critical to look at each workers' position in the administrative division of labour in order to examine variations in actual class position which may account for variations in actual class consciousness". These variations are likely to produce different types of identities, which return us to Gramsci's (1971, 302) powerful observation that "[t]he new methods of work are inseparable from a specific mode of living and thinking and feeling our life".

In tracing the effect of the transformation of assets on teachers and their work, I want to argue that an important consequence has been to further fracture the cohesiveness of teachers as a class beyond those divisions (gender, race, institution) which have historically divided teachers for much of the history of mass organised public education. The evidence, at this point, suggests that a range of new teacher identities are emerging, defined by their differential capacities to realise class assets and which are shaped by different market, work and status situations (see Table 9.1).

In addition to the service teachers, a number of new teacher identities have emerged: the *teacher bricoleur, teacher manager, teacher entrepreneur* and *temporary teacher*. The bricoleur, manager and entrepreneur arise with the imposition of the market and the restructuring of educational organisations. These three new identities can be used to secure for themselves additional economic assets as a result of their ability to realise cultural, organisational and social assets in the new environment. What defines each of these, as well, is a commitment to a new set of ideologies concerned with individualism, consumption and competence. In combination this new *troika* of post-Fordist workers present a potentially powerful alternative to the social trusteeship model of the post-war period embodied in the *service teacher*. The previous hegemonic class of teachers, the service workers for the welfare state and the welfare of the universal class interests, has been displaced as rigid and inflexible in an era that seeks flexibility, a market edge, innovation, problem solving and social efficiency. While the bricoleur works for a fee and the manager is paid on the basis of performance, the service teacher individually negotiates a salary on an increasingly precarious basis, given the potential erosion of teacher unions and collective employment contracts. The entrepreneur's innovations within the marketplace may be rewarded with various forms of 'bonus', whether it be reduced teaching time, additional salary or incentives. The most marginal teacher is the *temporary* teacher, whose economic assets are defined by the casual nature of his or her employment.

We can also discern shifts in the various cultural assets of each of the teacher identities. While the bricoleurs are able to use their multiple competencies to suit the situation at hand, the teacher managers are able to establish managerial credentials and skills as a new form of cultural capital. Service and temporary teachers remain committed to professional credentials, though these are under pressure from the state, which is able to control both the supply and demand sides of teacher labour. The entrepreneur embodies innovation—trading as much on personality and charisma as the service teacher trades on disembodied credentials. Each new teacher identity also realises organisational assets differently.

For the bricoleur, it is successive niche-filling within the organisation, dependent upon the needs of the organisation and the availability of

Table 9.1 Forms of Realisation of Teachers' Assets in the 1990s

Bases of Assets (Identity)	Teachers' Situations and Identities in the 1990s				
	Service ('Doing Good')	Bricoleur (Problem Solver)	Manager (Social Efficiency)	Entrepreneur ('Doing Well')	Temporary ('Filling-in')
Economic	Salary	Fee	Performance-related pay	Bonus	Casual wage
Cultural	Professional credentials	Fleeting multiple competencies	Managerial credentials and skills	Embodied innovator	Professional credentials
Organisational	Hierarchy	Successive niche-filling	Hierarchy	Niche creation	None—replaceable from labor pool
Social	Unions	External to internal networks	Professional association	Internal to external networks	Personal networking

economic resources. Both the teacher manager and service teacher derive their organisational assets from the organisational hierarchy. However, the teacher manager is increasingly able to direct the work of the service teacher within the organisational hierarchy. The service teacher also faces a major loss of occupational autonomy with the increased presence of managerialism and surveillance through auditing on all aspects of their work. In Bernstein's (1996) and Braverman's (1974) terms, service teachers have lost considerable control over their work. The boundaries defining teachers within the profession as different from other workers have been blurred. In that sense, we can say that the service teacher has lost considerable occupation power. This is not the case for the entrepreneur, who gains power and control from their organisational advantage: niche creation. Given their direct personal involvement, and the fact that the organisational knowledge is located in the individual person and not in the role, the entrepreneurial teacher is able to use these organisational assets in other settings. Temporary teachers, however, have no organisational assets. Their peripheral and excluded status makes it impossible to derive positional goods within the organisation. They are expendable—replaceable from a surplus pool of labour. This limits their capacity to acquire and utilise organisational assets as a set of class assets. The growing percentage of this group, the outcome of the state's flexible policy making, suggests that these teachers—as a group—have lost significant class assets as a result of the restructuring.

Finally, we can view these different teacher identities from the vantage point of the social assets that they are able to access. The temporary teacher is dependent largely on personal networks, becoming friendly with and getting along with key personnel in the school's administration. A change of personnel can result in the need to renegotiate the social relationships and social arrangements again. Managing this network requires a different set of skills: deference, a sense of being able to manage even the toughest class, of being on top of it, and always available. 'Filling in' is both a way of operating in the world and of understanding the world; it is like marking time and being marked by time. The entrepreneur develops and utilises external networks to create new niches and opportunities within the organisation. The bricoleur, in contrast, uses external and internal organisational networks in order to gain privileged information, access and particular outcomes. Teacher managers are more inclined to draw on associations of interest that further their own managerial expertise within the school, whether it be the traditional types of subject or managerial associations, or new types, such as the association of bulk-funded schools. These forms of associations carry with them access to particular types of knowledge and political power in the new environment. The service teacher, committed to unions, has historically benefited from this form of social asset when it has been mobilised to secure advantages for the whole of the group. As I have already argued, the squeeze on teacher unions as an illegitimate form of representation is given considerable weight in this new climate of individualism. 'Doing well', and social efficiency and 'problem solving' are viewed as more adequate teacher demeanours within the new competitive contractual state settlement.

These new teacher identities are necessarily abstract categories that have been developed on the basis of the theoretical lines of analysis and some empirical evidence that is available. What is now required is rigorous comparative work in a number of sites that attempts to operationalise the levels and lines of analysis that I have sought to lay out in this book. That clearly is the task for other books.

CONCLUDING COMMENTS

In this book I set out to understand better teachers' work as we move into a new century, framed by major changes in the global political economy. However, I needed to develop a set of categories that would help me to do this, as well as a way of thinking about change over time and space. This book has been an attempt to lay the theoretical groundwork and broad framework for how we might approach such a study. The ongoing theme has been to explore the changing relationship between teachers as an occupational group and their class location. As I have argued and sought to illustrate in the various chapters of this book, understanding teachers' market, work and status situations within a social formation and social settlement requires a process of mapping levels of activity and influence, from the global to the local. It also requires that we look at teachers' work within a social formation historically and politically, to discern the complex interweaving of ideology, institutional path dependency, regimes of accumulation, modes of regulation, the sites and spaces for resistance and transformation, and the production of new teacher identities. The form of analysis I have adopted in this book makes this possible.

If history can be read forward, there is a simple lesson to be learned about teachers and their class location in the new settlement. The conditions associated with fast capitalism, the rise of the competitive contractual state and the tendency toward individualism and 'doing well' have created new fissures and progressively fragmented teachers as a unified category of workers. Different types of teacher workers now compete with each other for diminished public and private resources, minimising the possibility of any form of collective mobility project. Ironically for teachers, though they have historically eschewed unionisation, it has mainly only been when they have mobilised these forms of social assets to secure state support for exclusive expertise, that teachers have achieved economic and cultural assets. Small wonder that they are under pressure to relinquish this particular social asset. In the new era of fast capitalism and fast schools, teachers will be placed in a new exploitative relationship with each other. If my analysis is correct, the rise of teachers as a professional class will be limited to the rise of more individualised occupational identities with their own vantage points and self-interested objectives.

References

Agger, B. (1991). *A Critical Theory of Public Life: Knowledge, Discourse and Politics in An Age of Decline*. Chicago: University of Illinois Press.

Aglietta, M. (1979). *A Theory of Capitalist Regulation*. London: New Left Books.

Altenbaugh, R. (1995). The irony of gender. In Mark Ginsburg (ed.), *The Politics of Educators' Work and Lives*. New York: Garland Publishing.

Amin, S. (1990). *Delinking: Toward a Polycentric World*. London: Zed Books.

Apple, M. (1982). Curricular form and the logic of technical control: Building the possessive individual. In M. Apple (ed.), *Cultural and Economic Reproduction in Education*. London: Routledge and Kegan Paul.

Apple, M. (1985). *Teachers and Texts: A Political Economy of Class and Gender Relations in Education*. New York: Routledge and Kegan Paul.

Apple, M. (1993). *Official Knowledge: Democratic Education in a Conservative Age*. New York: Routledge.

Apple, M. and Beane, J. (eds.). (1999). *Democratic Schools: Lessons from the Chalk Face*. Buckingham, U.K.: Open University Press.

Ashenden, D. (1992). Award restructuring and education. *QTU Professional Magazine*. Vol. 8 (1), pp. 8–13.

Atkinson, J. (1988). Manpower strategies for flexible organisation. *Personnel Management*. (August), pp. 27–31.

Ayres, L. (1909). *Laggards in Our School*. New York.

Bagguley, P., Lawson, J., Shapiro, D., Urry, J., Walby, S. and Warde, A. (1990). *Restructuring: Place, Class and Gender*, London: Sage Publications.

Ball, S. (1993). Culture, cost and control: Self-management and entrepreneurial schooling in England and Wales. In J. Smyth (ed.), *A Socially Critical View of the Self-Managing School*. Basingstoke: Falmer Press.

Ball, S. (1990). *Politics and Policymaking in Education: Explorations in Policy Sociology*. London:Routledge.

Ball, S. (1994). Education policy, power relations and teachers' work. In S. Ball (ed.), *Education Reform: A Critical and Post-Structural Approach*. Suffolk, U.K.: Open University Press.

Ball, S. and Goodson, I. (1985). Understanding teachers: Concepts and contexts. In S. Ball and I. F. Goodson (eds.), *Teachers' Lives and Careers*. London: Falmer Press.

Barber, B. (1995). *Jihad vs. McWorld*. New York: Times Books.

Barlow, M. and Robertson, H.-J. (1994). *Class Warfare: The Assault on Canada's Schools*. Ontario: Key Porter Books.

Bascia, N. (1997). Teacher unions and teacher professionalism in the U.S.: Reconsidering a familiar dichotomy. In B. Biddle, T. Good and I. Goodson (eds.), *International Handbook of Teachers and Teaching,* Vol. 1. Dordrecht: Kluwer Academic Publishers.

Bergen, B. (1988). Only a schoolmaster: Gender, class and the effort to professionalise elementary teaching in England 1970–1910. In J. Ozga (ed.), *Schoolwork: Approaches to the Labour Process of Teaching*. Milton Keynes: Open University Press.

Berliner, D. and Biddle, B. (1995). *The Manufactured Crisis: Myths, Fraud and the Attack on America's Schools*. New York: Addison Wesley.

Bernstein, B. and Davies, B. (1969). Some sociological comments on Plowden. In Richard Peters (ed.), *Perspectives on Plowden*. London: Routledge and Kegan Paul.

Bernstein, B. (1971). *Class, Codes and Control,* Vol. 1. London: Routledge and Kegan Paul.

Bernstein, B. (1996). *Pedagogy, Symbolic Control and Identity: Theory, Research, Critique*. London: Taylor and Francis.

Bessant, B. and Spaull, A. (1972). *Teachers in Conflict*. Melbourne: Melbourne University Press.

Bhaskar, R. (1978), *A Realist Theory of Science*. Sussex, U.K.: Harvester.

Bhaskar, R. (1986). *Scientific Realism and Human Emancipation*. Bristol, U.K.: Verso.

Bidwell, C. Frank, K. and Quiroz, P. (1997). Teacher types, workplace controls, and the organisation of schools. *Sociology of Education*. Vol. 70, October, pp. 285–307.

Block, F. (1990). *Postindustrial Possibilities: A Critique of Economic Discourse.* Los Angeles: University of California Press.

Bourdieu, P. (1984). *Distinction: A Social Critique of the Judgement of Taste.* New York: Routledge and Kegan Paul.

Bourdieu, P. (1997). The forms of capital. In A. H. Halsey, H. Lauder, P. Brown and A. S. Wells (eds.), *Education, Economy and Society.* Oxford: Oxford University Press.

Bourdieu, P. and Passeron, J.C. (1977). *Reproduction in Education, Society and Culture.* London: Sage.

Boyer, R. (1990). *The Regulation School: A Critical Introduction.* New York: Columbia University Press.

Boyer, R. (1997). French statism at the crossroads. In Colin Crouch and Wolfgang Steeck (eds.), *Political Economy of Modern Capitalism: Mapping Convergence and Diversity.* London: Sage.

Braudel, F. (1994). *A History of Civilizations* [trans. Richard Mayne]. New York: A. Lane.

Braverman, H. (1974). *Labor and Monopoly Capitalism: The Degradation of Work in the Twentieth Century.* New York: Monthly Review Press.

Bryk, A., Lee, V. and Smith, J. (1990), High school organisation and its effects on teachers and students. In. W. Clune and J. Witte (eds.), *Choice and Control in American Education, Vol. 1: The Theory of Choice and Control in American Education.* Philadelphia: Falmer Press.

Brint, S. (1994). *In an Age of Experts: The Changing Role of Professionals in Politics and Public Life.* Princeton: Princeton University Press.

Brunhes, B. (1989). Labour flexibility in enterprises: A comparison of firms in four European countries. In Organisation for Economic and Co-operative Development, *Labour Market Flexibility.* Paris: Organisation for Economic and Co-operative (OECD).

Burawoy, M. (1985). *The Politics of Production: Factory Regimes Under Capitalism.* London: Verso.

Caldwell, B. (1995). *The Impact of Self-management and Self-government on Professional Cultures of Teaching. A Strategic Analysis of the 21st Century.* Paper presented to the Re-thinking U.K. Education: What Next, sponsored by the Roehampton Institute, London.

Callahan, R. (1962). *Education and the Cult of Efficiency: A Study of the Social Forces That Have Shaped the Administration of the Public Schools.* Chicago: University of Chicago Press.

Carlson, D. (1992). *Teachers and Crisis: Urban School Reform and Teachers' Work Culture.* New York: Routledge.

Carmichael, L. (1989). After the revolution: Micro-chips with everything. *Australian Left Review*. Vol. 110, pp. 23–28.

Carnoy, M. and Levin, H. (1985). *Schooling and Work in the Democratic State*. Stanford: Stanford University Press.

Cerny, P. (1990). *The Changing Architecture of the Politics: Structure, Agency and the Future of the State*. Wiltshire, G. B. Sage Publications.

Cerny, P. (1995). Globalisation and the changing logic of collective action. *International Organisation*. Vol. 49, No. 4, pp. 595–625.

Cerny, P. (1997). Paradoxes of the competition state: The dynamics of political globalisation. *Government and Opposition*. Vol. 32, No. 2, Spring, pp. 251–274.

Chadbourne, R. (1992). *The National School's Project in Western Australia: A Formative View of the First Year*. Perth, Australia: IIPAS.

Chen, S. (1997). *Opening Doors, Opening Minds: A Study of the Perceptions of Chinese Speaking Foreign Full Fee Paying Students in Selected New Zealand Secondary Schools*. Master of Arts Thesis, University of Auckland, New Zealand.

Chubb, J. and Moe, T. (1990). *Politics, Markets and America's Schools*. Washington: Brookings Institute.

Chubb, J. and Moe, T. (1997). Politics, markets and the organisation of schools. In A. H. Halsey, H. Lauder, P. Brown and A. Stuart Wells (eds.), *Education: Culture, Economy and Society*. Oxford: Oxford University Press.

Clifford, G. (1975). *The Shape of American Education*. Englewod Cliffs, N.J.: Prentice Hall, Inc.

Clifford, G. (1987). 'Lady teachers' and politics in the United States, 1850–1930. In M. Lawn and G. Grace (eds.), *Teachers: The Culture and Politics of Work*. Basingstoke: Falmer Press.

Clune, W. and Witte, J. (1990). *Choice and Control in American Education*. London: Falmer Press.

Codd, J. (1993). Managerialism, market liberalism and the move to self-managing schools in New Zealand. In J. Smyth (ed.), *A Socially Critical View of the Self-Managing School*. Basingstoke: Falmer Press.

Codd, John, Gordon, L. and Harker, R. (1997). Education and the role of the state: Devolution and control post-Picot. In A. H. Halsey, H. Lauder, P. Brown and A. Stuart Wells (eds.), *Education: Culture, Economy and Society*. Oxford: Oxford University Press.

Cole, S. (1969). *The Unionization of Teachers: A Case Study of the UFT*. New York: Praeger Publishers.

Coleman, J. (1990). In William Clune and John Witte (eds.), *Choice and Control in American Education*. London: Falmer Press.

Concise Oxford Dictionary 6th edition (1976). *The Concise Oxford Dictionary of Current English* [Ed. J. B. Sykes]. Oxford, U.K.: Clarendon Press.

Connell, R. (1995). Transformative labour. In Mark Ginsburg (ed.), *The Politics of Educators' Work and Lives*. New York: Garland Publishing.

Considine, M, (1996). Market bureaucracy? Exploring the contending rationalities of contemporary administrative regimes. *Labour and Industry*. Vol. 7, No. 1, June, pp. 1–27.

Copiat, B. (1995). Incentives, bargaining and trust: Alternative scenarios for the future of work. *International Contributions to Labour Studies*. Vol. 5, pp. 131–151.

Cox, R. and Sinclair, T,. (1996). *Approaches to World Order*. Cambridge: Cambridge University Press.

Cremin, L. (1961). *Transformation of the School: Progressivism in American Education 1876–1957*. New York: Alfred A. Knopf.

Cuban, L. (1993). *How Teachers Taught: Constancy and Change in American Classrooms 1880–1990*. 2nd ed. New York: Teachers College Press.

Dale, R. (1982). Education and the capitalist state: Contributions and contradictions. In M. Apple (ed.), *Cultural and Economic Reproduction in Education*. Oxford, U.K.: Routledge and Kegan Paul.

Dale, R. (1987). *Open University Course E333, Education Policy Studies, Unit 2*. Milton Keynes: Open University Press.

Dale, R. (1993). The McDonalization of schooling and the street-level bureaucrat. (Review Essay). *Curriculum Studies*. Vol. 2, No. 2, pp. 249–262.

Dale, R. (1994). Applied education politics or political sociology of education?: Contrasting approaches to the study of recent reform in England and Wales. In D. Halpin and B. Troyna (eds.), *Researching Education Policy: Ethical and Methodological Issues*. Basingstoke, U.K.: Falmer Press.

Dale, R. (1997). The state and the governance of education: An analysis of the restructuring of the state-education relationship. A. H. Halsey, H. Lauder, P. Brown and A. Stuart Wells (eds.), *Education: Culture, Economy and Society*. Oxford: Oxford University Press.

Dale, R. (forthcoming). Globalisation and education: demonstrating a 'common world educational culture' or locating a 'globally structured educational agenda'? *Education Theory*.

Dale, R. and Robertson, S. (1996). 'Resting' the nation, 'reshaping' the state: Globalization effects on education policy. In M. Olssen and K. Morris Matthews (eds.), *Education Policy in New Zealand*. Palmerston North: Dunmore.

Dale, R. and Robertson, S. (1998). *Competitive Contractualism and New Social Settlements: Contours and Consequences*. A paper presented to the Inaugural Development Studies Conference, University of Auckland, New Zealand. February 26–28.

Danylewycz, M. and Prentice, A. (1988). Teachers' work: changing patterns and perceptions in the emerging school systems of nineteenth- and early twentieth-century central Canada. In J. Ozga (ed.), *Schoolwork: Approaches to the Labour Process of Teaching*. Milton Keynes: Open University Press.

Darling-Hammond, L. (1997). *The Right to Learn: A Blueprint for Creating Schools that Work*. San Francisco: Jossey Bass Publishers.

Davis, G., Sullivan, B. and Yeatman, A. (eds.) (1997). *The New Contractualism?* Australia: Macmillan Education.

Deal, T. and Jenkins, W. (1994). *Managing the Hidden Organisation: Strategies for Empowering Your Behind-the-Scenes Employees*. New York: Warner.

Delamont, S. (1976). *Interaction in the Classroom*. London: Methuen.

Delhi, K. (1996). Between 'market' and 'state'? Engendering education change in the 1990s. D*iscourse: Studies in the Cultural Politics of Education*. Vol. 17, No. 3, pp. 363–376.

Dicken, P. (1992). *Global Shift: The Internationalisation of Economic Activity*. 2nd ed. London: Paul Chapman Publishing Company.

Doshe, K., Jurgens, U. and Malsch, T. (1985). From Fordism to Toyotaism: The social organisation of the labour process in the Japanese automobile industry. *Politics and Society*. Vol. 14, No. 2, pp. 115–146.

Drucker, P. (1993). *Post Capitalist Society*. New York: Harper.

du Gay, P. (1994). Colossal immodesties and hopeful monsters: Pluralism and organisational conduct. *Organisation*. Vol 1, No. 1, pp. 125–148.

Edwards, R. (1979). *Contested Terrain: The Transformation of the Workplace in the Twentieth Century*. New York: Basic Books.

Fine, B. (1995). From political economy to consumption: A review of new studies. In Daniel Miller (ed.), A*cknowledging Consumption*. London: Routledge.

Florida, R. and Kenny, M. (1994). Institutions and economic transformation: The case of post-war Japanese capitalism. *Growth and Change*. 25 (Spring), pp. 247–262.

Franklin, B. (1986). *Building the American Community*. Barcombe, Lewes, U.K.: Falmer Press.

Fraser, J. (1989). Agents of democracy. In D. Warren (ed.), *American Teachers: Histories of a Profession at Work*. New York: Macmillan.

Fukuyama, F. (1989). The end of history. *The National Times*. Vol. 16, Summer, pp. 8–14.

Singh, G. M. (1996). Studying Asia for the national economic interest: An-analysis of the Australian government's strategy for schools. *Discourse: Studies in the Cultural Politics of Education.* Vol. 17, No. 2, pp. 153–170.

Gee, J. (1994). New alignments and old literacies: Critical literacy, postmodernism and fast capitalism. In P. O'Connor (ed.), *Thinking Work Vol. 1: Theoretical Perspectives on Worker Literacies.* Sydney: ALBSAC.

Gee, J. (1996). On mobots and classrooms: The converging languages of the new capitalism and schooling. *Organisation.* Vol. 3, No. 3, pp. 385–407.

Gee, J. and Lankshear, C. The new work order: Critical language awareness and 'fast capitalism' texts. *Discourse: Studies in the Cultural Politics of Education.* Vol 16, No. 1, pp. 5–20.

Gee, J., Hull, G. and Lankshear, C. (1996). *The New Work Order.* Boulder, CO: Westview.

Gerstner, L., Semerand, R., Doyle, P. and Johnston, W. (1994). *Reinventing Government: How the Entrepreneurial Spirit Is Transforming the Public Sector.* New York: Dutton.

Gewirtz S., Ball, S. and Bowe, R. (1995). *Markets, Choice and Equity.* Milton Keynes: Open University Press.

Giddens, A. (1972). *Emile Durkheim: Selected Writings.* (A Giddens, ed. trans). Bristol, U.K.: Cambridge University Press.

Ginsburg, M. (1988). *Contradictions in Teacher Education and Society: A Critical Analysis.* London: Falmer Press.

Ginsburg, M., Kamat, S., Raghu, R. and Weaver, J. (1995). Educators and politics: Interpretations, involvement and implications. In Mark Ginsburg (ed.), *The Politics of Educators' Work and Lives.* New York: Garland Publishing.

Ginsburg, M. and Lindsay, B. (eds.). (1995). *The Political Dimension in Teacher Education: Comparative Perspectives on Policy Formation, Socialisation and Society.* London: Falmer Press.

Goldthorpe, J. (1982). On the service class: Its formation and future. In A. Giddens and C. McKenzie (eds.), *Social Class and the Divisions of Labour.* Cambridge: Cambridge University Press.

Goodson, I. (1992). Studying teachers' lives: An emerging field of enquiry. In Ivor Goodson (ed.), *Studying Teachers' Lives.* London: Routledge.

Gordon, L. (1993). *A Study of Boards of Trustees in Canterbury Schools.* Christchurch, U.K.: Educational Policy Research Unit.

Gordon, L. (1997). *'Tomorrow's Schools'* today: School choice and the education quasi market. In M. Olssen and K. Morris Matthews (eds.), *Education Policy in New Zealand: The 1990s and Beyond.* Palmerston North: Dunmore.

Gouldner, A. (1979). *The Future of Intellectuals and the Rise of the New Class.* London: Macmillan.

Grace, G. (1987). Teachers and the state in Britain: A changed Britain. In M. Lawn and G. Grace (eds.), *Teachers: The Culture and Politics of Work.* East Sussex, U.K.: Falmer Press.

Gramsci, A. (1971). *Selections from the Prison Notebooks of Antonio Gramsci.* New York: International Publishers.

Green, A. (1993). *Education and State Formation: The Rise of Education Systems in England, France and the United States.* New York: St. Martin's Press.

Habermas, J. (1979).*Communication and the Evolution of Society* [trans. T. McCarthy]. Boston: Beacon Press.

Hall, P. (1989). *The Political Power of Economic Ideas: Keynesianism Across Nations.* Princeton: Princeton University Press.

Hall, S. (1988). Brave new world. *Marxism Today* (October), pp. 24–29.

Hamilton, D., (1989). *Toward a Theory of Schooling.* East Sussex, U.K.: Falmer Press.

Hammersley, M. and Woods, P. (1976). *The Process of Schooling.* London: Routledge and Kegan Paul.

Hargreaves, A. (1994). *Changing Teachers, Changing Times: Teachers' Work and Culture in the Postmodern Age.* London: Cassell.

Harris, K. (1980). *Teachers and Classes: A Marxist Analysis.* London: Routledge and Kegan Paul.

Harris, K. (1993). *The Commercialisation and Deprofessionalisation of Teachers' Work in the 1990s.* A paper presented to the Third International Teacher Development Conference, Adelaide.

Harvey, D. (1989). *The Condition of Postmodernity.* Oxford: Oxford University Press.

Hay, C. (1996). *Restating Social and Political Change.* Buckinghamshire, U.K.: Open University Press.

Helleiner, E. (1996). Post-globalisation: Is the financial liberalisation trend likely to be reversed? In R. Boyer and D. Drache (eds.), *States Against Markets: The Limits of Globalisation.* London and New York: Routledge.

Henig, J. (1995). *Rethinking School Choice: Limits of the Market Metaphor.* Princeton: Princeton University Press.

Hirsch, F. (1977). *The Social Limits to Growth.* London: Routledge and Kegan Paul.

Hirsch, J. (1991). Fordism and post-Fordism: The present social crisis and its consequences. In W. Bonefeld and J. Hollowaty (eds.), *Post-Fordism and*

Social Form: A Marxist Debate on the Post-Fordist State. Hong Kong: Macmillan.

Hobsbawm, E. (1987). *The Age of Empire, 1875–1914.* London: Weidenfeld and Nicolson.

Hobsbawm, E. (1994). *The Age of Extremes: The Short Twentieth Century 1914–91.* London: Abacus.

Hodgson, G. (1988). *Economics and Institutions.* Cambridge: Polity.

Hogan, D. (1982). Education and class formation: The peculiarities of the Americans. In M. Apple (ed.), *Cultural and Economic Reproduction in Education.* Oxford, U.K.: Routledge and Kegan Paul.

Hogan, D. (1985). *Class and Reform: School and Society in Chicago 1930–1998.* Philadelphia: University of Pennslyvania Press.

Hogan, D. (1997). The social economy of parent choice and the contract state. In G. Davis, B. Sullivan and A. Yeatman (eds.), *The New Contractualism?* Australia: Macmillan Education.

Holloway, J. (1987). The red rose of Nissan. *Capital and Class.* Vol. 32, pp. 147–165.

Holloway, J. (1994). Global capital. *The Socialist Register 1994.* London: The Merlin Press.

House, E. (1991). Realism in research. *Educational Researcher.* Vol. 20, No. 6, pp. 2–9.

ICEM. (1996). *Power and Counter-power: The Union Response to Globalisation.* London: Pluto Press.

International Labour Organisation, (1996). *Impact of Structural Adjustment on the Employment and Training of Teachers.* Report for discussion at the Joint Meeting on the Impact of Structural Adjustment on Educational Personnel. Geneva: International Labour Office.

Jameson, F. (1984). Postmodernism or the Cultural Logic of Late Capitalism. *New Left Review.* July-August, pp. 53–93.

Jesson, J. (1993). *The PPTA and the State: From Militant Professionals to Bargaining Agents.* Doctor of Philosophy Thesis, University of Auckland, New Zealand.

Jessop, B. (1989). Conservative regimes and the transition to post-Fordism: The cases of Great Britain and West Germany. In M. Gottdiener and N. Komninos (eds.), *Capitalist Development and Crisis Theory: Accumulation, Regulation and Spatial Restructuring.* New York: St. Martin's Press.

Jessop, B. (1990). Regulation theories in retrospect and prospect. *Economy and Society.* Vol. 19, No. 2, pp. 153–216.

Jessop, B. (1993). Toward a Schumpeterian workfare state? Preliminary remarks on the post-Fordist political economy. *Studies in Political Economy.* Vol. 40, Spring, pp. 7–39.

Johnson, R. (1976). Notes on the schooling of the English working class 1780–1850. R. Dale, G. Esland and M. MacDonald (eds.), *Schooling and Capitalism: A Sociological Reader.* Milton Keynes: The Open University Press.

Joyce, P. (1995). *Class.* Oxford: Oxford University Press.

Kean, H. (1989). Teachers and the State 1900–30. *British Journal of Sociology of Education.* Vol. 10, No. 2, pp. 141–154.

Kenney, M. and Florida, R. (1988). Beyond mass production and the labour process in Japan. *Politics and Society.* Vol 16, No. 1, pp. 121–158.

Kenway, J. (1995). *The Marketisation of Education: Mapping the Contours of a Feminist Perspective.* A paper presented to the ECER Conference, Bath, U.K.

Kenway, J. and Epstein, D. (1996). Introduction: The marketisation of school education: Feminist studies and perspectives. *Discourse: Studies in the Cultural Politics of Education.* Vol. 17, No. 3, pp. 301–314.

Kenway, J. and Fitzclarence, L. (1997). *Devolved Institutions with Design: Consuming Children.* Paper presented to the AERA, March. Chicago.

Kern, H. and Schumann, M. (1987). Limits of the division of labour: New production and employment concepts in West German industry. *Economic and Industrial Democracy.* Vol. 8, No. 3, pp. 151–170.

Labaree, D. (1989). Career ladders and the early public high school teacher. In D. Warren (ed.), *American Teachers: Histories of a Profession at Work.* New York: Macmillan.

Larson, M. S. (1977). *The Rise of Professionalism: A Sociological Analysis.* Berkeley: University of California Press.

Lasch, C. (1995). *The Revolt of the Elites and the Betrayal of Democracy.* New York: W. W. Norton and Company.

Lash, S. and Urry, J. (1987). *The End of Organised Capitalism.* Oxford: Oxford University Press.

Lauder, H. et al. (1994). *The Creation of Market Competition for Education in New Zealand: An Empirical Analysis of a New Zealand Secondary School Market 1990–93.* Wellington: Ministry of Education.

Lawn, M. (1985). *The Politics of Teacher Unionism: International Perspectives.* London: Croom Helm.

Lawn, M. (1987). *Servants of the State: Contested Control of Teaching 1900–1930.* East Sussex, U.K.: Falmer Press.

Lawn, M. (1988). Skill in schoolwork: Work relations in the primary school. In Jenny Ozga (ed.), *Schoolwork: Approaches to the Labour Process of Teaching*. Milton Keynes: Open University Press.

Lawn, M. (1996). *Modern Times? Work, Professionalism and Citizenship in Teaching*. London: Falmer Press.

Lawn, M and Grace, G. (1987). *Teachers: The Culture and Politics of Work*. East Sussex, U.K.: Falmer Press.

Levin, H. (1990). The theory of choice applied to education. In W. Clune and J. Witte (eds.), *Choice and Control in American Education. Vol. 1: The Theory of Choice and Control in Education*. Basingstoke: U.K.: Falmer Press.

Lipietz, A. (1992). *Toward a New Economic Order: Post-Fordism, Ecology and Democracy*. Oxford: Polity Press.

Lipietz, A. (1986). New tendencies in the international division of labour: Regimes of accumulation and modes of regulation. In A. Scott and M. Storper (eds.), *Production, Work and Territory: A Geographical Anatomy of Industrial Capitalism*. Boston: Allen and Unwin.

Livingtone, D. (1996). Searching for missing links: Neo-Marxist theories of education. *British Journal of Sociology of Education*. Vol. 16, No. 1, pp. 53–73.

Lockwood, D. (1958). *The Blackcoated Worker*. London: Unwin University Books.

Lortie, D. (1969). The balance of control and autonomy in elementary school teaching. In A. Etzioni (ed.), *The Semi-Profession and Their Organizations*. New York: Free Press.

Lortie, D. (1975). *School Teacher: A Sociological Study*. London: The University of Chicago Press.

March J. and Olsen J. (1996). An institutionalist approach to political institutions. *Governance*. Vol. 9, No. 3, pp. 247–263.

Marchak, P. (1993). *The Integrated Circus: The New Right and the Restructuring of Global Markets*. Montreal: McGill-Queens University Press.

Martell, G. (1995). *A New Education Politics: Bob Rae's Legacy and the Response of the Ontario Secondary School Teachers' Federation*. Toronto: James Lorimar.

Martin, B. (1998). Knowledge, identity and the middle class: From collective to individualised class formation? *The Sociological Review*. Vol. 46, No. 4, pp. 653–686.

Marx, K. (1932). The Communist Manifesto. In Karl Marx, *Capital and Other Writings of Karl Marx*. New York: Random House.

Mathews, J. (1989). *Tools for Change: Technology and the Democratisation of Work*. Sydney: Pluto Press.

Mattingly, P. (1975). *The Classless Profession: American Schoolmen in the Nineteenth Century*. New York: New York University Press.

Menter, I., Muschamp, Y., Nicholls, P., Ozga, J. and Pollard, A. (1997). *Work and Identity in the Primary School: A Post-Fordist Analysis*. Bristol, U.K.: Open University Press.

Meyer, J. W. and Hannan, M. T. (eds.). (1979). *National Development and the World System*. Chicago: University of Chicago Press.

Meyer, J. W., Boli, J., Thomas, G. M. and Ramirez, F. O. (1997) World Society and the Nation-State. *American Journal of Sociology*. Vol. 103, No. 1, pp. 144–181.

Meyer, J. W., Kamens, D. H. and Benavot, A. (eds.). (1992). *School Knowledge for the Masses: World Models and Curricular Categories in the Twentieth Century*. London: Falmer Press.

Middleton, S. and May, H. (1997). *Teachers' Talk Teaching: Early Childhood, Schools and Teachers Colleges, 1915–1995*. Palmerston North: Dunmore.

Mishra, R. (1990). *The Welfare State in Capitalist Society: Policies of Retrenchment and Maintenance in Europe North America and Australia*. London: Harvester, Wheatsheaf.

Molnar, A. (1996). *Giving Kids the Business: The Commercialization of America's Schools*. Boulder, CO: Westview Press.

Morris, N. (1972). State paternalism and *laissez faire* in the 1860s. In B. Cosin (ed.), *Education, Structure and Society*. Middlesex, U.K.: Penguin Books and the Open University Press.

Muschamp, Y., Menter, Y., Nicholls, I. Ozga, P. and Pollard, A. J. (1995). *The market and the school. Confidences about the real work of teachers*. Paper presented to the American Education Research Association, San Francisco.

Offe, C. and Ronge, V. (1970). Theses on the theory of the State. In C. Offe, *Contradictions of the Welfare State*. Wiltshire, U.K.: Huchinson and Company.

Organisation for Economic and Co-operative Development (OECD). (1990a). *The Teacher Today*. Paris: OECD.

Organisation for Economic and Co-operative Development (OECD). (1990b). *Quality in Teaching*. Paris: OECD.

Organisation for Economic and Co-operative Development (OECD). (1995). *Education at a Glance*. Analysis. Paris: OECD/CERI.

Organisation for Economic and Co-operative Development (OECD). (1996). *Education at a Glance*. Analysis. Paris: OECD/CERI.

Ontario Secondary School Teachers' Federation (OSSTF). (1995). *Commercialisation in Ontario Schools: A Research Report*. Toronto: OSSTF.

Ozga, J. (ed.). (1988). *Schoolwork: Approaches to the Labour Process of Teaching*. Milton Keynes: Open University Press.

Ozga, J. and Gewirtz, S. (1994). Sex lies and audio-tape: Interviewing the education policy élite. In David Halpin and Barry Troyna (eds.), *Researching Education Policy: Ethical and Methodological Issues*. London: Falmer Press.

Ozga, J. and Lawn, M. (1981). *Teachers, Professionalism and Class: A Study of Organised Teachers*. London: Falmer Press.

Palmer, B. (1995). Capitalism Comes to Napanee High. *Our Schools/Our Selves*. Vol. 6, No. 3, pp. 14–41.

Panitch, L. (1994). Globalisation and the State. *The Socialist Register 1994*. London: Merlin Press.

Parkin, F. (1974). Strategies of social closure in class formation. In F. Parkin (ed.), *The Social Analysis of Class Structure*. London: Tavistock.

Perkin, H. (1989). *The Rise of Professional Society: England Since 1880*. London: Routledge.

Peters, T. (1994). *The Tom Peters Seminar: Crazy Times Call for Crazy Organisations*. New York: Vintage.

Piore, M. and Sabel, C. (1984). *The Second Industrial Divide: Possibilities for Prosperity*. New York: Basic Books.

Plowden Report [see Report of the Central Advisory Council for Education].

Polanyi, K. (1944). *The Great Transformation: The Political and Economic Origins of Our Time*. Boston: Beacon Press.

Popkewitz, T. (1991). *Political Sociology of Educational Reform: Power/ Knowledge in Teaching, Teacher Education and Research*. New York: Teachers' College Press.

Poster, M. (1990). *The Mode of Information—Post Structuralism and Social Context*. Chicago: University of Chicago Press.

Poulantzas, N. (1978). *State, Power, Socialism*. London: New Left Books.

Price, J. (1994). Lean production at Suzuki and Toyota: A historical perspective. *Studies in Political Economy*, 45, Fall, pp. 66–99.

Ranson, S. (1993). Markets or democracy for education. *British Journal of Education Studies*. Vol. XXXXI, No. 4, pp. 333–352.

Reich, R. (1997). Why the rich are getting richer. In A. H. Halsey, H. Lauder, P. Brown and A. Stuart Wells (eds.), *Education: Culture, Economy and Society*. Oxford: Oxford University Press.

Reich, R. (1992). *The Work of Nations*. New York: Vantage Books.

Report of the Central Advisory Council for Education (1967). *Children and Their Primary School [The Plowden Report]*. London: England.

Ritzer, G. (1993). *The McDonaldization of Society*. Newbury Park, CA: Pine Forge Press.

Roberts, W. (1994). The Toronto Board takes the Pepsi challenge . . . and loses. *Our Schools/Our Selves*. Vol. 5, No. 3, pp. 8–15.

Robertson, H.-J. (1995). *Traders and Travellers: Public Education in a Corporate Dominated Culture.* A discussion paper prepared for the Canadian Teachers' Federation.

Robertson, S. (1995). *Fast Capitalism and Fast Schools: New Realities and New Truths.* American Education Research Association Conference, San Francisco, 18–22 April.

Robertson, S. and Woock, R. (1991). The political economy of educational "reform" in Australia. In M. Ginsburg (ed.), *Understanding Educational Reform in Global Context: Economy, Ideology and the State.* New York: Garland Publishing.

Robertson, S. (1993). The politics of devolution, self-management and post-Fordism in schools. In J. Smyth (ed.), *A Socially Critical View of the Self-Managing School.* London: Falmer Press.

Robertson, S. (1994). Teachers' labour and post-Fordism: An exploratory analysis. In J. Kenway (ed.), *Economising Education: The Post-Fordist Directions.* Geelong: Deakin University Press.

Robertson, S. (1997). Restructuring teachers' labour: 'Troubling' post-Fordisms. In B. Biddle, T. Good and I. Goodson (eds.), *International Handbook of Teachers and Teaching,* Vol. 1. Dordrecht: Kluwer Academic Publishers.

Robertson, S. (1998). Quality, contractualism and control: Orchestrating the sectoral settlement in teachers' work in New Zealand. *New Zealand Journal of Educational Studies.* Vol. 33, No. 1, pp. 5–22.

Robertson, S. and Chadbourne, R. (1998). Banning voluntary labour: A study of teachers' work in the context of changing industrial relations regimes. *Discourse: Studies on the Cultural Politics of Education.* Vol. 19, No. 1, pp. 19–39.

Robertson, S. and Dale, R. (1998). *Centring the Margins: Locating Education in a Theory of Social Settlements.* A paper presented at the Sociological Association of New Zealand Annual Conference, Nov. 27–29. Hawks Bay, New Zealand.

Robertson, S. and Smaller, H. (eds.). (1996). *Teacher Political Activitsm in the 1990s.* Toronto: James Lorimar.

Robertson, S., Dale, R., Thrupp, M., Vaughan, K. and Jacka, S. (1997). *A Review of ERO: Final Report to the PPTA.* Wellington: Post-Primary Teachers Association.

Robertson, S., Soucek, V., Pannu, R. and Schugurensky, D. (1995). Chartering new waters: The Klein revolution and the privatisation of education in Alberta. *Our Schools/Ourselves.* Vol. 7 (2), No. 44, pp. 80–106.

Robins, K. and Webster, F. (1989). *The Technical Fix: Education, Computers and Industry.* London: Macmillan.

Romanish, B. (1991). *Empowering Teachers: Restructuring Schools for the 21st Century*. London: University Press of America.

Royal Commission on Learning, Ontario. (1994). *For the Love of Learning: Report of the Royal Commission on Learning (Vol III)*. Ontario: Government of Ontario.

Rury, J. (1989). Who became teachers? The social characteristics of teachers in American history. In D. Warren (ed.), *American Teachers: Histories of a Profession at Work*. New York: Macmillan.

Salant, W. (1989). The spread of Keynesian doctrines and practices in the United States. In Peter Hall (ed.), *The Political Power of Economic Ideas: Keynesianism Across Nations* Princeton: Princeton University Press.

Sarup, M. (1996). *Identity, Culture and the Postmodern World*. Edinburgh: Edinburgh University Press.

Saunders, P. (1986). *Social Theory and the Urban Question*, 2nd ed. London: Hutchinson.

Savage, M., Barlow, J., Dickens, P. and Fielding, T. (1992). *Property, Bureaucracy and Culture*. London: Routledge.

Sayer, A. (1992). *Method in Social Science: A Realist Approach,* 2nd Ed. London: Routledge.

Sayer, A. (1995). *Radical Political Economy: A Critique*. Oxford, U.K.: Blackwell.

Schools Council. (1992). *Developing Flexible Strategies in the Early Years of Schooling*. Canberra: AGPS.

Seddon, T. (1991). Restructuring teachers and teaching: Current Australian development and future prospects. *Discourse: The Australian Journal of Educational Studies*. Vol. 12, No. 1, October, pp. 1–23.

Seddon, T. (1993). An historical reckoning: Education and training reform. *Education Links*. Vol. 44, pp. 5–9.

Simon, B. (1974). *The Politics of Educational Reform 1920–1940*. London: Lawrence and Wishart.

Simon, B. (1987). Systematisation and segmentation in education: The case of England. In Detlef Muller, Fritz Ringer and Brian Simon (eds.), *The Rise of the Modern Educational System*. Cambridge: Cambridge University Press.

Sinclair, J., Seifert, R. and Ironside, M. (1995). Market-driven reforms in education: Performance, quality and industrial relations in schools. In Ian Kirkpatrick and M. M. Lucio (eds.), *The Politics of Quality in the Public Sector*. London: Routledge.

Smith, G. H. (1997). *The Development of Kaupapa Maori: Theory and Practise*. Doctoral dissertation, University of Auckland, New Zealand.

Smyth, J. (1991). *International perspectives on teacher collegiality: A labour process approach*. Paper presented at the annual meeting of the Comparative and International Education Society, March. Pittsburgh.

Smyth, J. (ed.). (1993). *A Socially Critical View of the Self-Managing School*. London: Falmer Press.

Soucek, V. (1994). Flexible education and the new standards of competence. In J. Kenway (ed.), *Economising Education: Post-Fordist Directions*. Geelong: Deakin University Press.

Soucek, V. and Pannu, R. (1996). Globalising education in Alberta: Teachers' work and the options to fight back. In S. Robertson and H. Smaller (eds.), *Teacher Political Activism in the 1990s*. Toronto: James Lorimar.

Sparkes, A. and Bloomer, M. (1993). Teaching cultures and school-based management. In J. Smyth (ed.), *A Socially Critical View of the Self-Managing School*. Basingstoke: Falmer Press.

Taylor, F. W. (1911). *Scientific Management*. Westport, CT: Greenwood Press.

Teeple, G. (1995). *Globalisation and the Decline of Social Reform*. Toronto: Garamond Press.

Thrupp, M. (1999). *Schools Making a Difference: Let's Be Realistic: School Mix, School Effectiveness and the Social Limits of Reform*. Buckingham, U.K.: Open University Press.

Tickell, A. and Peck, J. (1995). Social regulation after Fordism: Regulation theory, neo-liberalism and global-local nexus. *Economy and Society*. Vol. 24, No. 3, pp. 357–386.

Torres, C. (1991). State corporatism, educational policies and students and teachers' movements in Mexico. In M. Ginsburg (ed.), *Understanding Educational Reform in Global Context: Economy, Ideology and the State*. New York: Garland Publishing.

Tropp, A. (1957). *The School Teachers: The Growth of the Teaching Profession in England and Wales from 1800 to the Present Day*. London: William Heinemann Ltd.

Tyack, D. (1974). *One Best System: History of American Urban Education*, Cambridge, MA: Harvard University Press.

Tyack, D., and Hansot, E. (1982). *Managers of Virtue: Public School Leadership in America, 1820–1980*. New York: Basic Books.

Tyack, D., Lowe, R. and Hansot, E. (1984). *Public Schools in Hard Times: The Great Depression and Recent Years*. Cambridge, MA: Harvard University Press.

Urban, W. (1989). Teacher activism. In D. Warren (ed.), *American Teachers: Histories of a Profession at Work*. New York: Macmillan.

Wade, R.. (1996). Japan, the World Bank and the Art of Paradigm Maintenance. *New Left Review*. No. 217, pp. 3–36.

Waller, W. (1932). *The Sociology of Teaching*. New York: Wiley.

Warren, D. (ed.). (1989). *American Teachers: Histories of a Profession at Work*. New York: Macmillan.

Watkins, P. (1993). Pushing crisis and stress down the line. In J. Smyth (ed.), *A Socially Critical View of the Self-Managing School*. London: Falmer Press.

Watkins, P. (1994). The Fordist/Post-Fordist debate: The educational implications. In J. Kenway (ed.), *Economising Education: The Post-Fordist Directions*. Greelong: Deakin University Press.

Weir, M.. (1989). Ideas and politics: the acceptance of Keynesianism in Britain and the United States. In P. Hall (ed.), *The Political Power of Economic Ideas: Keynesianism Across Nations*. Princeton: Princeton University Press.

Wexler, P. (1995). *Becoming Someone. Toward a Social Psychology of Schools*. London: Falmer Press.

Whitty, G. (1997). Marketisation, the state and the re-formation of the teaching profession. In A. H. Halsey, H. Lauder, P. Brown and A. Stuart Wells (eds.), *Education: Culture, Economy and Society*. Oxford: Oxford University Press.

Whitty, G., Power, S. and Halpin, D. (1998). *Devolution and Choice in Education: The School, the State and the Market*. Buckingham, U.K.: Open University Press.

Wilson, M.. (1997). New contractualism and the employment relationship in New Zealand. In G. Davis, B. Sullivan and A. Yeatman (eds.), *The New Contractualism?* Macmillan Education Australia.

Wood, S. (1989). The transformation of work? In. S. Wood (ed.), *The Transformation of Work?* London: Unwin.

Woods, P. (1979). *The Divided School*. London: Routledge and Kegan Paul.

Wotherspoon, T. (1996). Regulating teaching. *Studies in Political Economy*. Vol. 46, Spring, pp. 119–152.

Wright, E. O. (1985). *Classes*. London: Verso.

Wright, E. O. (1997). *Class Counts*. London: Verso.

Young, M. (ed.). (1971). *Knowledge and Control: New Directions for the Sociology of Education*. London: Collier-Macmillan.

Index